IMAGES
of America

ABERDEEN

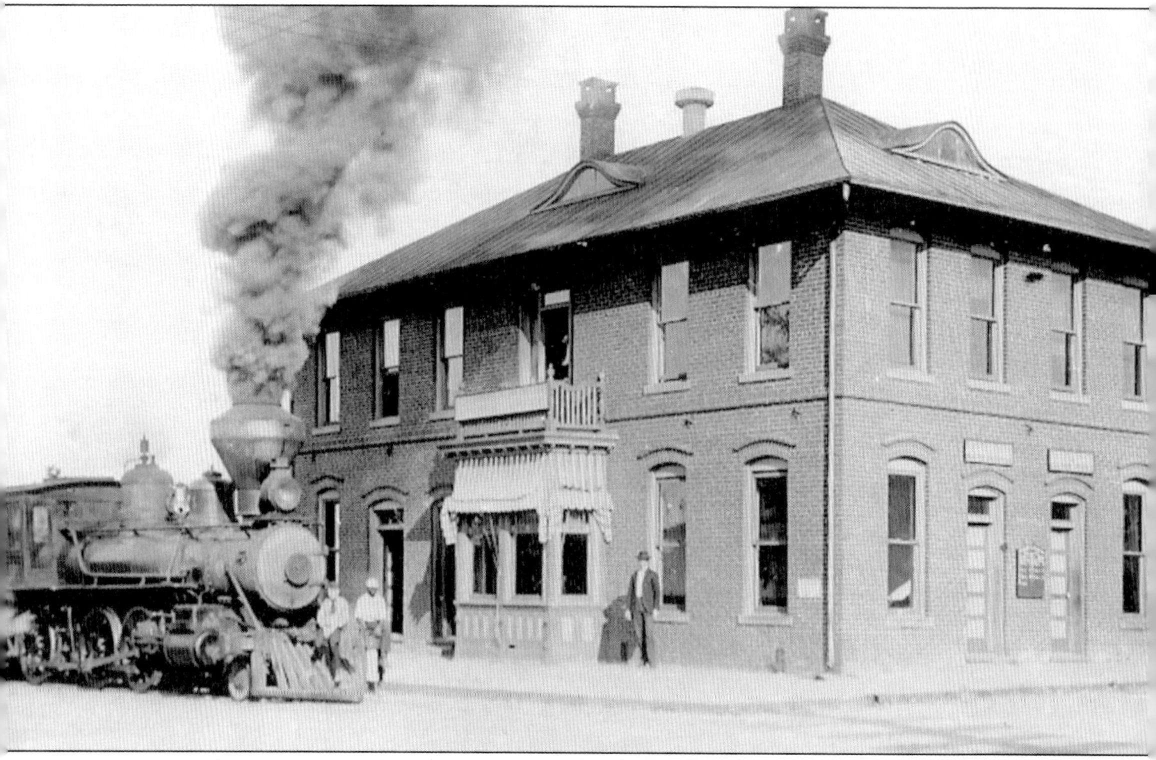

For more than a century after the arrival of the first railroad in the Sandhills region of North Carolina, Aberdeen continues as a pivotal center of transportation and commerce in the area. With a major north-south main line and two short line railroads extending rails east and west, Aberdeen is the hub of an extensive rail network that establishes it as an important commercial, industrial, and railroad center for the region. A wood-burner, Aberdeen & Rockfish Railroad No. 4, belches smoke while waiting for orders in front of the railroad offices in this c. 1910 photograph. Built by Baldwin Locomotive in 1901, it continued in service until sold in 1913. The building looks today much as it did when constructed in 1904. (Courtesy of Herbert Clifton Blue.)

ON THE COVER: Summertime in the 1950s meant a day at Aberdeen Lake for many citizens of Aberdeen and surrounding areas. When swimming pools were a luxury for the few and a trip to the ocean a two-hour excursion, the lake was a popular substitute that was filled with swimmers and sunbathers from the first of June to the end of August. Finding a parking spot near the lake was especially difficult on weekends when many families from out of town would make a day trip to the lake to enjoy the water, concession stand, and open beaches. (Author's collection.)

IMAGES
of America

ABERDEEN

Robert A. Farrell

ARCADIA
PUBLISHING

ISBN 978-0-7385-9815-4

Published by Arcadia Publishing
Charleston, South Carolina

Printed in the United States of America

Library of Congress Control Number: 2012945457

For all general information, please contact Arcadia Publishing:
Telephone 843-853-2070
Fax 843-853-0044
E-mail sales@arcadiapublishing.com
For customer service and orders:
Toll-Free 1-888-313-2665

Visit us on the Internet at www.arcadiapublishing.com

To Laura, for all her encouragement and support,
and to Robert and Stephen, my inspiration

Contents

ACKNOWLEDGMENTS

This book would not be possible without the generous support of the citizens of Aberdeen who have given of their time and resources for this project. Special thanks go to John and Lynn Blue for the use of their extensive archive of photographs and to Don and Matt McKenzie of McKenzie Photography for their patience in tirelessly scanning images for this book. The support and assistance of Susan Pockmire and the Moore County Historical Society have been invaluable. I also wish to thank John and Harriett Sloan, Lee and Louise Buchan, Martha Swaringen, Forrest and Eldiweiss Lockey, Betsy Mofield, employees of the Town of Aberdeen, Page Memorial Library, Margaret McLeod, Betsy Ingraham, Faye Honeycutt, John Burns, Joe Rosy, David Keith, Gloria Cruce, Jeanie Crockett, Richard Styers, Frank McNeill, Tony Huntley, Caroline Eisenstein, Beverly Warren-Leigh, and many others who supplied me with photographs and postcards and their knowledge of Aberdeen history. To all the past members of the Aberdeen Bicentennial Committee, who paved the way in making this book possible, as well as Mary Edmondson and other friends who provided encouragement and moral support, I owe a debt of gratitude.

INTRODUCTION

Long after the Native Americans and the bear and buffalo no longer inhabited the pine barrens and sandy soil of the Sandhills region of North Carolina, a migration of hardy Highland Scots began to appear. Looking to escape persecution in their native land after their failed rebellion against the English in 1746, many looked for a new start in the colonies of America. As the settlements along the coast expanded, many Highlanders, united with a Gallic language and kinship, moved up the Cape Fear River valley along its tributaries and into the southeastern section of present-day Moore County.

By the 1760s, settlers inhabited large tracts of land with expansive pine forests in what would be called the Bethesda Community. Because the soil of this community was not fertile except in the bottomlands, the Highlanders eked out a living growing corn and grains and hunting small game and deer that were abundant in the area. With their loyalties to the Crown during the American War of Independence, many Highlanders suffered hardships and reprisals during the conflict. After a new nation emerged in 1784, they continued to settle lands of western Cumberland County, which were later formed into Moore County. A gristmill for converting corn into meal was established on Ray's Mill Creek, and the community started to grow as local citizens began to engage in commerce with surrounding settlements.

A common bound among the Scotsmen was their Presbyterian faith, and soon a rudimentary church covered by pine branches was established near the head of Rockfish Creek. As membership grew out of this first church, a larger one was constructed near what was named the Devil's Gut, a flowing stream bounded on the east and west by rolling, sandy hills covered by vast tracts of longleaf pine trees. It is this location and the natural resource of the stands of trees that gave rise to the establishment of a community called Blue's Crossing.

Malcolm McMillan Blue was the son of a Scottish immigrant who had settled along Crain's Creek in Cumberland County. Purchasing land near the Devil's Gut, he built a home for his family in 1825 along a trading route known as the Pee Dee Road. By the 1850s, Blue had acquired large tracts of land and began tapping the pine trees for their tar, pitch, and turpentine. As the cutting of trees and the shipping of naval stores grew, the area began to prosper and more settlers were drawn to the region looking for work in the growing timber industry.

By 1859, the Presbyterian congregation had outgrown their smaller church on the Devil's Gut Creek and began construction of a large frame church made from heart pine sawn from the abundant pine forests. The church was dedicated in 1862, and the settlement around the church continued to grow. The War Between the States briefly touched the lives of the citizens in the area of Bethesda Church. In 1865, a unit of federal cavalry under the command of Gen. Judson Kilpatrick paused overnight at the home of Malcolm Blue on their way to Fayetteville, North Carolina.

After the war, the manufacturing and shipping of turpentine, tar, and pitch to market was greatly influenced by the arrival in the mid-1870s of the Raleigh & Augusta Railroad. Along with the laying of the tracks, railroad stations were constructed along the route and one was built where the Raleigh & Augusta Railroad tracks crossed the Pee Dee Road. This was known as Blue's Crossing.

The year 1880 marked a turning point for the settlement when Allison Francis Page began to acquire large tracks of land and established a lumber mill on Devil's Gut Creek. As his business prospered and the volume of products continued to grow, he constructed a rail line extending west from a junction with the Raleigh & Augusta tracks and named it the Aberdeen & West End Railroad. The availability of large tracts of virgin pine forests also drew John Blue, a lumberman from Cumberland County, to Blue's Crossing. He began to acquire large tracts of land and in 1892 built the Aberdeen & Rockfish Railroad east from a juncture with the Raleigh & Augusta Railroad.

In 1893, Blue's Crossing was incorporated by the North Carolina General Assembly and named Aberdeen, for its Scottish heritage. At the turn of the 20th century, Aberdeen had a population of approximately 1,000 people as well as retail stores, sawmills, and drying kilns, a foundry and machine shop, and two hotels. As the town grew, many of the older wooden buildings gave way to brick and masonry structures and a growing downtown business district emerged. By the 1920s, Aberdeen had established itself as an important regional center for commerce, banking, and transportation.

The wealth and success of two of the leading families of Aberdeen, the Pages and the Blues, were seen in the homes and buildings erected by both families. The Blues built the Aberdeen & Rockfish Railroad Building in 1904, and the Page family constructed Page Memorial Library in 1907 and Page Memorial Methodist Church in 1913. These structures have endured and are a testament to their design and construction as well as a legacy of the builders.

As the lumber industry drew to a close, Aberdeen began to diversify with a central business district of stores, banks, and a large hotel. Situated on a major north-south rail line with two branch lines extending east and west and the heavily traveled Federal Highway 1 that ran through the heart of town, Aberdeen became a major rail and commercial center for Moore County. As the effects of the Great Depression were overcome by the flurry of activity preceding and during World War II, Aberdeen became a hub for military transportation and two United Service Organizations offices were opened, one in town and the other at Aberdeen Lake, to service the thousands of soldiers at nearby Camp Mackall and surrounding encampments.

Postwar Aberdeen has emerged as a vibrant shopping destination and commercial center with a strong retail core along with industrial development that rivals other communities in the region. In the late 1940s, Highway 1 was moved to bypass the center of town and that realignment opened up a new area of development. The first commercial shopping center built in Moore County was built in Aberdeen in the early 1960s on the Highway 1 corridor between Aberdeen and nearby Southern Pines, North Carolina. The opening of the shopping center drew many long-established businesses away from downtown, and in the 1970s, the central core consisted of mostly boarded-up storefronts. With redevelopment of the downtown district taking place during the 1990s, there has been a resurgence of activity, with retail stores and shops catering to a wide variety of shoppers.

As the 20th century came to a close, Aberdeen had grown in stature and population. New families arrived and established homes, and many local and national retail businesses opened new stores along the major highways through town. The 2010 census revealed a population of 6,350 citizens. With a temperate climate, close proximity to larger cities in the state, a few hours drive time to the coast or mountains of North Carolina, and a rich history, Aberdeen begins a new century of development and prosperity.

One

Turn of the Century

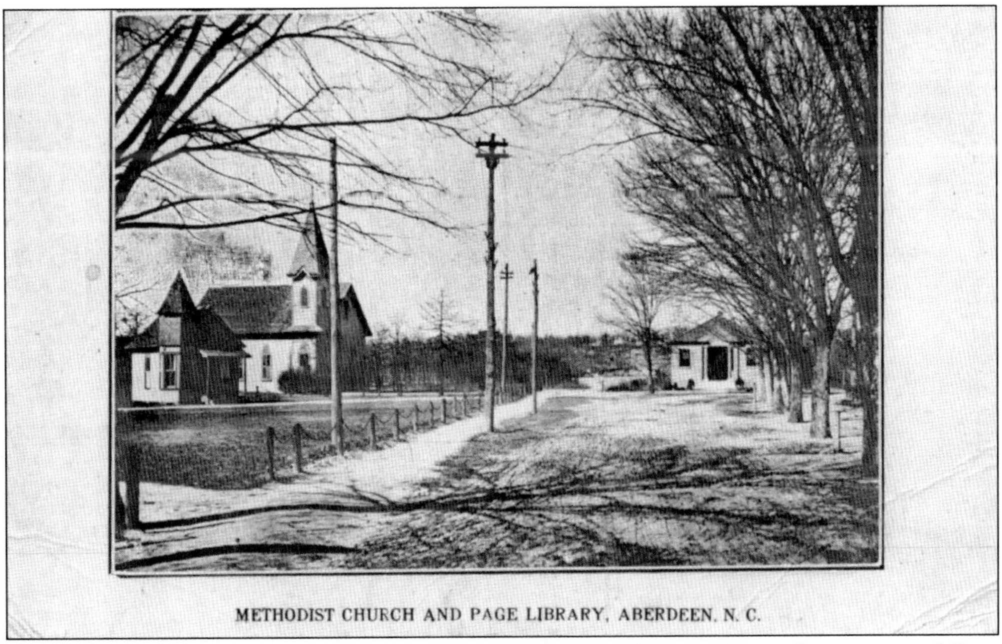

Main Street, looking west, is seen in this c. 1907 photograph with the newly constructed Page Memorial Library at the end of the street. The clear-cutting of the pine forests around Aberdeen is evident by the lack of trees visible in the background. Utility poles can be seen in front of the frame buildings on the left. I.F. Chandler was the first to bring a limited supply of electricity to Aberdeen in 1907, and by 1920, most of the homes in Aberdeen had electricity. (Author's collection.)

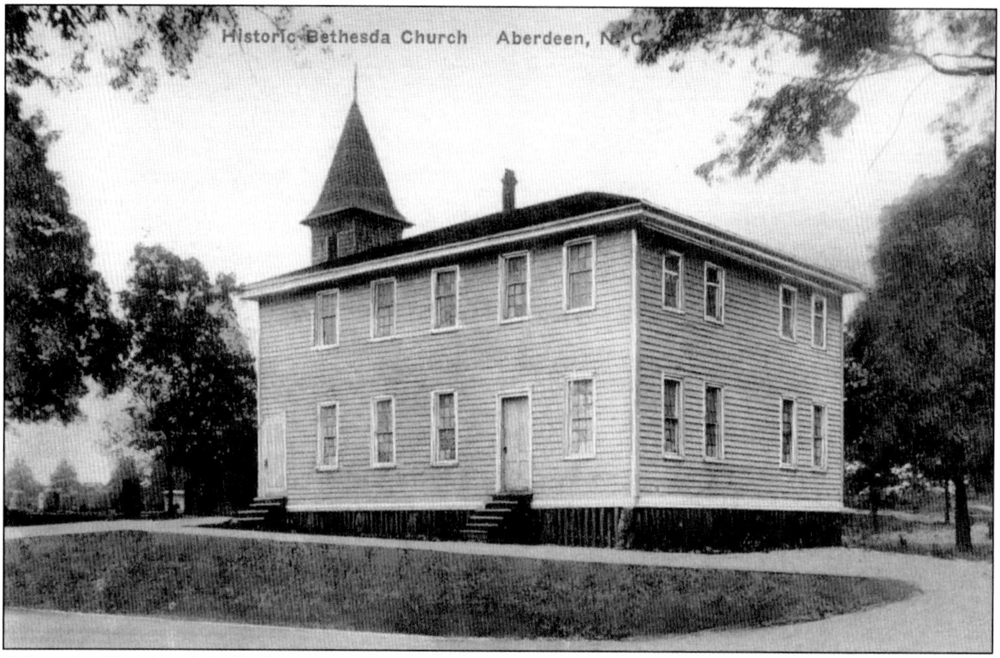

After the Battle of Culloden in 1746 and subsequent persecution of the Scottish Highlanders, a migration began to America, with many settling in the coastal regions of North Carolina. The Highland Scots brought their Presbyterian faith to the area, and in the early 1800s, a church was organized. By 1859, the Bethesda congregation had outgrown an earlier structure and constructed a new church that was dedicated in May 1862. Today, Bethesda Presbyterian Church is the oldest surviving church in Aberdeen and has been preserved in much of its original appearance. The upstairs gallery was reserved for slaves who worshipped along with their masters. In 1907, the congregation moved to a larger sanctuary in town, and the church is now used for homecoming gatherings, weddings, and special events. (Both, author's collection.)

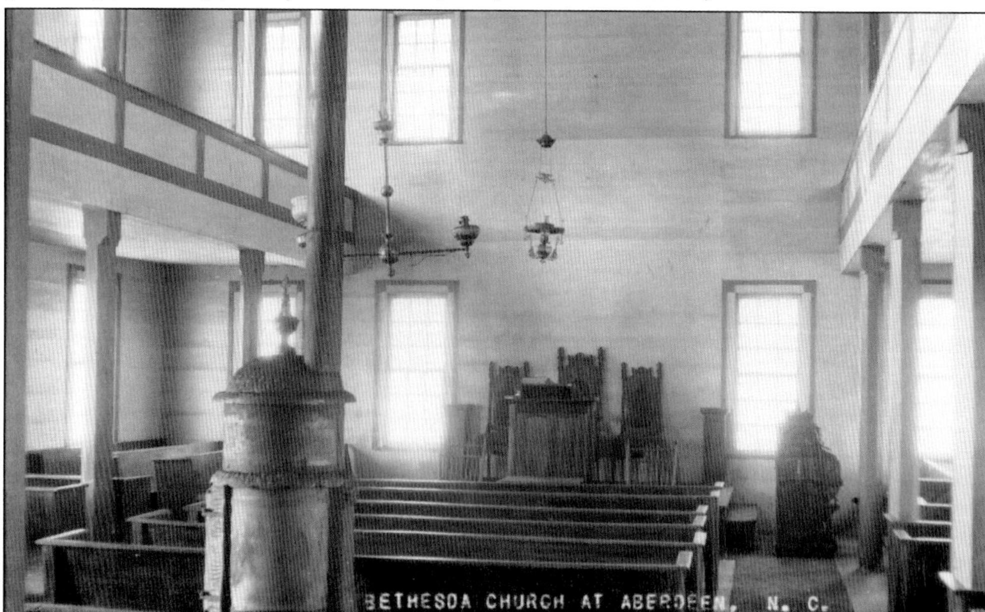

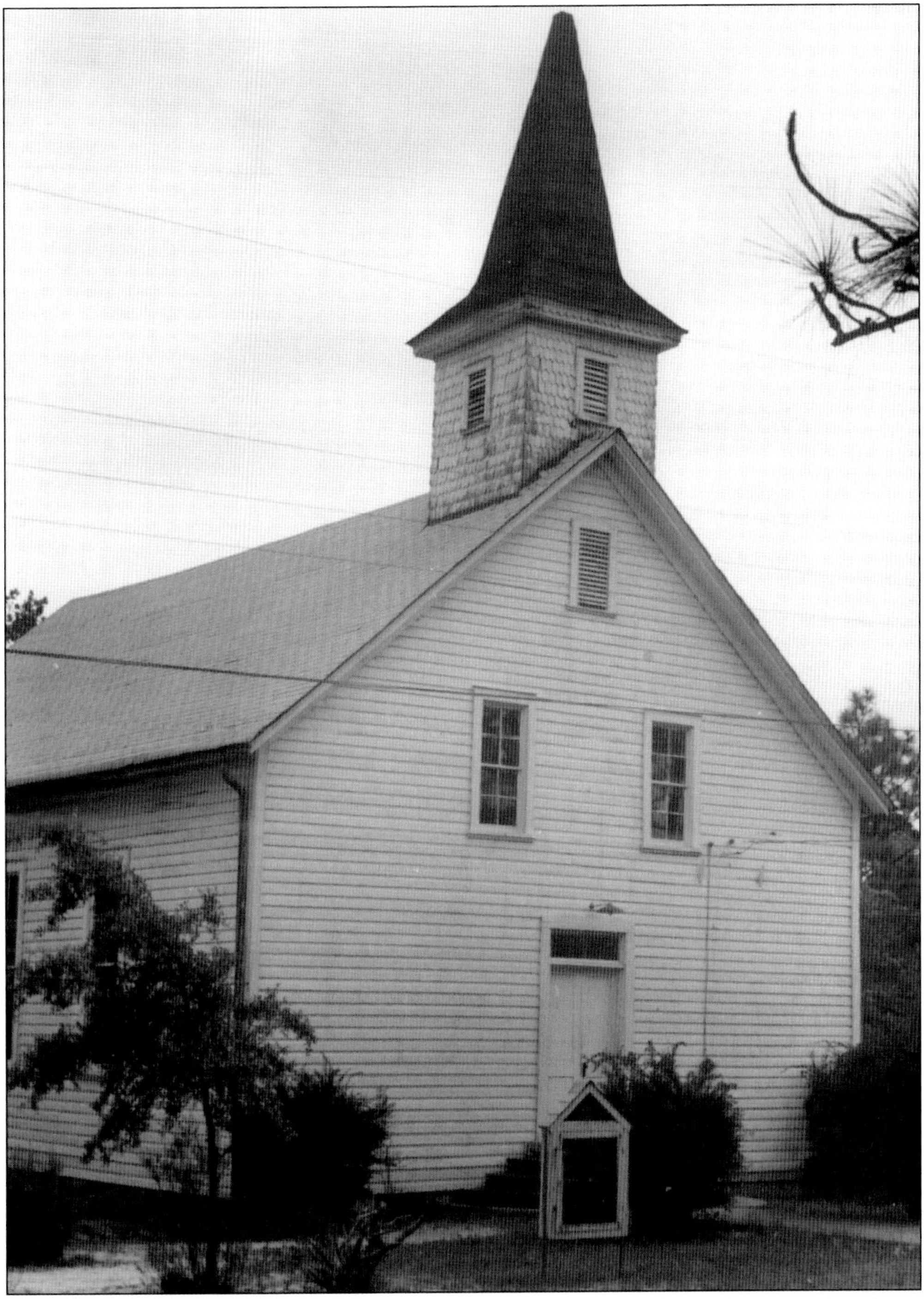

Faith Presbyterian Church on Bethesda Avenue was founded by Rev. W.H. Hood and was constructed about 1867 by freed slaves. Faith Presbyterian Church resembles nearby Bethesda Presbyterian Church where the parishioners attended worship prior to the end of the War Between the States. It is the oldest African American church in Aberdeen and is still used as a house of worship. (Courtesy of Aberdeen Centennial Committee.)

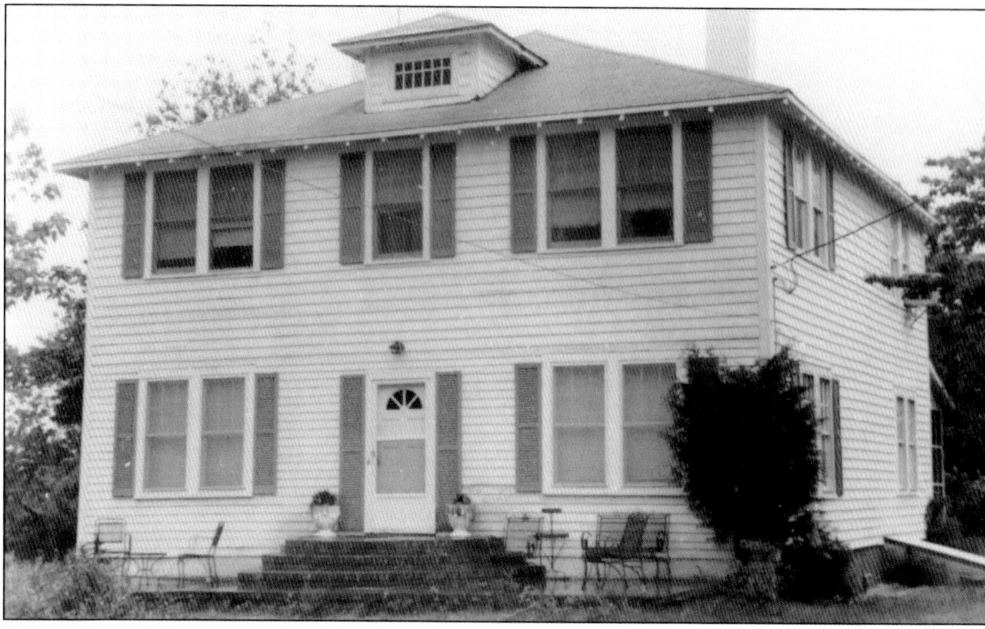

Allison Francis Page moved to Aberdeen from Cary, North Carolina, in 1881 and built this large frame home for his family using local lumber cut by his sawmilling operations. Lacking roads in the area, the house, seen from the rear, was built facing the Raleigh & Augusta Railroad tracks north of present-day downtown Aberdeen. It was the Edna Maurer home for a number of years and was demolished in 2008 for a new subdivision. (Courtesy of John Blue.)

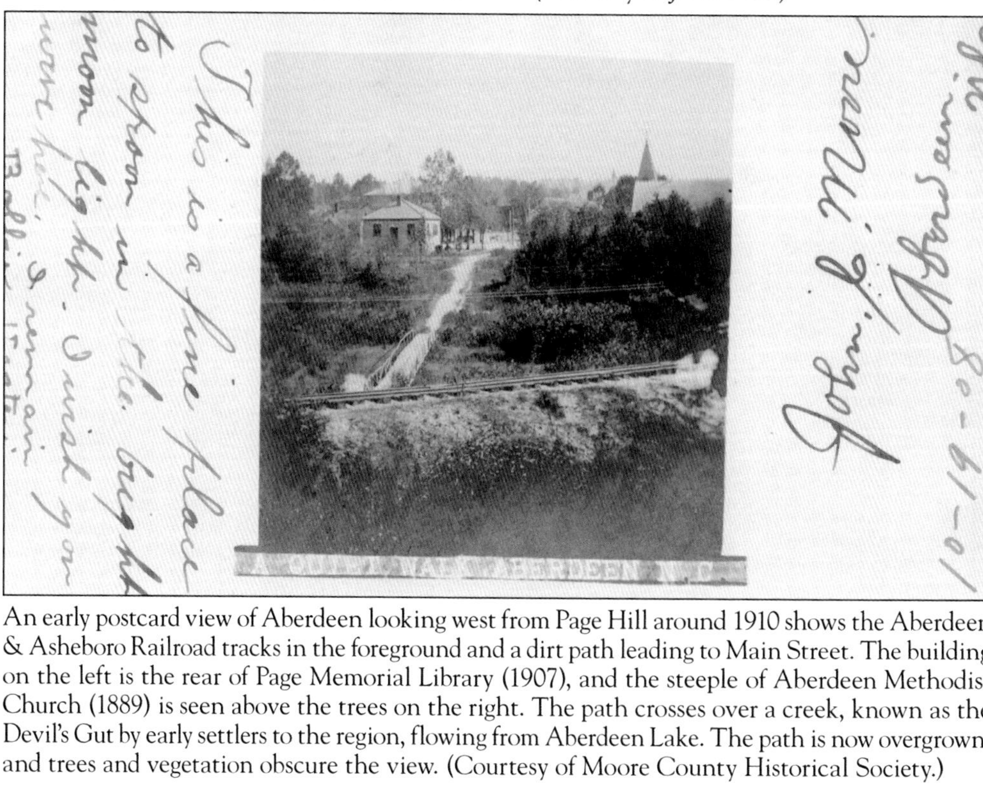

An early postcard view of Aberdeen looking west from Page Hill around 1910 shows the Aberdeen & Asheboro Railroad tracks in the foreground and a dirt path leading to Main Street. The building on the left is the rear of Page Memorial Library (1907), and the steeple of Aberdeen Methodist Church (1889) is seen above the trees on the right. The path crosses over a creek, known as the Devil's Gut by early settlers to the region, flowing from Aberdeen Lake. The path is now overgrown, and trees and vegetation obscure the view. (Courtesy of Moore County Historical Society.)

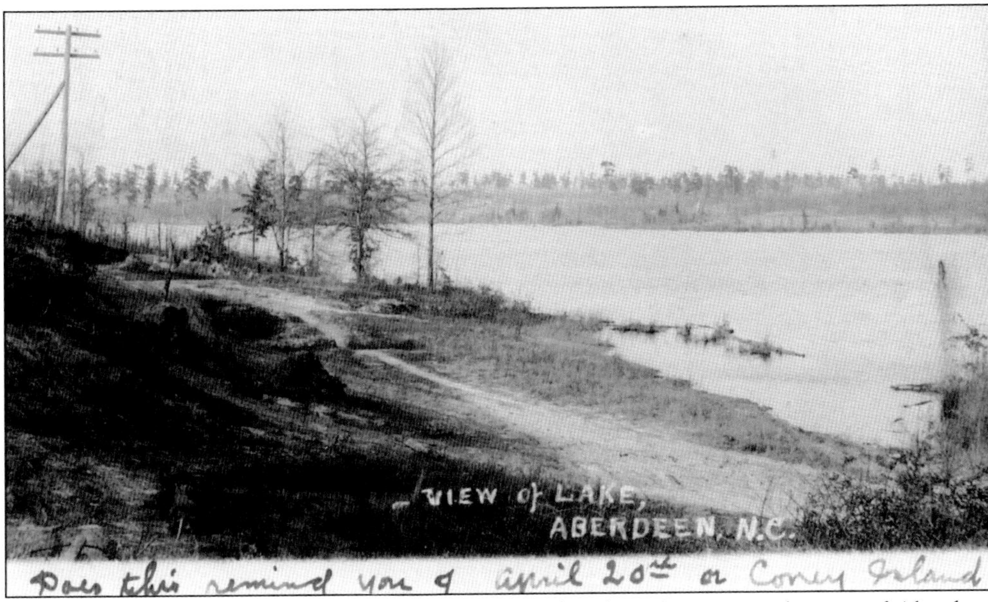

Looking north from the Aberdeen & Asheboro Railroad tracks is an early view of Aberdeen Lake. The tracks climbed the steep grade on the western side of the lake. The lake was created in 1882 when Allison Page, who owned large tracts of timber, built a dam at Aberdeen Creek, formerly known as Devil's Gut. The dam provided power for a sawmill and gristmill. Of note is the clear-cutting of trees around the lake by the extensive logging industry at the turn of the 20th century. (Author's collection.)

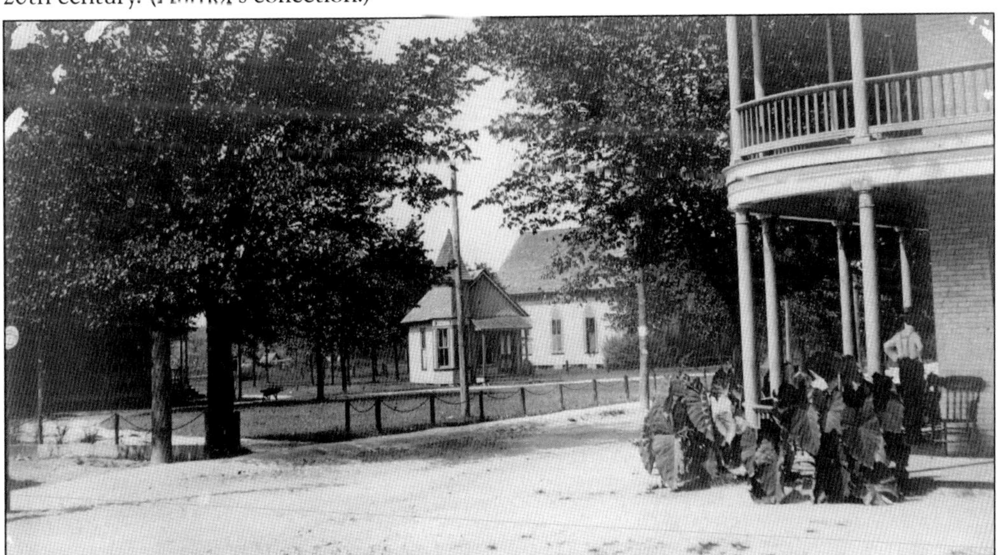

A penny postcard view of Main Street is seen in this c. 1905 photograph. The small building on the left is the Heckart Real Estate office that was later moved to Sycamore Street next to where Aberdeen Feed and Seed Company is located today. It was moved to clear the way for construction of the Aberdeen & Asheboro Railroad Building. In the center is Aberdeen Methodist Church, which was demolished around 1910 to clear the site for a new church building. On the right is a corner of the Aberdeen Hotel with its covered verandas where guests could escape the heat of the day. (Author's collection.)

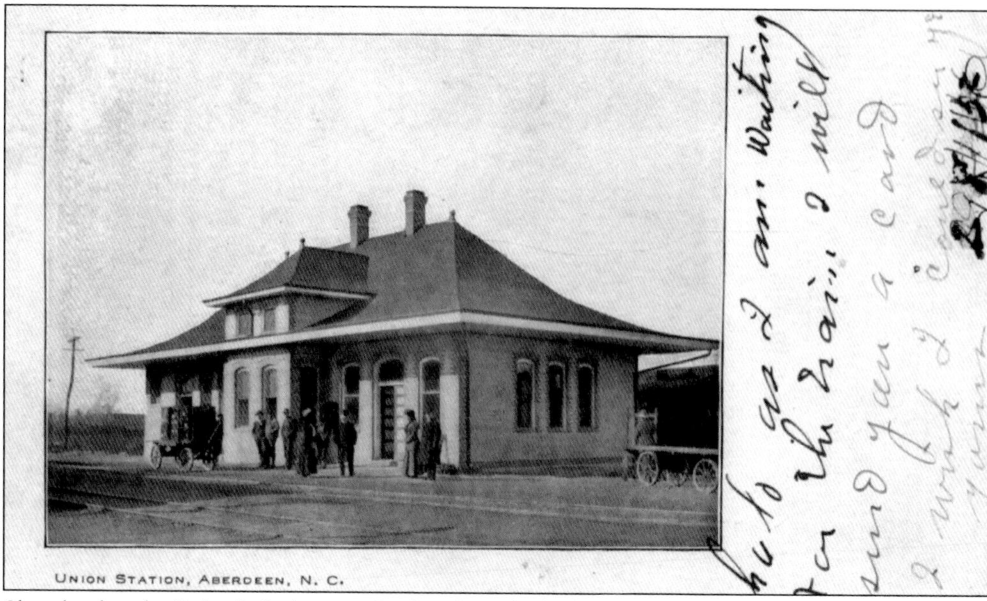

Shortly after the Raleigh & Augusta Railroad reached what is now Aberdeen, it became necessary to build a train station. When the Seaboard Air Line Railway acquired the Raleigh & Augusta Railroad, it contracted with T.B. Creel to build a brick station to a standard design provided by the Seaboard Air Line Railway. Opened in 1906, Union Station was used by the Seaboard Air Line Railway and Aberdeen & Asheboro Railroad. In the 1950s, an addition was added on the south elevation to accommodate the Railway Express offices. Passenger service was phased out in the 1970s, and the Town of Aberdeen took ownership of the building. Today, it is used as a museum and model railroad club. (Author's collection.)

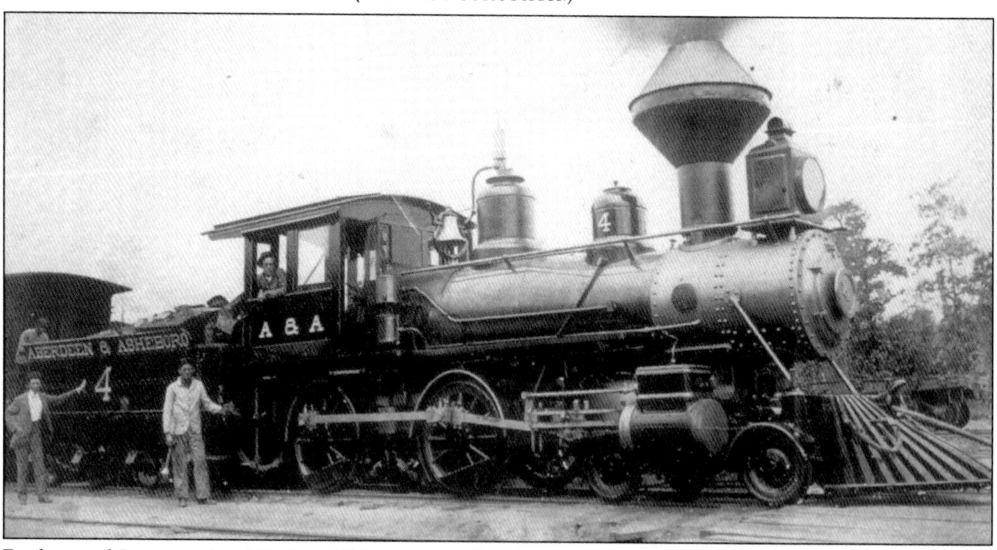

Richmond Locomotive Works of Virginia built Aberdeen & Asheboro No. 4, seen in this early photograph. The Aberdeen & Asheboro Railway was originally the Aberdeen & West End Railroad until the tracks were extended to Biscoe, North Carolina. Used mainly to transport lumber products between Aberdeen and points west, it merged with the Norfolk & Southern Railroad in 1912 and began passenger service to Pinehurst and Jackson Springs, North Carolina. (Courtesy of John Sloan.)

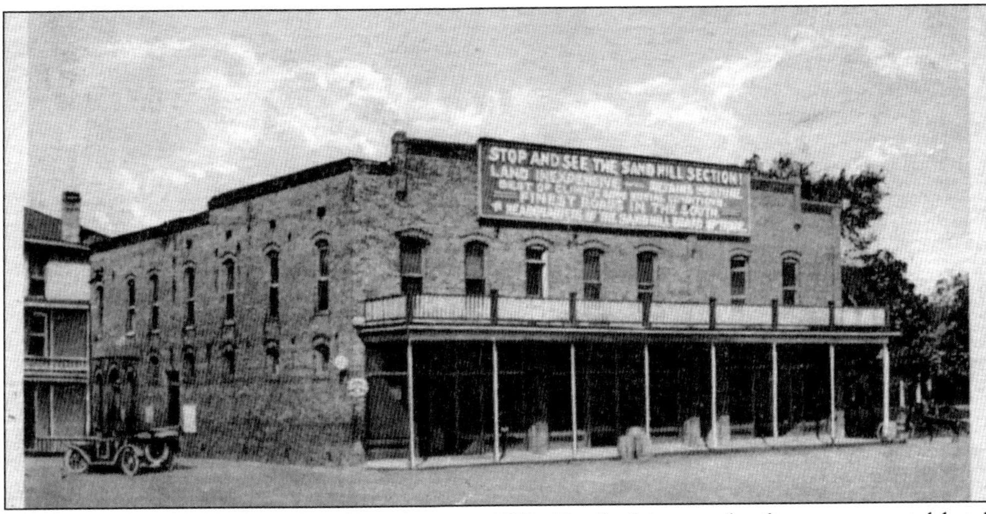

Originally constructed in 1900 by contractor T.B. Creel, this was the first commercial brick building in Aberdeen. Known as Farrell Dry Goods, in 1907 it would become the Wilson and Farrell General Store. In 1912, a nearly identical addition was built, and it became the largest structure in town for many years. Taking advantage of its proximity to Union Station, a large billboard was erected on the front of the building to entice rail passengers to stop and inquire about the Sandhills. The sign reads: "Stop and see the Sandhill section, land inexpensive, retains moisture, best of climate and social conditions, finest roads in the south and headquarters of the Sandhills Board of Trade." The building has been used for various businesses over the years and is now a home furnishings store. (Author's collection.)

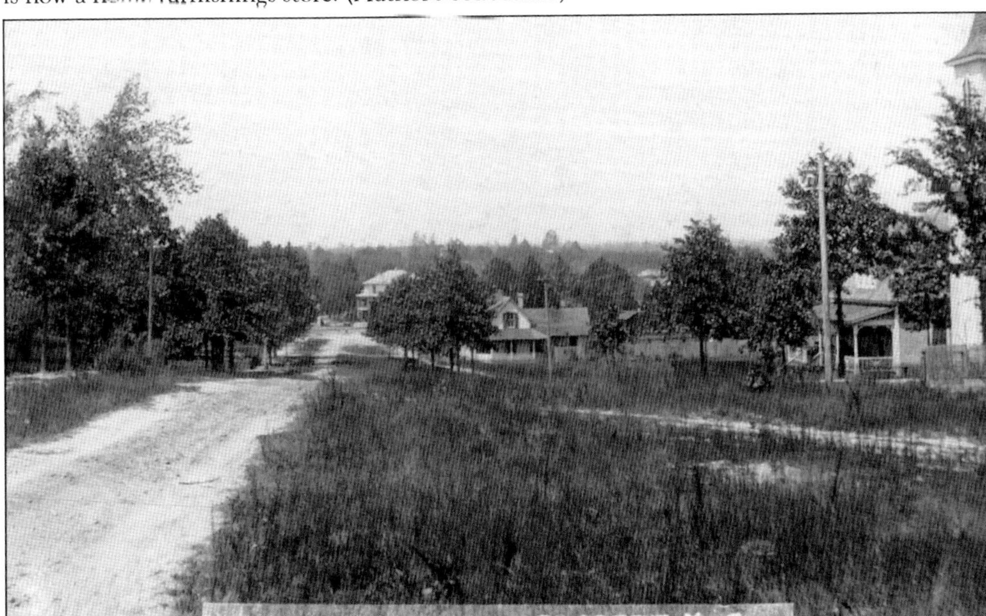

Looking west from where present-day Main and Blue Streets intersect, a single-lane dirt road leads to downtown Aberdeen. This scene is from a postcard postmarked 1909 and mailed from Aberdeen to Waynesburg, Pennsylvania. The Aberdeen Hotel can be seen on the left. The house to the left of Aberdeen Baptist Church was the first office of the Aberdeen & Asheboro Railroad. Both the offices and the church are private residences today. (Author's collection.)

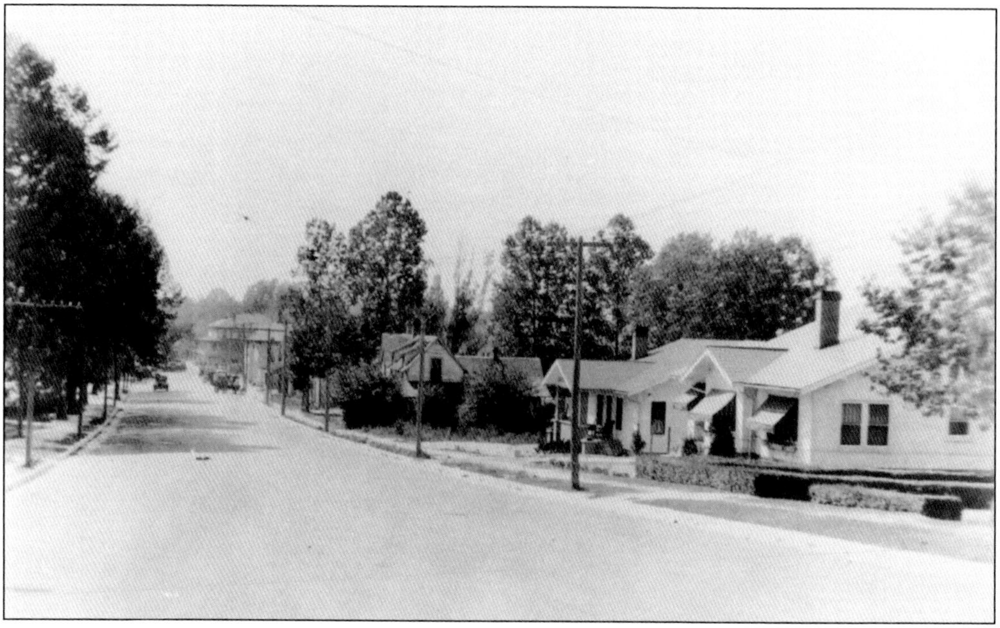

Main Street, looking west, is seen in this c. 1940 image showing curbing, sidewalks, and utility poles on both sides of the street. The sidewalks were installed by the Work Progress Administration in 1937; later, the WPA installed the sidewalks on Poplar Street. The large building visible on the right is the Aberdeen Hotel. Today, many of the homes shown are included in the Aberdeen Historic District. (Courtesy of Aberdeen Centennial Committee.)

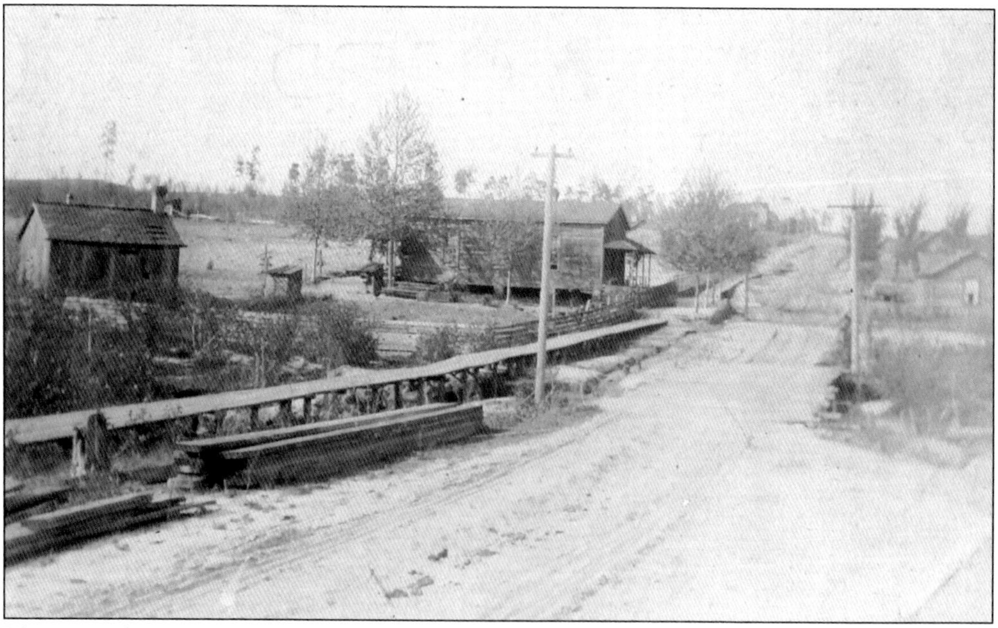

This scene shows an early Aberdeen road that would later be Poplar Street. The view is facing north from where present-day Poplar and Maple Streets intersect. The sandy road is seen spanning the creek from Ray's Mill Pond. The home of the William Hurley (1858–1945) family is facing the road on the left. He operated an iron foundry that cast ornamental and structural building materials still seen in many buildings in Aberdeen today. (Courtesy of Moore County Historical Society.)

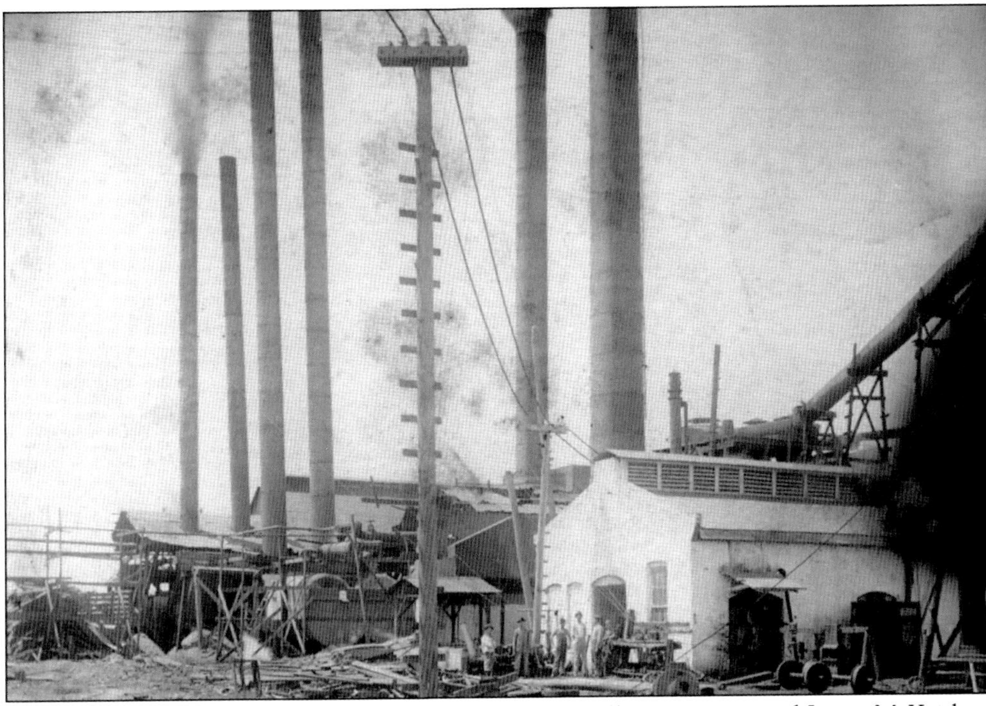

Organized around 1900 by John Blue, Joseph Allred, William Maurer, and James McKeithen, the Aberdeen Sash and Blind Company manufactured window treatments from lumber sawn by local sawmills. Located between the Seaboard Air Line Railway and Aberdeen & Rockfish Railroad tracks, the company made daily shipments by rail to Baltimore and New York. At one time one of the largest industries in Aberdeen, the depletion of the local pine forests eventually made the procurement of raw materials unprofitable, and the business ceased operations in the 1920s. (Both, courtesy of Moore County Historical Society.)

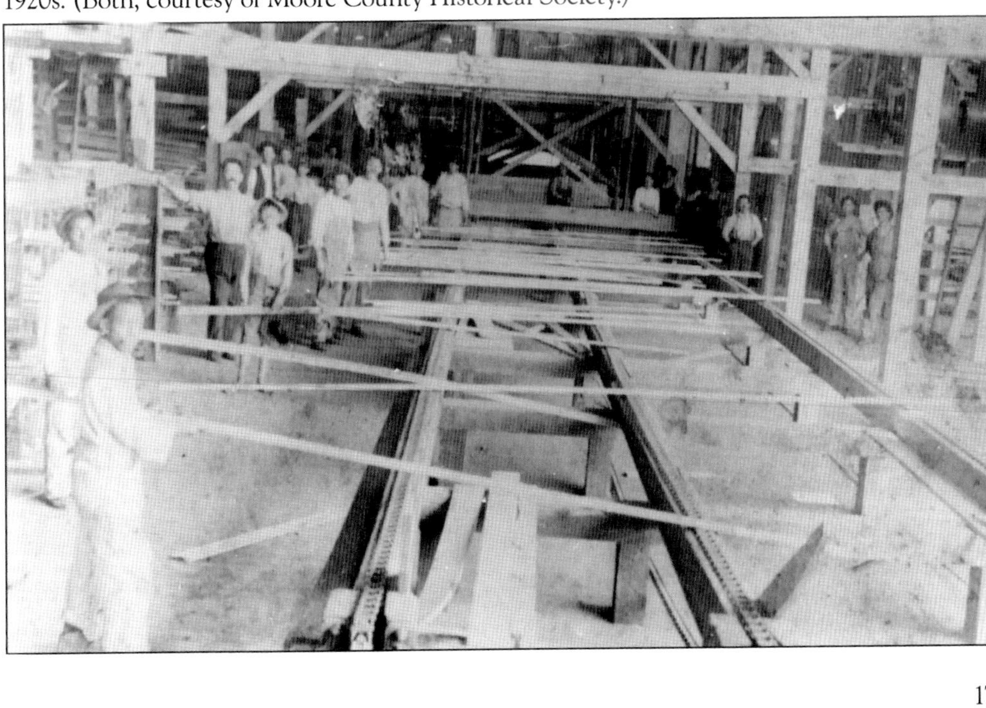

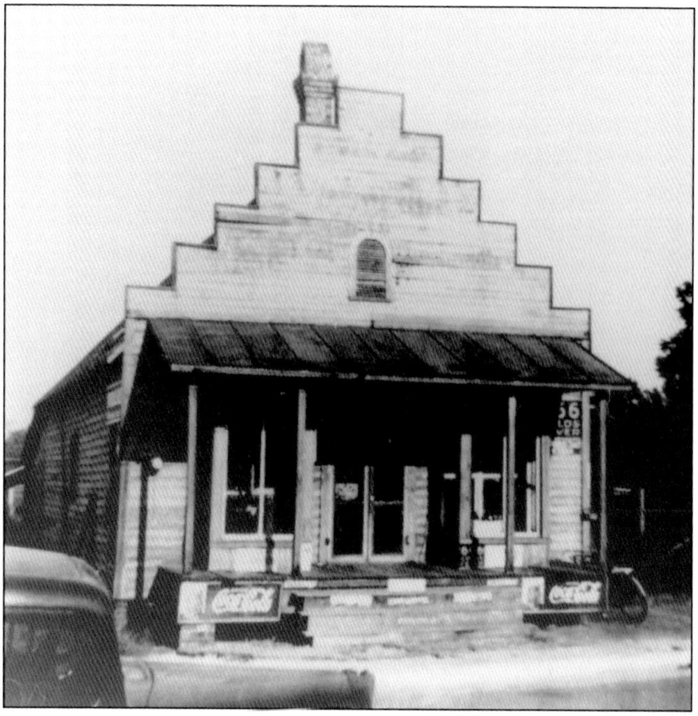

Mark Wimberley opened a general merchandise store on Sycamore Street facing the Seaboard Air Line Railway tracks around 1900. It was one of the oldest general stores built in early Aberdeen. The store motto was: "We have it, you need it, come get it." After much difficulty crossing over railroad tracks, the building was moved to Blue Street in the 1960s and reopened. The combination of age and the stress of being moved caused the building to later be demolished. (Courtesy of Aberdeen Centennial Committee.)

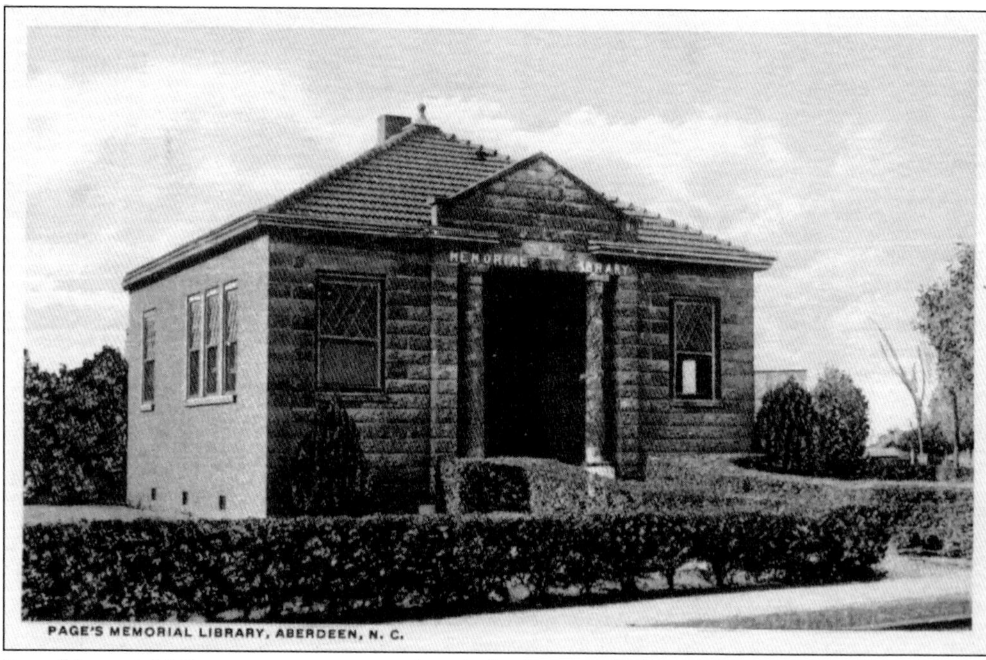

Page Memorial Library was constructed with funds provided by Mary Page in memory of her parents, Allison Francis and Catherine Robeteau Page. The building was constructed in 1907 and stands on the corner of Main and Poplar Streets. The charming diminutive building was constructed of rock-faced concrete blocks with a pyramidal slate roof. Noted builder T.B. Creel was contracted for the project. Today, it is a member of the countywide library system and is one of the oldest continuously operated public libraries in North Carolina. (Author's collection.)

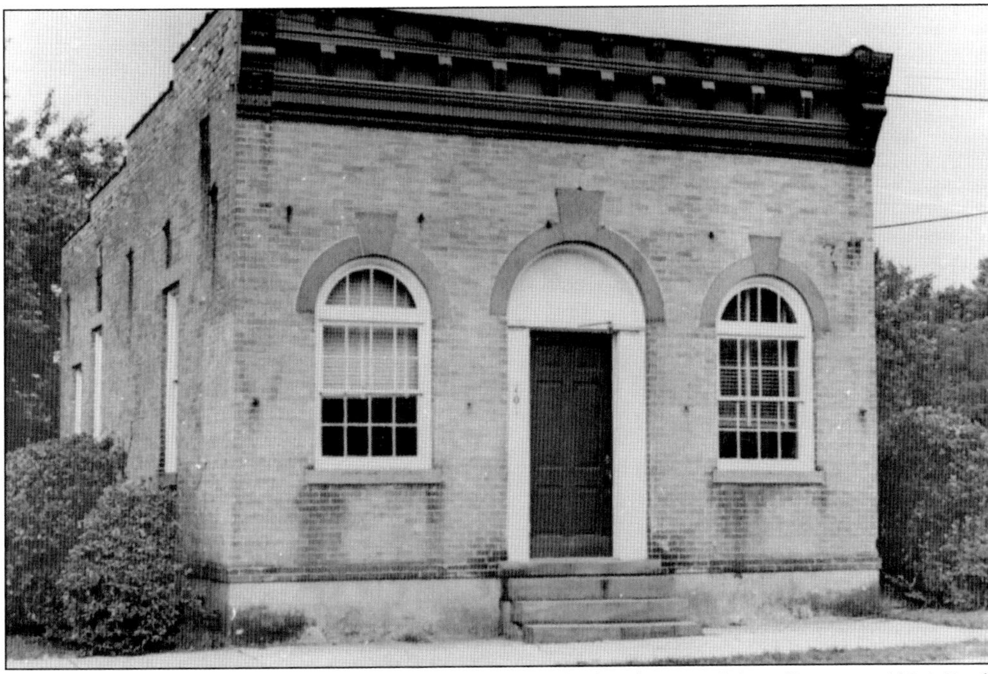

Members of the Blue families established the Bank of Aberdeen on Main Street in 1904. Built in the Romanesque Revival style by noted contractor and brick mason T.B. Creel, it would later house the Merchants and Farmers Bank. The building today is no longer used as a bank but remains unchanged in appearance from when it was constructed. It is in the Aberdeen Historic District. (Courtesy of Aberdeen Centennial Committee.)

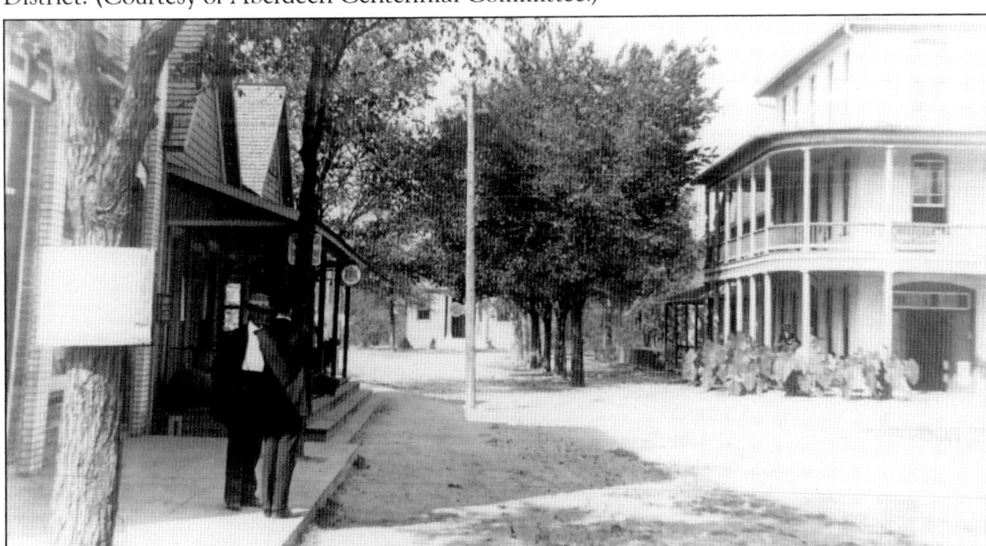

Main Street is viewed looking from Union Station, built in 1906, toward Page Memorial Library, erected in 1907. Before the construction of the library, a wooden building stood on the site where James McNeill Johnson operated a drugstore. Johnson would later become an attorney in Aberdeen. The building was moved to East Main Street and became R.G. Farrell's Livery Stable. Keith Dry Goods and Grocery occupied the wooden building on the left. The Aberdeen Hotel is seen on the right. (Courtesy of Aberdeen Centennial Committee.)

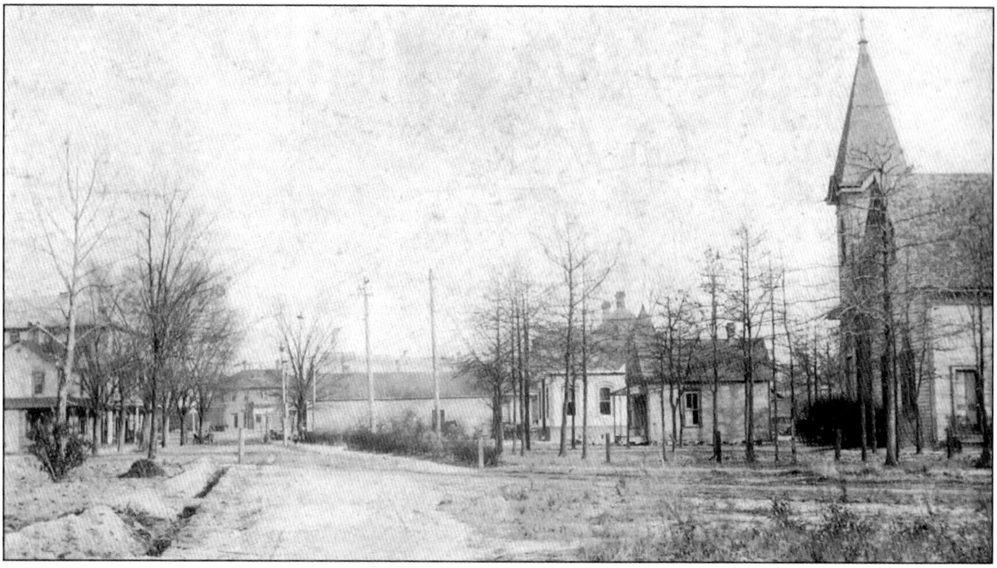

A wintry view of Main Street, looking east around 1910, shows the early development in the commercial center of Aberdeen. Prominent is the unpaved street with an open ditch for drainage. Seen on the left partially hidden behind trees is the Aberdeen Hotel before it was brick veneered. The offices of the Aberdeen & Rockfish Railroad are at the end of the street. On the right (from left to right) are the brick Aberdeen & Asheboro Railroad offices, the Heckart Reality office, and the wooden Aberdeen Methodist Church. The long wooden building was the first store operated by Hugh Keith. A close examination reveals an early automobile parked next to the hotel and horses standing beside the Keith Building. (Courtesy of Elease Goodwin.)

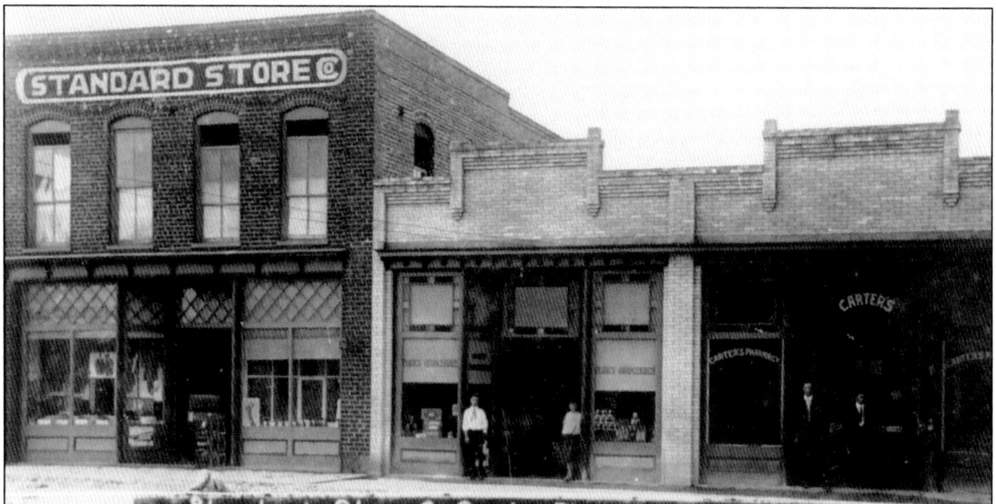

Located on East Main Street, the Standard Store, Allred's Grocery, and Carter's Pharmacy are seen in this c. 1910 image. The Standard Store was a major commercial center in early Aberdeen. Contractor and brick mason T.B. Creel, who moved to Aberdeen in 1891, built this block. Later, a fish market opened in the Allred's Grocery Building, and Keith's Deluxe Cleaners occupied the pharmacy building until it became the offices of the *Sandhill Citizen* newspaper in 1937. Today, the buildings are located in the Aberdeen Historic District. (Courtesy of Aberdeen Centennial Committee.)

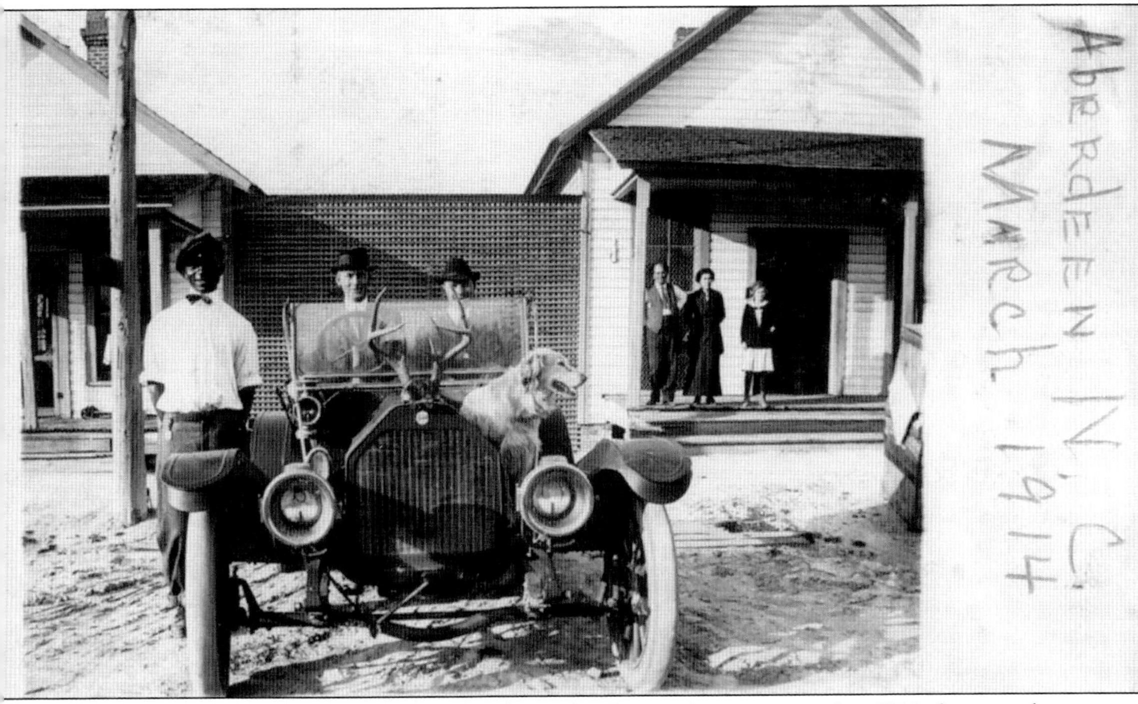

Early Aberdeen motorists are enjoying a ride on the dirt roads in town in this 1914 photograph. The wooden structures in the background were on the north side of Main Street and adjacent to the Bank of Aberdeen building. W.T. Bobbitt operated a general store at this location. The first automobile in Aberdeen was an E-M-F, owned by Clifton N. Blue. The E-M-Fs were built in Detroit between 1909 and 1912 and sold by Studebaker wagon dealerships. (Courtesy of Moore County Historical Society.)

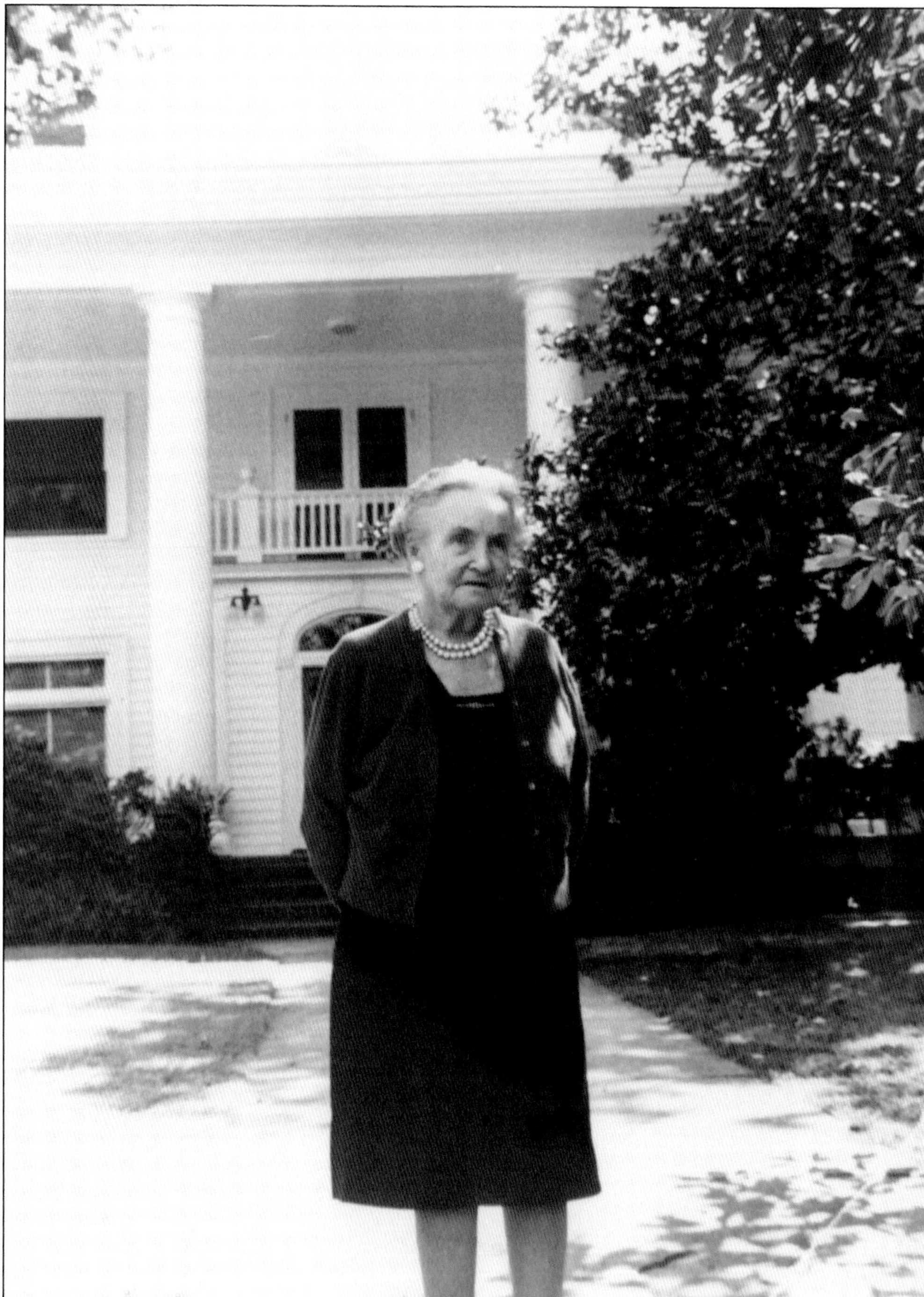

Frances Louise Blue was one of five children born to John and Frances Blue. She is standing in front of her home on Blue Street. Her father established the Aberdeen & Rockfish Railroad to serve his turpentine and timber enterprises near Aberdeen. Known as Miss Louise Blue about town, she was always seen in the finest of attire and maintained the elegance of the Blue home throughout her life. (Courtesy of Aberdeen Centennial Committee.)

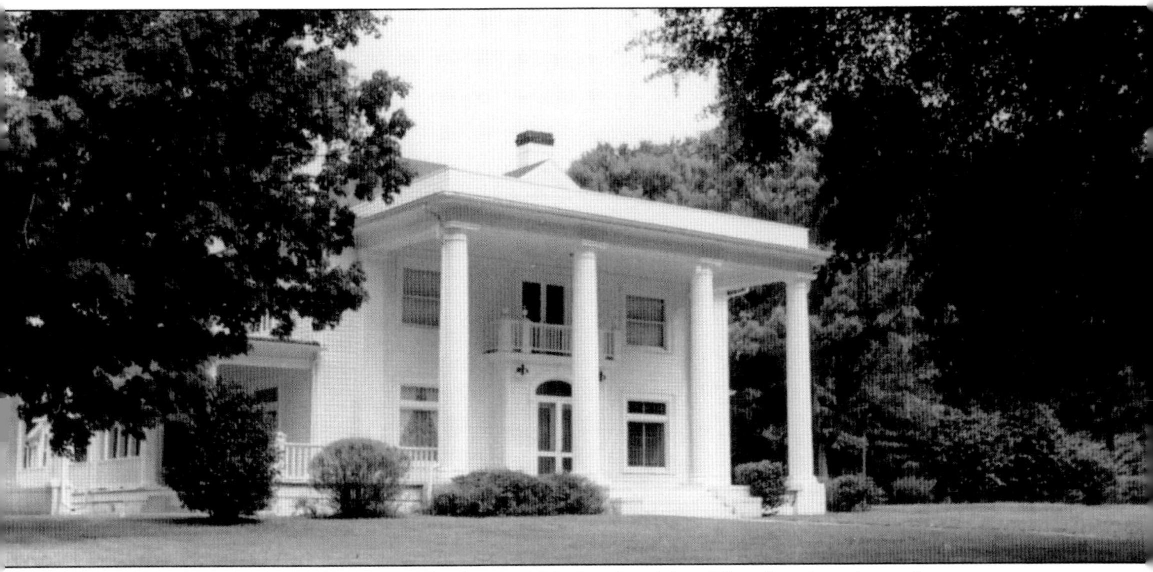

This large two-story residence was built in 1888 for the John Blue family, whose fortunes were made in the lumber and railroading industries. Located on what would later be named Blue Street, noted Charlotte, North Carolina, architect Charles C. Hook extensively renovated this Neoclassical Revival house in 1903. It remained unchanged in appearance until a tragic fire in 1999 gutted the interior. The ruins were demolished several years later. Placed in the National Register of Historic Places, the last of this elegant home is still in evidence by the remains of the brick front steps. (Courtesy of John Blue.)

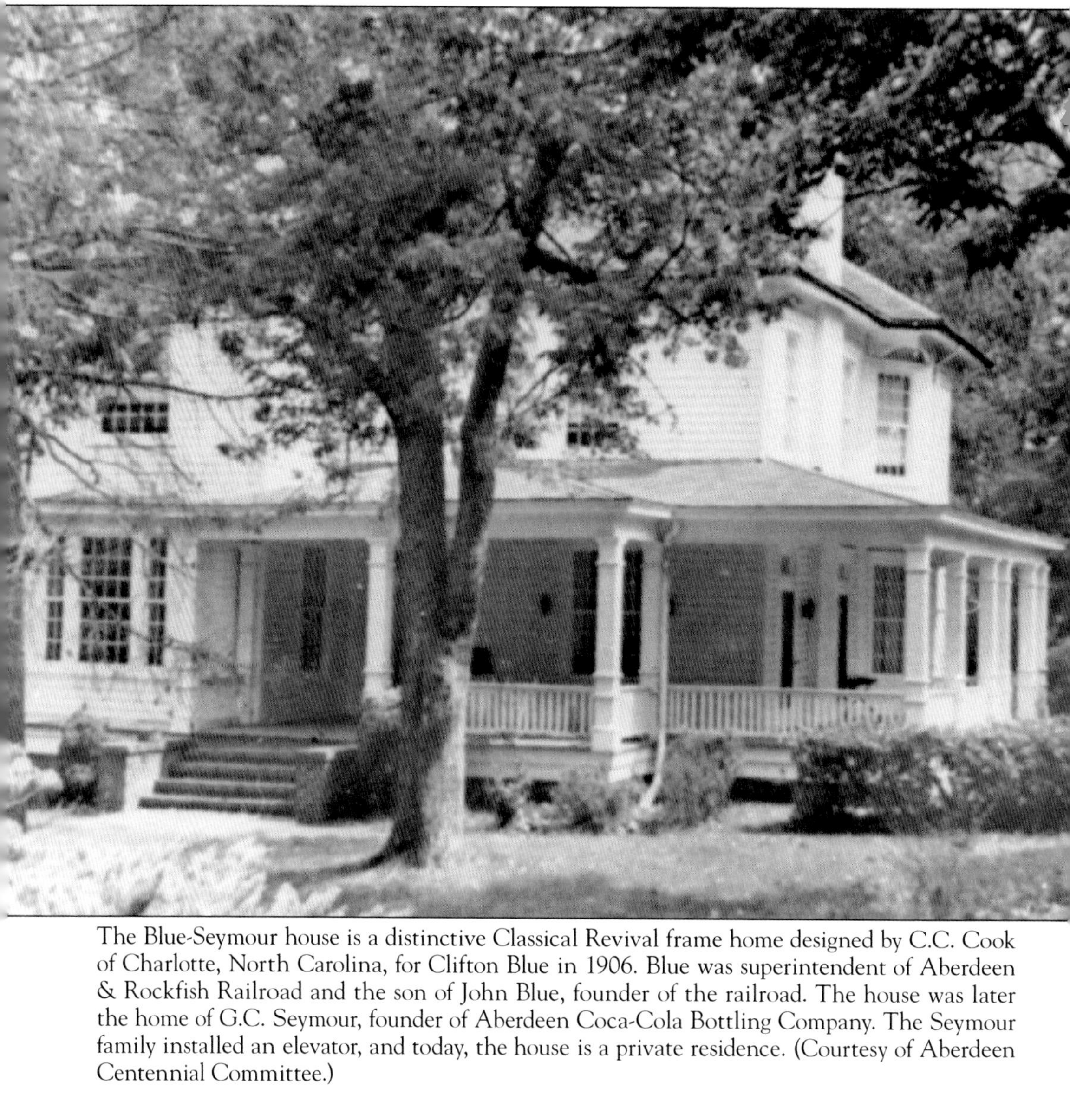

The Blue-Seymour house is a distinctive Classical Revival frame home designed by C.C. Cook of Charlotte, North Carolina, for Clifton Blue in 1906. Blue was superintendent of Aberdeen & Rockfish Railroad and the son of John Blue, founder of the railroad. The house was later the home of G.C. Seymour, founder of Aberdeen Coca-Cola Bottling Company. The Seymour family installed an elevator, and today, the house is a private residence. (Courtesy of Aberdeen Centennial Committee.)

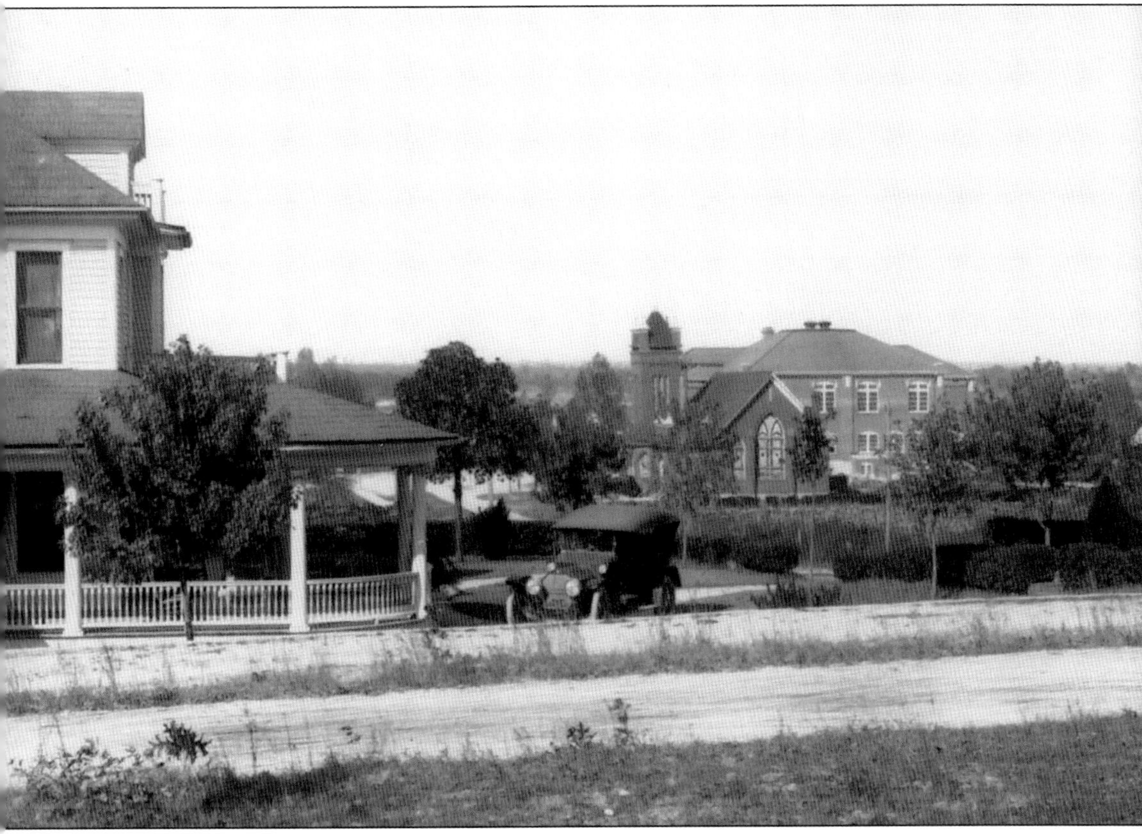

Located on the south side of Blue Street, this large frame house with a sweeping covered porch was the home of W.A. Blue, known as Will Blue. Blue was the son of John Blue, founder of the Aberdeen & Rockfish Railroad in 1902. Upon his father's death in 1922, Blue was elected president and chairman of the board of the family-owned railroad. He was a capitalist and peach grower The house remains much as it did when built and is a private residence today. The 1907 Bethesda Presbyterian Church can be seen on the north side of the street, and the brick Aberdeen school is behind the church. (Courtesy of Aberdeen Centennial Committee.)

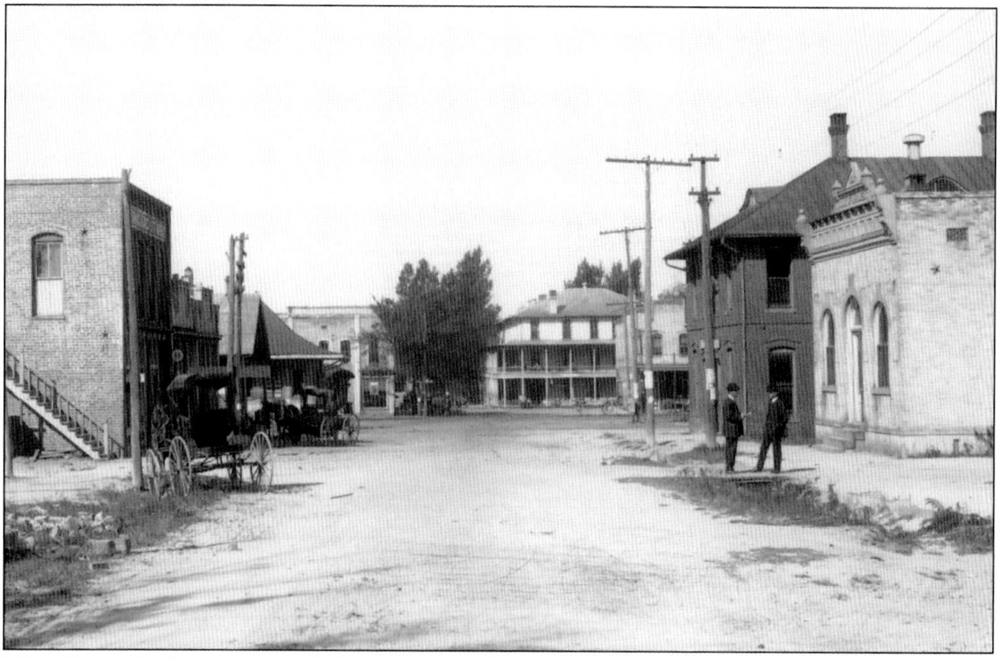

Main Street, looking west, includes many early buildings with horse-drawn buggies in view. The two men on the right are standing in front of the Bank of Aberdeen, and the building behind them houses the offices of Aberdeen & Rockfish Railroad. Across the railroad tracks, the Farrell Building and the Aberdeen Hotel can be seen. The buggies are parked in front of the Standard Store on the left. The photograph was taken between 1910 and 1915. (Author's collection.)

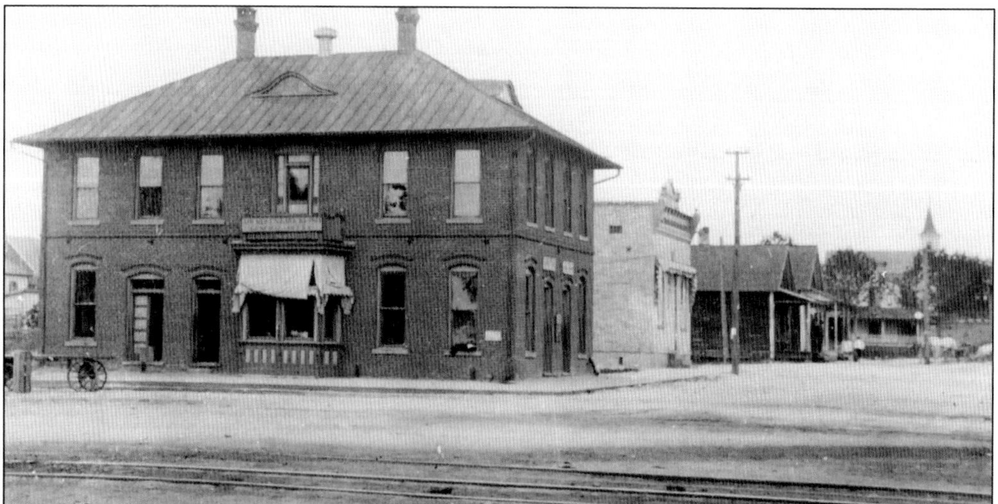

An early view looking east on Main Street shows, from left to right, the Aberdeen & Rockfish Railroad Building, the Bank of Aberdeen, a feed store, and a store operated by W.T. Bobbitt. The railroad building was designed and constructed in 1904 by T.B. Creel. Minor alterations have been made to the building, including the ticket window bay being replaced with a Colonial Revival entrance and a door on the west elevation being converted to a window. The Aberdeen & Rockfish Railroad was organized in 1892 and is one of the oldest continuously operated railroads in the United States. (Courtesy Moore County Historical Society.)

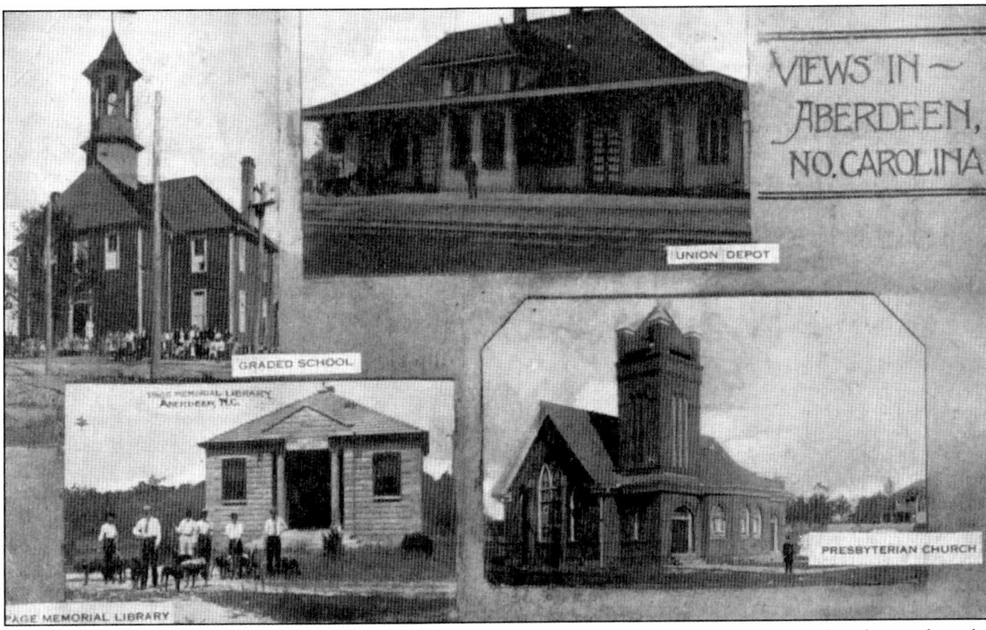

An early postcard depicts four prominent buildings that attest to the growth of Aberdeen after the turn of the 20th century. Pictured from left to right (clockwise) are the following: Union Station, built in 1906; Bethesda Presbyterian Church, built in 1907; Page Memorial Library, built in 1907; and Aberdeen School and Community Center, built in 1897. (Author's collection.)

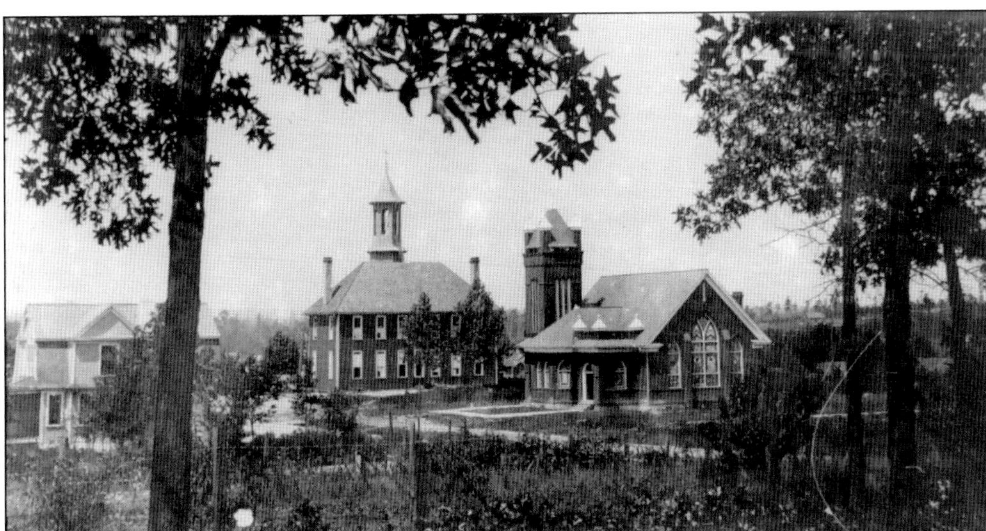

Pictured on the left in this early photograph is the former home of Ralph and Zadie Leach. He was owner and manager of the Aberdeen Hotel. In the center is the first Aberdeen school (c. 1893), which was removed in 1913. Pictured on the right is Bethesda Presbyterian Church. (Courtesy of John Blue.)

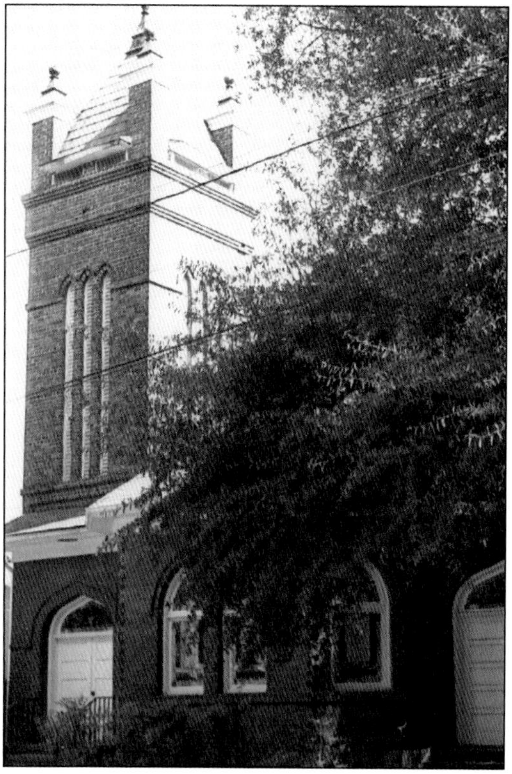

Constructed in 1906–1907 to replace the original wooden Bethesda Presbyterian Church (c. 1860), this fine example of Gothic Revival architecture located at 307 High Street was built to accommodate a growing congregation at the turn of the century. Many a youth on Sundays vied to pull the ropes that rang the tower bells. After many years of service, the congregation moved in 1972 to a new church on Highway 1. It is now the home of Aberdeen Church of Christ. (Courtesy of John Blue.)

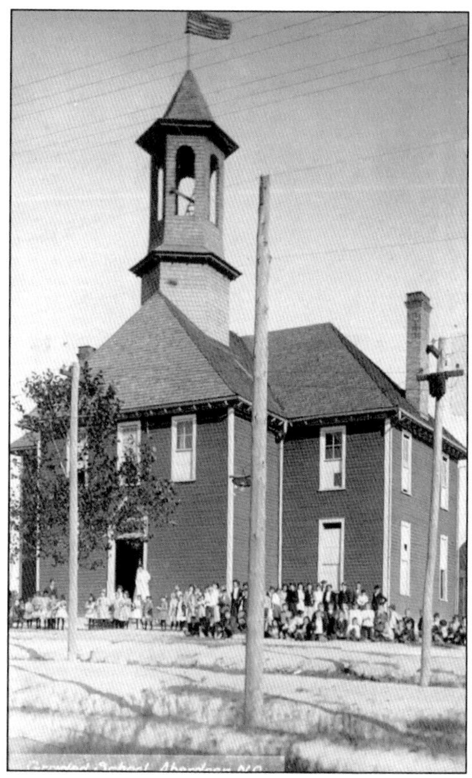

The first school in Aberdeen was constructed in 1893 on High and Pine Streets. Classrooms were located on the first floor, and an auditorium on the second floor served the school and community events. It was removed in 1913 and replaced with a two-story brick school. (Courtesy of Aberdeen Centennial Committee.)

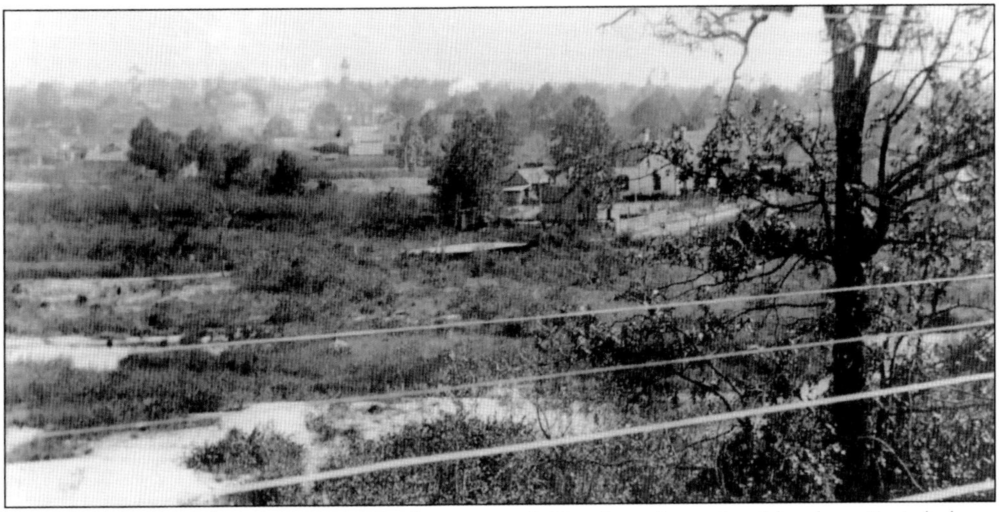

Here is an early-20th-century view looking east of Aberdeen from the Aberdeen & Asheboro Railroad tracks. In the foreground is the creek flowing from the spillway on Page's Lake. The lake was dammed to create power for sawing the timber harvested in the area. The spire of the first Aberdeen school is visible in the distance. The wires are carrying telegraph signals to the station at the end of the rail line. (Courtesy of Moore County Historical Society.)

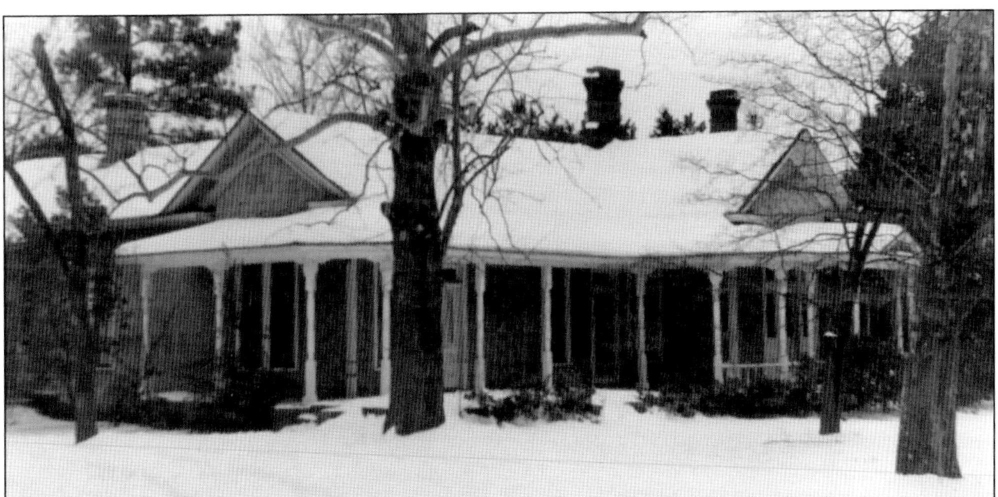

The home of Gordon and Iris Keith is pictured under a fresh snowfall. Robert N. Page originally built the house for his pending marriage to Flora Shaw in 1888. Page was in the lumber and railroading business. As treasurer of Aberdeen & Asheboro Railroad, he moved to Bisco, North Carolina, the western terminus of the railroad in 1897. He was the first mayor of Aberdeen and served in the US Congress from 1903 to 1917. Hugh A. Keith Sr. purchased the house about 1902, and his son Gordon inherited it in 1928. Located on Keith Street, the house retains much of its original appearance and remains in the Keith family today. (Courtesy of John Blue.)

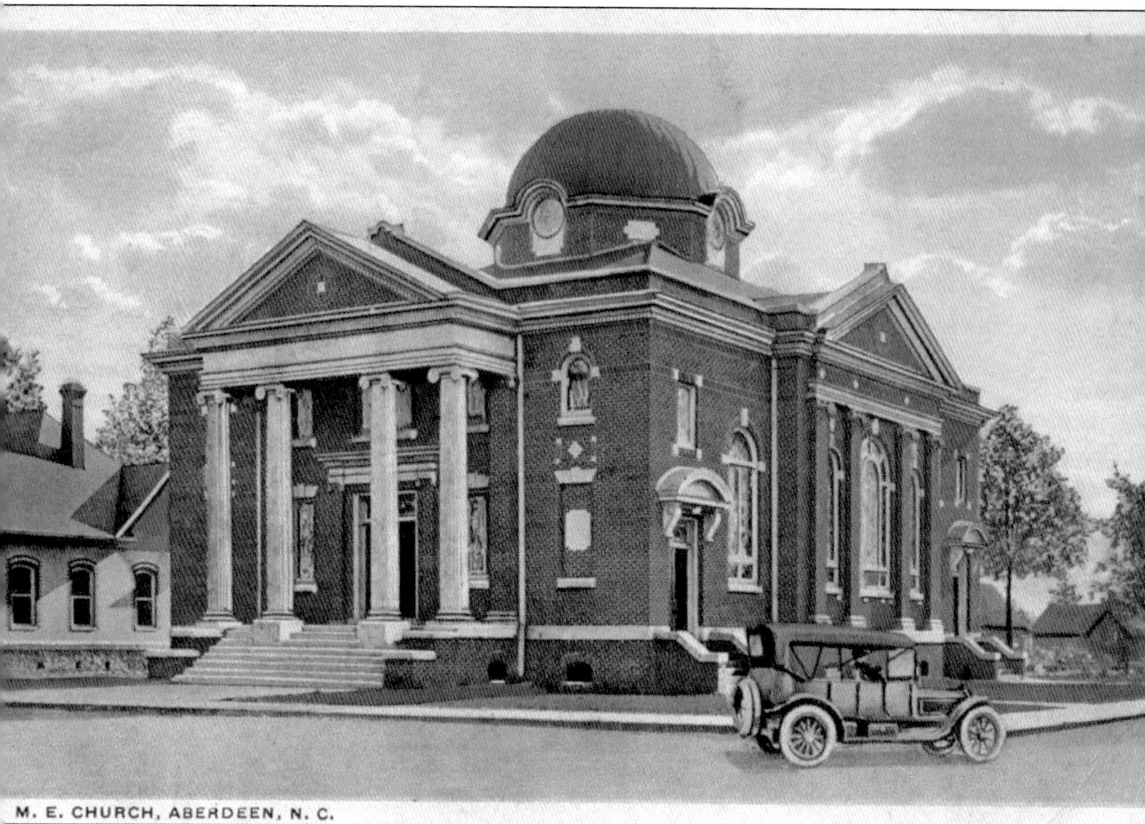

With generous funding provided by the Allison Francis Page family, a new Methodist church was erected on the site of a wooden church built in 1889. The brick Neoclassical Revival sanctuary was designed by noted architect J.M. McMichael and built by T.B. Creel. It was dedicated in 1913 and named Page Memorial Methodist Church. Located on Main Street, it is noted for the four majestic iconic columns, a large lighted dome, and the arched stained-glass windows constructed by the George Hardy Payne Studios of Patterson, New Jersey. (Author's collection.)

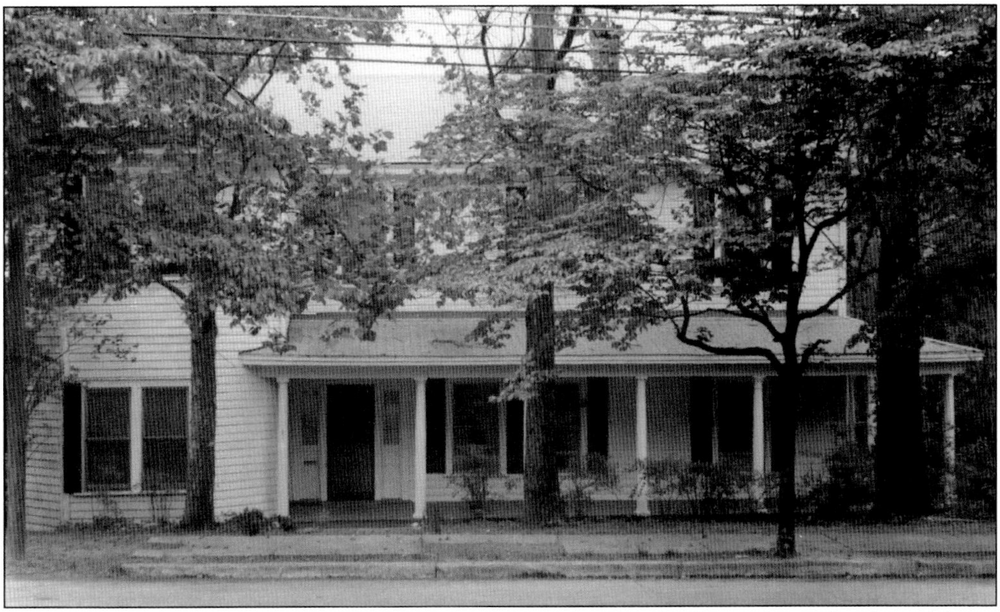

Built in 1891 as the parsonage for the Aberdeen Methodist Church, this traditional L-shaped frame house, with recessed bays spanning a one-story porch supported by Tuscan columns, is located on the corner of Main and Blue Streets. Rev. L.M. Chafin and his family were the first occupants. Later, the house was sold to Bethesda Presbyterian Church and was used as a manse for a number of years. Today, it is a private residence. (Courtesy of Aberdeen Centennial Committee.)

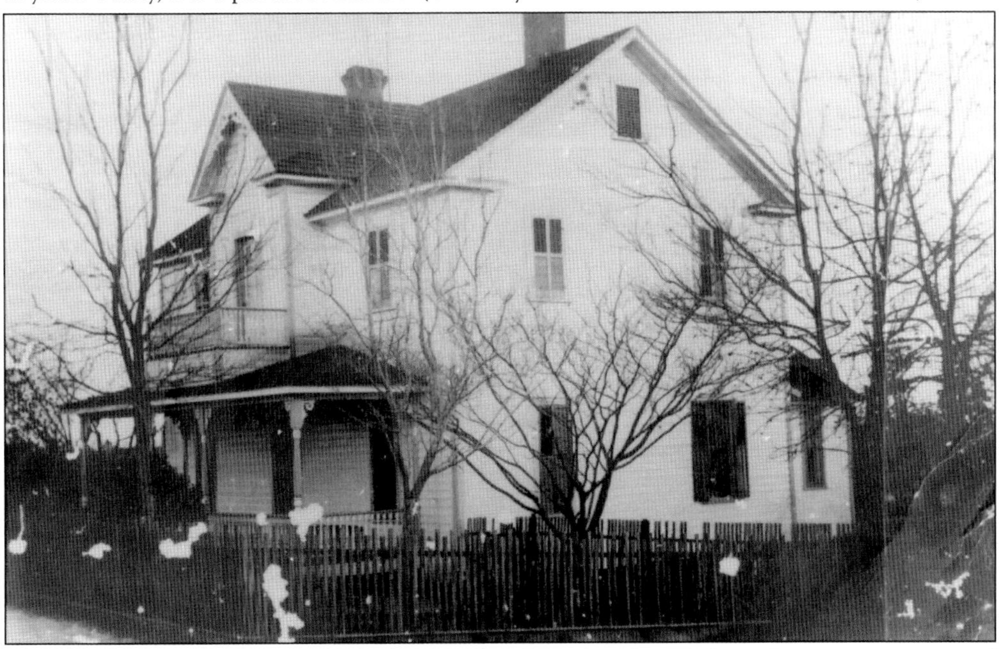

The John B. Graham house was built around 1891 as a one-story frame house on an unpaved Main Street. The second floor was added about 1900, and the porch was later removed. The house is now clad in asbestos siding. Graham was a schoolteacher and banker. Today, it is the residence of John and Harriett Sloan. Sloan is the great-grandson of John Graham. (Courtesy of Aberdeen Centennial Committee.)

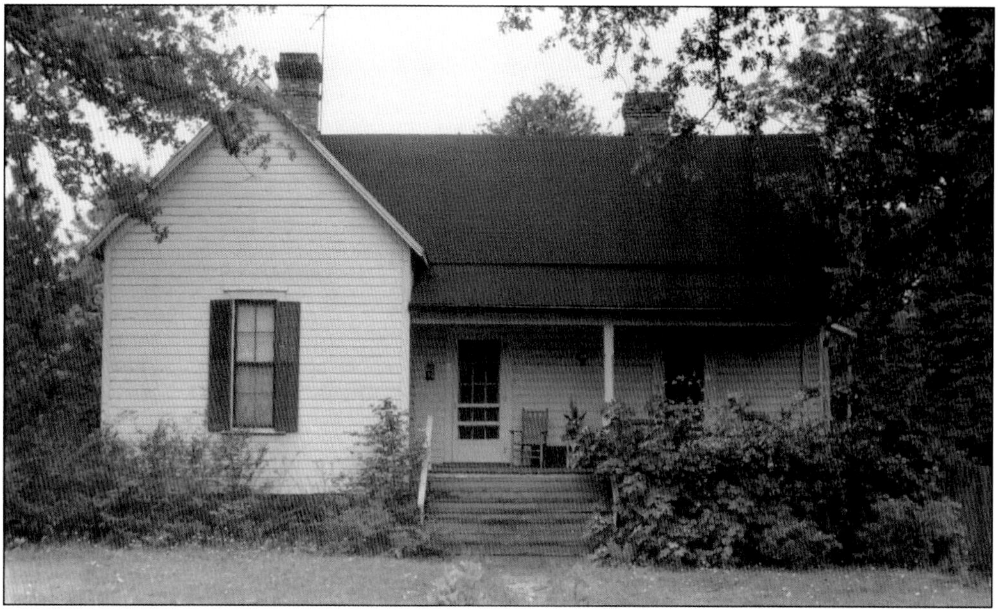

This gable-roofed, T-shaped frame house on East Main Street was built for Dr. Herbert Williams in 1894. In 1922, John Blue purchased it from the Williams estate. The house is within the Aberdeen Historic District. (Courtesy of Aberdeen Centennial Committee.)

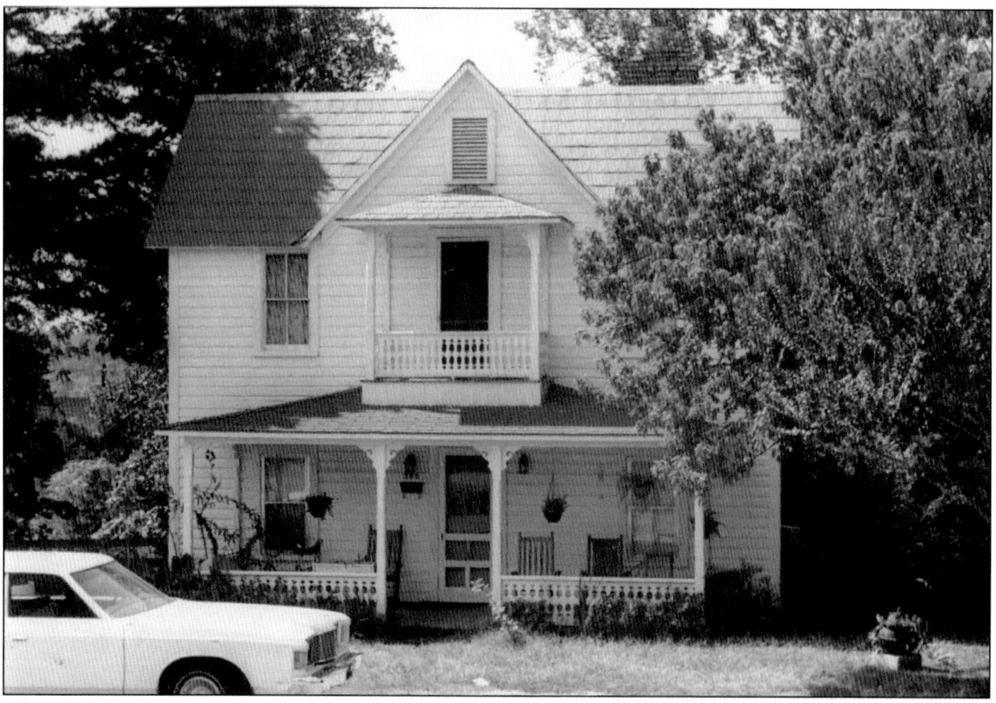

The A.T. McFarland home at 205 North Pine Street was built around 1904 as a traditional gable-roofed frame house. It was originally clad in German siding but is now covered with vinyl. McFarland was one of the first to own an automobile in Aberdeen. As a master mechanic, he operated a garage and sold gasoline at a location on Poplar Street. (Courtesy of Aberdeen Centennial Committee.)

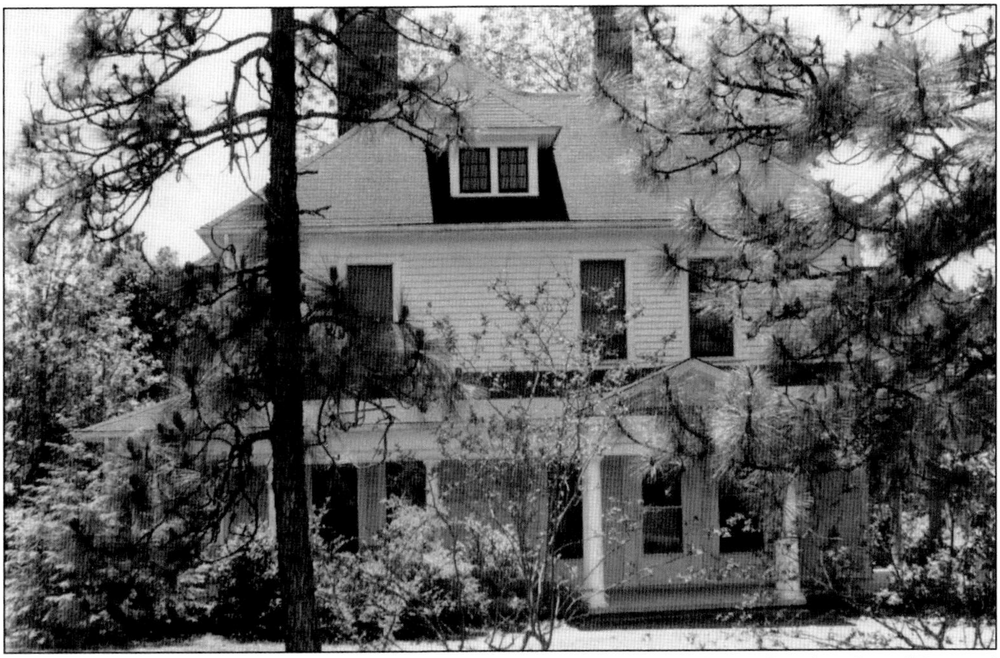

The John Graham house on High Street was built about 1909 in a Classical and Colonial Revival design. Topped with a pyramidal roof, the one-story wraparound porch is supported by Tuscan columns. Graham was an officer with the Bank of Aberdeen, founded in 1904. He also served as chairman of the Moore County Board of Education. The house is in the Aberdeen Historic District. (Courtesy of Aberdeen Centennial Committee.)

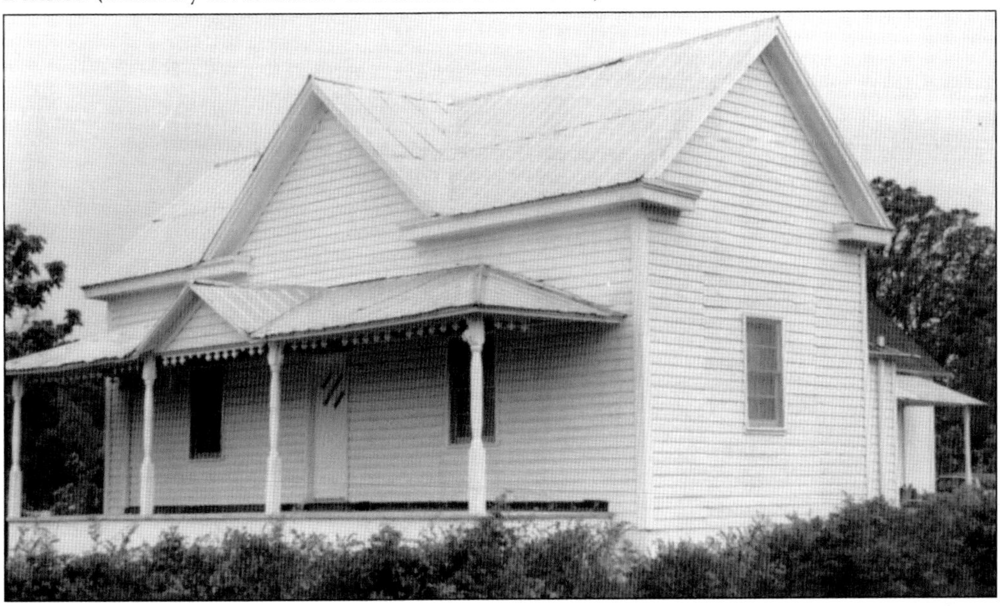

The Furman Yates house was built around 1900 in the French Colonial style. Yates was an employee of the Moore County Railroad, a logging operation that ran from Aberdeen to Craigrownie, an unincorporated community west of town. The house today looks much as it did when constructed after being restored by the Sam Bowden family. It fronts Roseland Road, which was laid on the former track bed of the railroad. (Courtesy of Aberdeen Centennial Committee.)

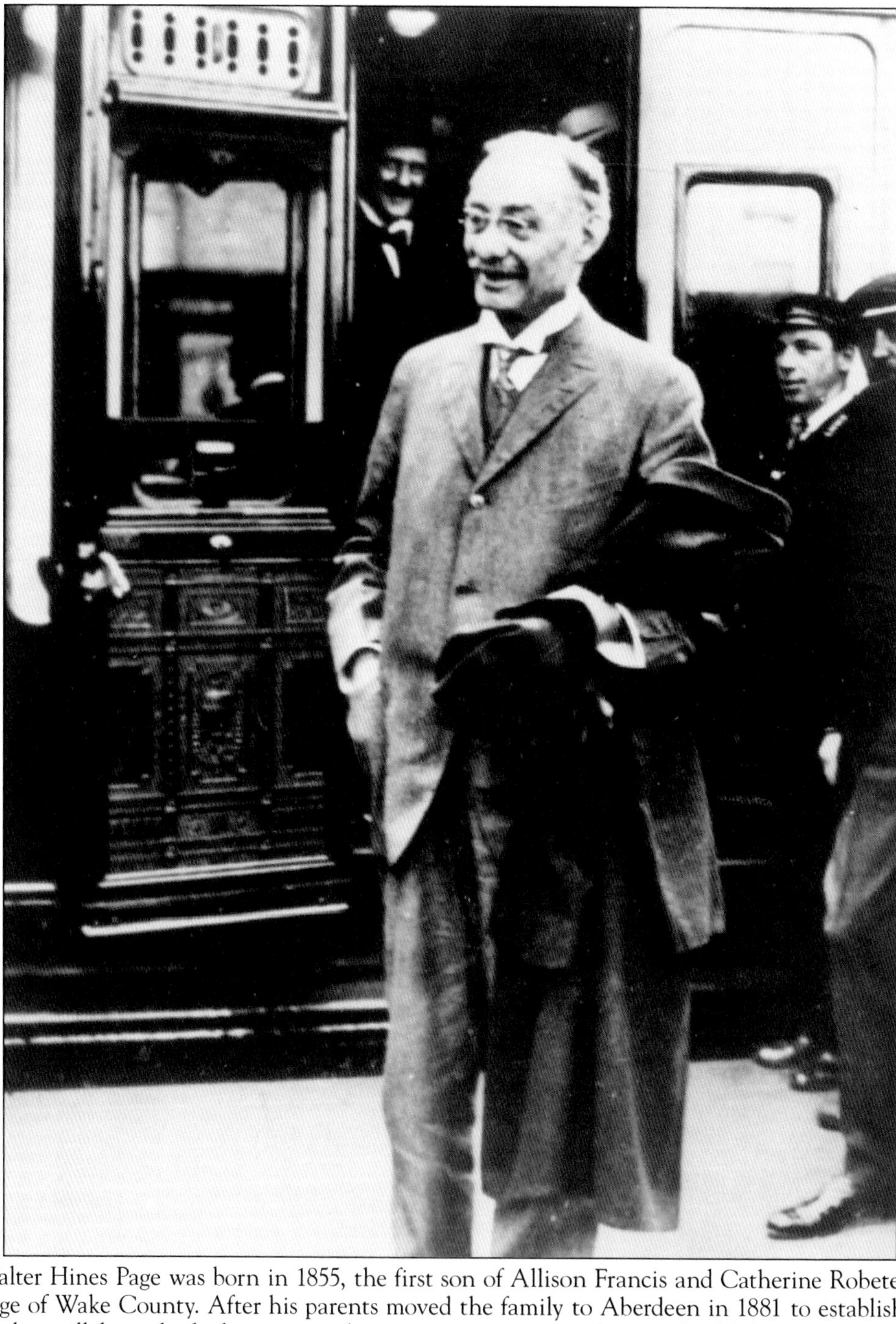

Walter Hines Page was born in 1855, the first son of Allison Francis and Catherine Robeteau Page of Wake County. After his parents moved the family to Aberdeen in 1881 to establish a lumber mill, he embarked on a journalistic career as a writer, editor, and publisher. He took over the prestigious *Atlantic Monthly* in 1898 and in 1900 joined with Frank Doubleday to create the Doubleday, Page, and Company publishing house. In 1913, Pres. Woodrow Wilson appointed him ambassador to the United Kingdom where he served during World War I. Due to declining health, he returned home and passed away in 1918. His funeral was held at Page Methodist Episcopal Church with burial in Bethesda Cemetery. (Courtesy of Aberdeen Centennial Committee.)

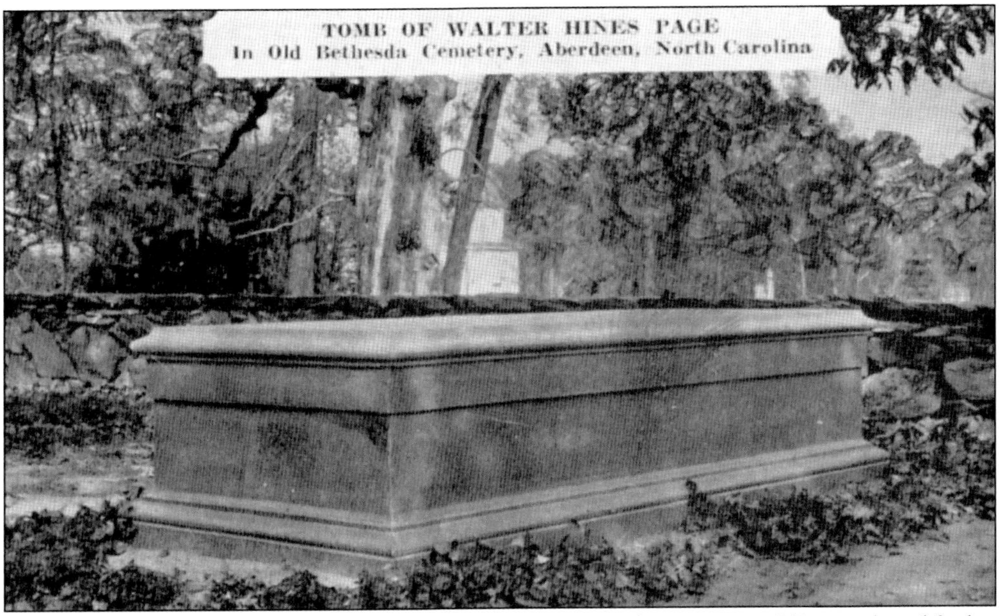

The tomb of Walter Hines Page (1855–1918) is commemorated on a postcard. Remembered for his role as ambassador, he was also known as a proponent of public education and industrialization of the South to overcome the effects of the Civil War. Many dignitaries, local citizens, and the extended Page family attended his funeral and interment in Bethesda Cemetery. (Author's collection.)

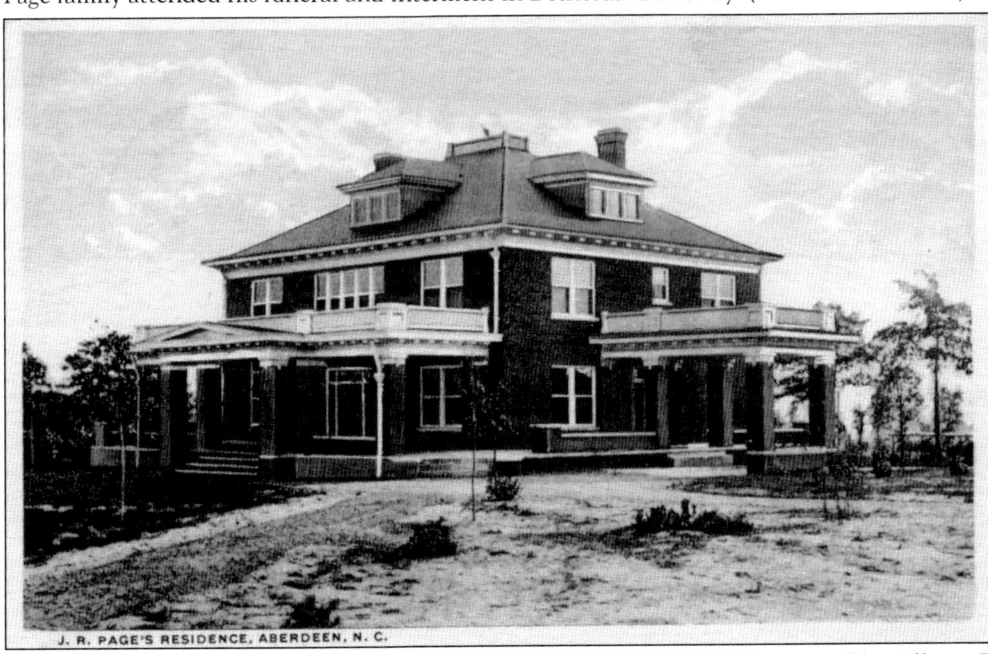

Noted Charlotte, North Carolina, architect J.M. McMichael, who was retained by Allison F. Page to design Page Memorial Methodist Church, designed the Junius R. Page residence. It was constructed around 1913 by T.B. Creel who also built the church. Located on Page Street, this home has many interior features similar to ones found in the church. Page was a banker, farmer, and businessman. Today, the home is a private residence and remains essentially unchanged in a grove of trees overlooking downtown Aberdeen. (Author's collection.)

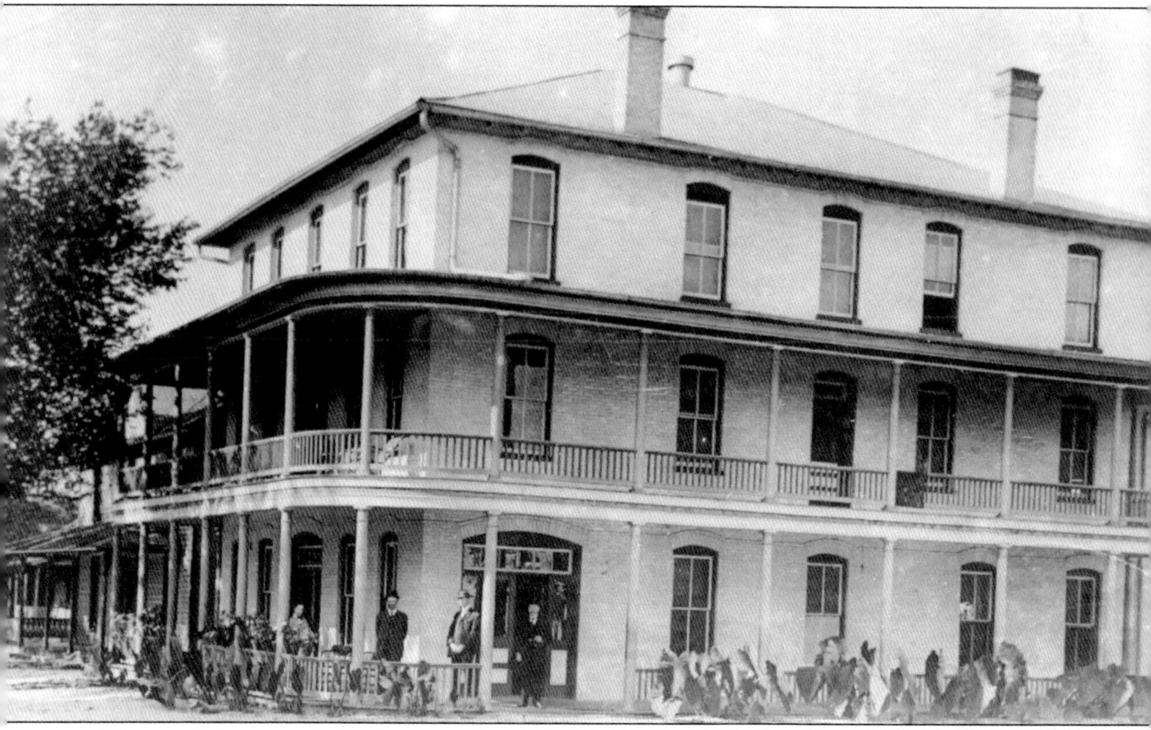

This c. 1920 view of the Aberdeen Hotel includes the wraparound verandas where Aberdeen locals gathered to discuss news of the day. Originally a wooden structure, it was brick veneered by Ralph Leach Sr., who owned and operated the hotel prior to his death. Main Street to the left is unpaved, and large trees can be seen in the background. The hotel burned in 1941 and was rebuilt as the Sandhill Hotel. (Courtesy of Herbert Clifton Blue.)

Two

THE BUILDING YEARS

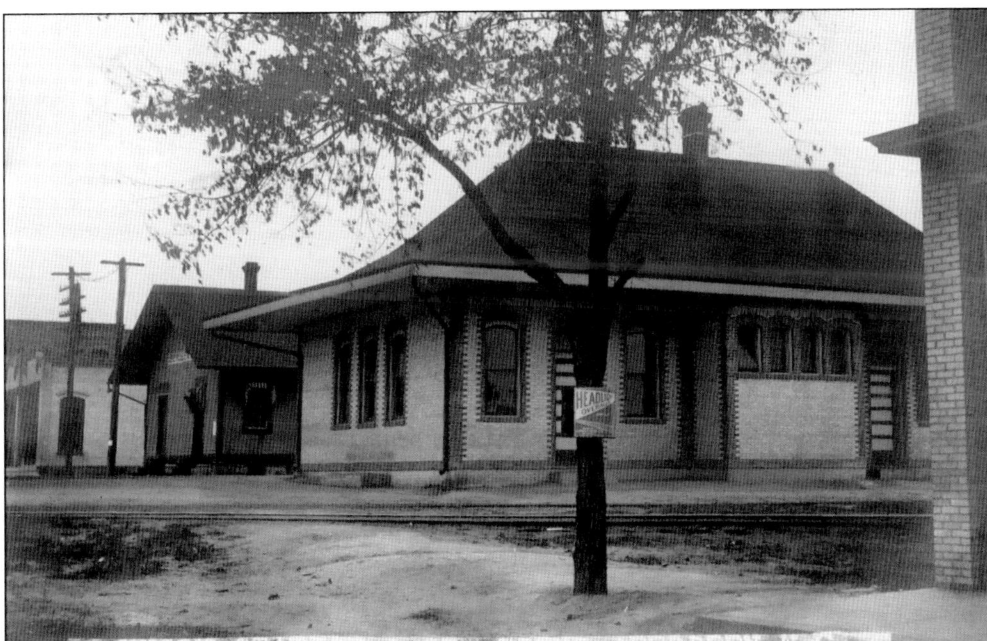

An early penny postcard view of Main Street, looking east, shows Union Station (right) and a partial view of the original Raleigh & Augusta Railroad station. Aberdeen's first telegraph office was located in the R&A Railroad depot. Main Street is unpaved, and Sycamore Street has yet to be built connecting Main and South Streets. The wooden depot would later be the Seaboard Air Line Railway offices. It was torn down in the 1950s. A sign advertising Headlight Overalls has been nailed to a tree in the middle of the street. The overalls company made denim work clothes and advertised them to railroad and factory workers. Founded in 1884, the Sarnia Woolen Mills Company was located in Ontario, Canada. The Larned, Carter, and Company of Detroit, Michigan, sold the brand. (Author's collection.)

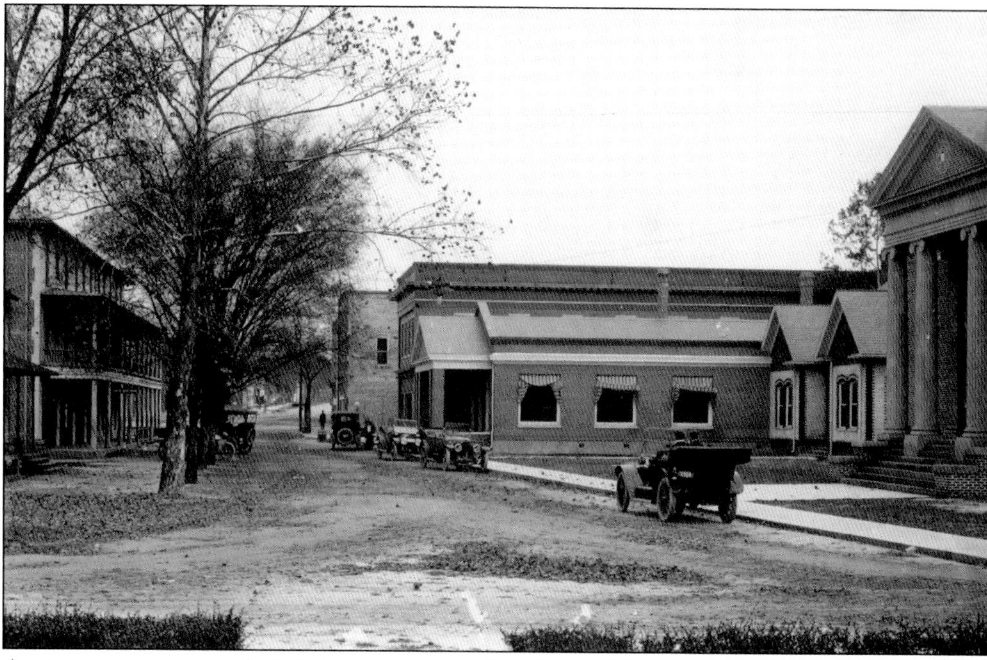

A wintery scene around 1915 shows a dirt road in the middle of town with automobiles parked along the curb in front of Page Memorial Methodist Church and Page Trust Company farther down the road. Photographed from the steps of Page Memorial Library, the Aberdeen Hotel can be seen to the left of the trees. Viewed from the same location in the early 1930s, Main Street has been paved and the trees removed. The one-story brick building on the right was erected in 1920 between the Keith Building and Aberdeen Hardware Building that closed an alleyway. The building was originally used as an automobile dealership and is a fabric and millinery shop today. (Both, author's collection.)

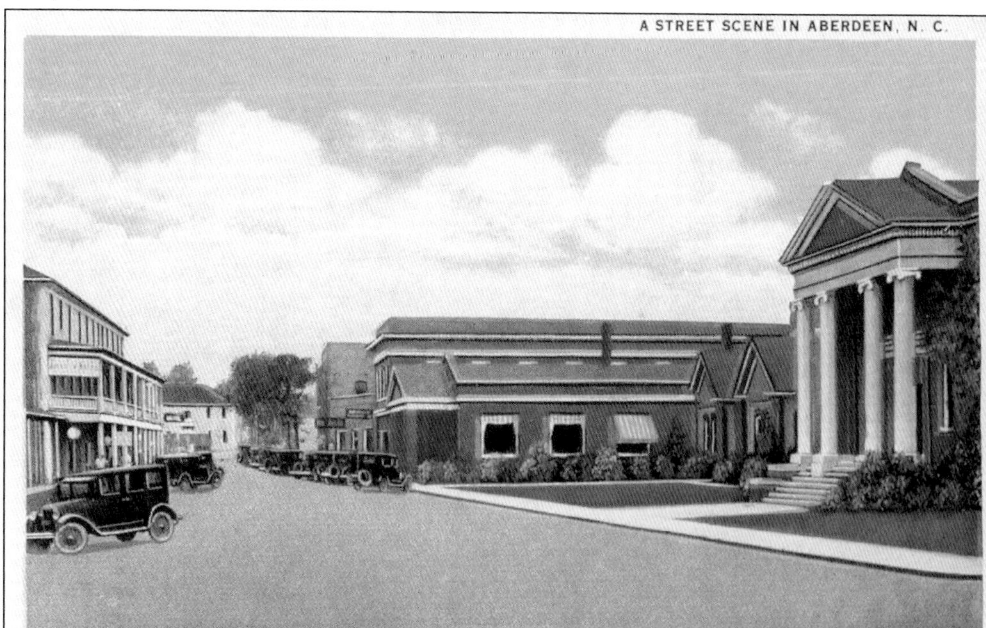

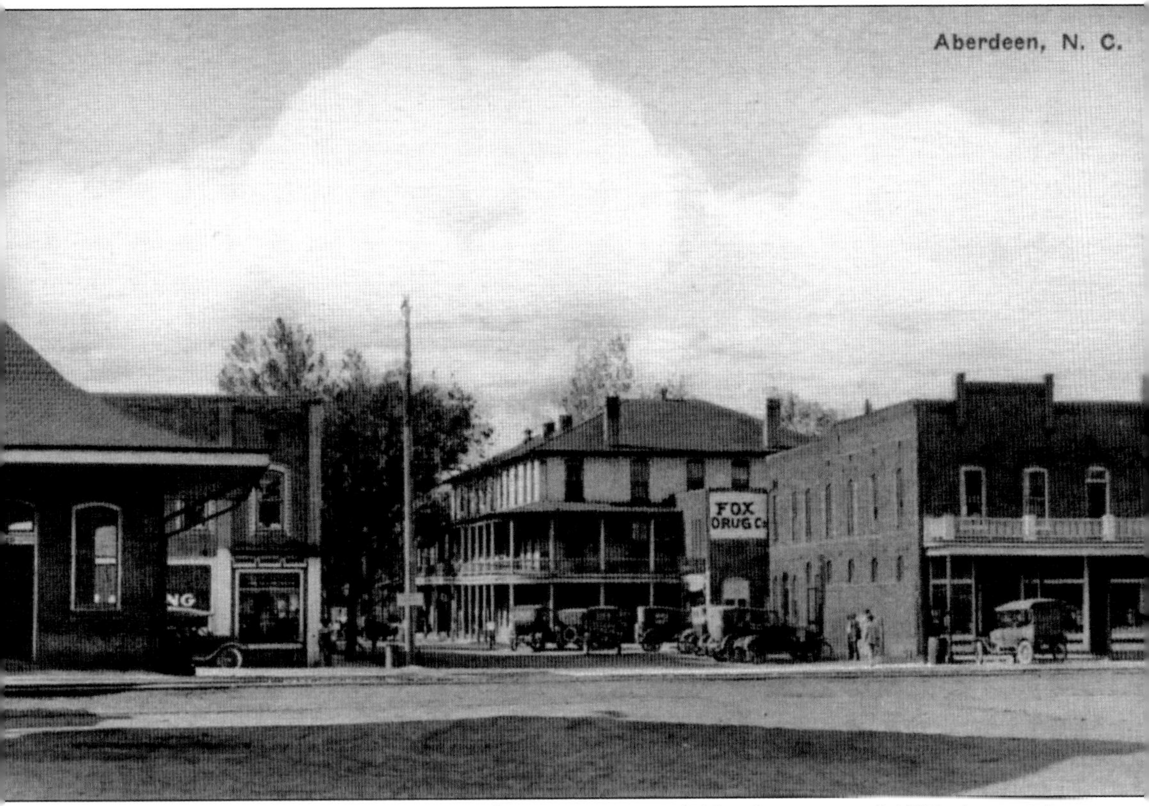

A penny postcard depicts a prosperous downtown view of Aberdeen around 1930. A partial view of Union Station is on the left, and the five-sided Eva Page Building is seen behind the station. The Farrell Building is seen on the right with the Fox Drug company located in the hotel annex next door to the Aberdeen Hotel. This postcard, sold in many locations in town, was originally in black and white but was hand colored, giving the impression of a color photograph. (Author's collection.)

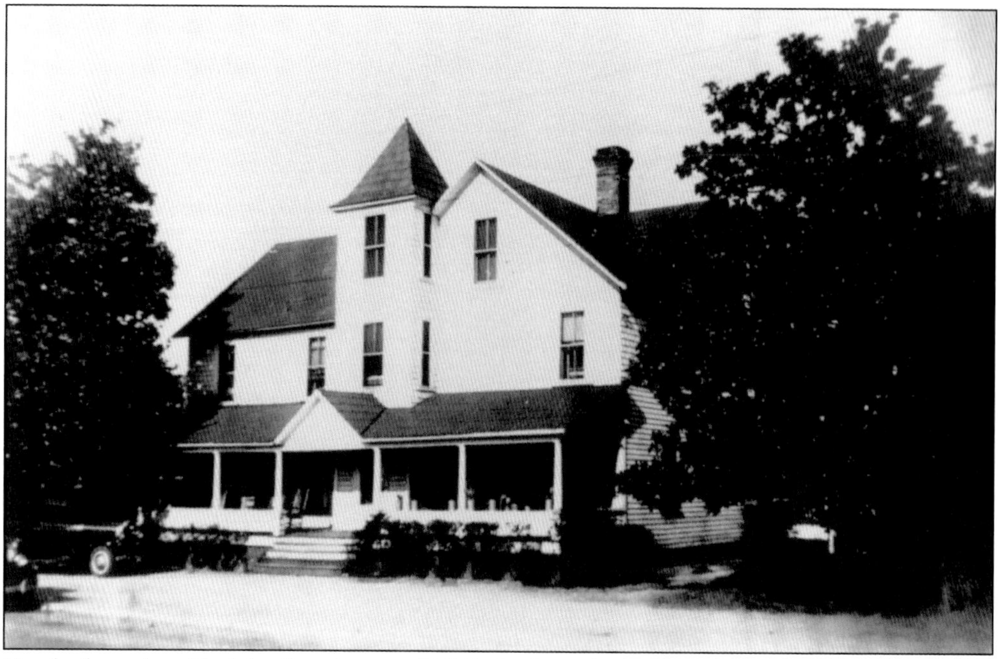

First built as a hotel by John Powell around 1895, this large frame house located on North Sycamore Street was later the home of Dr. Alexander Bethune. Run as a boardinghouse for many years by Maggie Lewis, it also served as a teacherage for single schoolteachers. Torn down in the 1960s, the site is now a grocery store and parking lot. (Courtesy of Aberdeen Centennial Committee.)

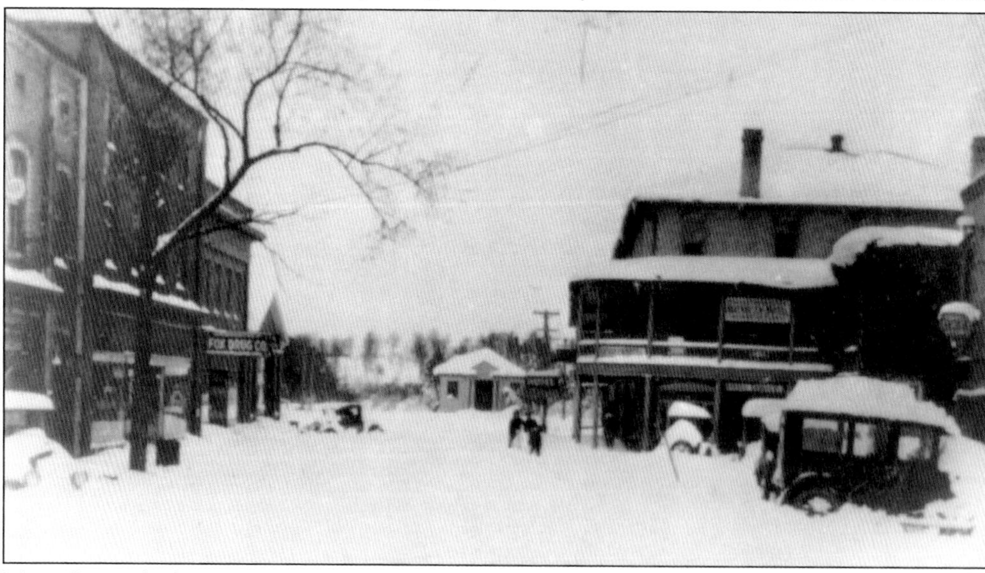

Main Street, looking east, is seen under a record snowfall from a March 2, 1927, winter storm that dumped over 26 inches on Aberdeen and the Sandhills. The accumulations brought road and rail traffic to a halt for several days, stranding tourists in the local hotels and bringing all commerce to a halt. James Bushway, visiting from New Jersey, and local resident Helen Huggins were driving south of town when their automobile became snowbound. Attempting to seek shelter for the night, they tried to walk back to Aberdeen but were found the next day having perished in the snow. (Courtesy of Aberdeen Centennial Committee.)

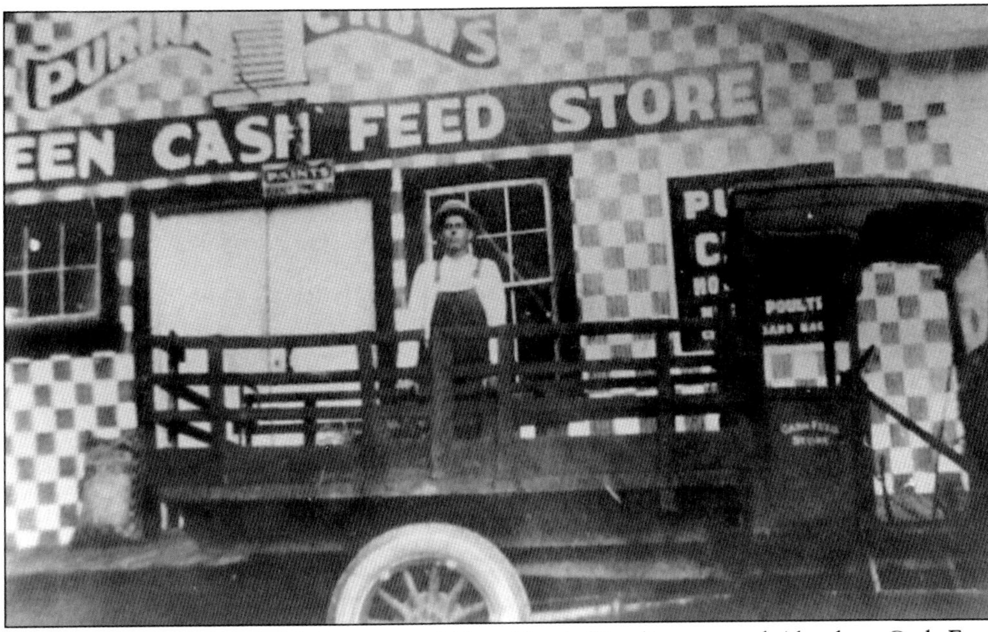

In the early 1930s, Dunk McCrimmon of Vass, North Carolina, started Aberdeen Cash Feed Store at the corner of Knight and Sycamore Streets. It was later named Aberdeen Supply, and Emerson Oldham ran the business after World War II. Peter Vuncannon has been the proprietor since taking over the business in the 1970s. Today, it is well known for supplying hay to the large equine communities surrounding Aberdeen. (Courtesy of Aberdeen Centennial Committee.)

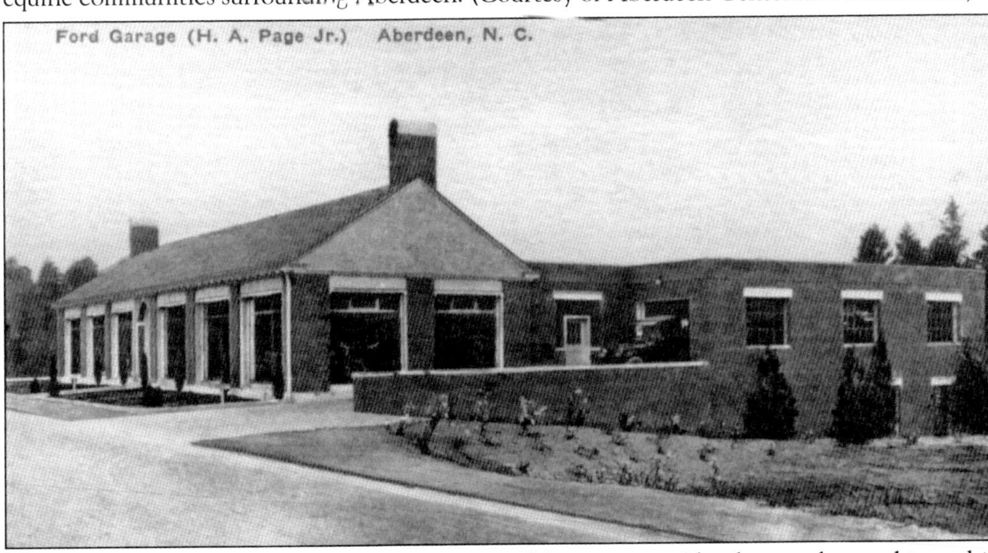

Henry A. Page Jr. sold Ford automobiles at several locations in Aberdeen and moved into this Colonial-style building in the early 1930s where the Pinebluff and Pinehurst Roads crossed Aberdeen Creek. The showroom and offices were on ground level with the road, and the rear was two stories for automobile repair and storage. The style of architecture reflected many of the buildings constructed by the Page families in Aberdeen. After his death, Page's dealership was owned in partnership with Mrs. Henry Page, Make Pleasants, and Ralph Leach. The dealership closed in the 1970s, and the building was demolished. The site was later filled to street level and today is a used vehicle sales lot. (Author's collection.)

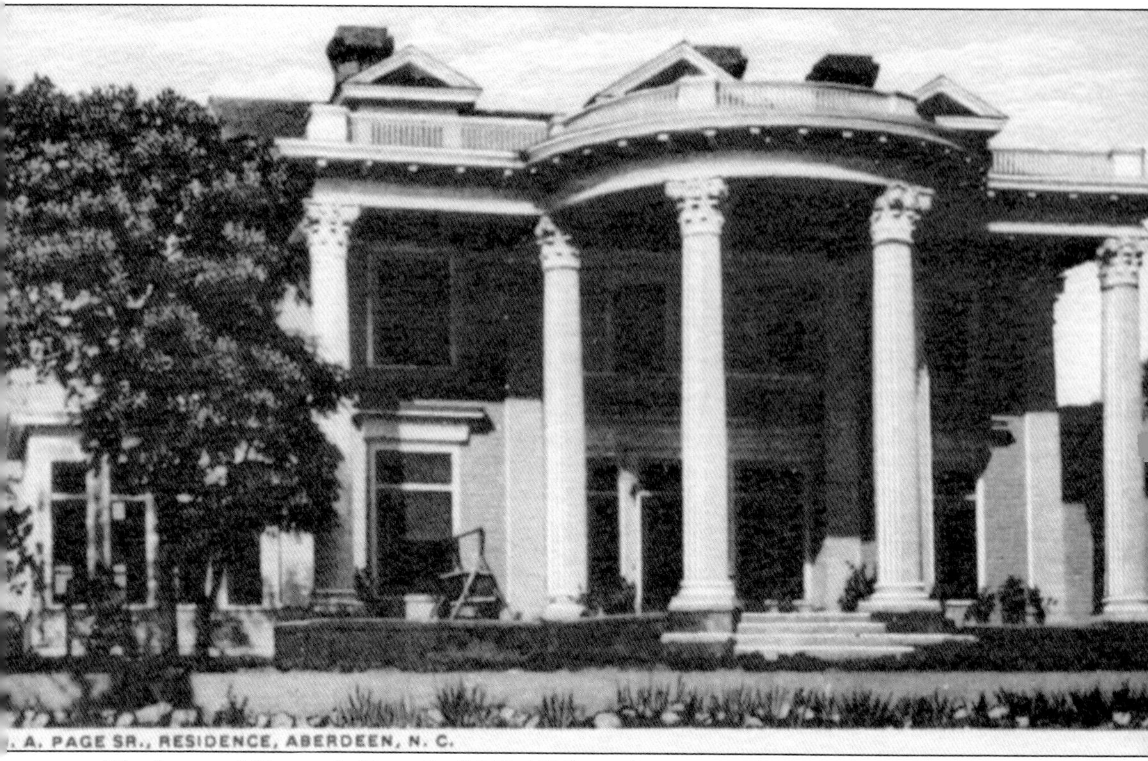

The home of Henry A. Page Sr. (1862–1935), with its magnificent columned portico, held a dominating view overlooking Aberdeen. Built about 1889, the house displayed the wealth and sophistication of the Page families in early Aberdeen. As many as 11 homes associated with the family were built on the west side of town above Aberdeen Lake on what was known as Page Hill. Henry Page was a member of the North Carolina House of Representatives, serving from 1913 to 1919. The house was destroyed by fire in the 1960s. (Courtesy of Moore County Historical Society.)

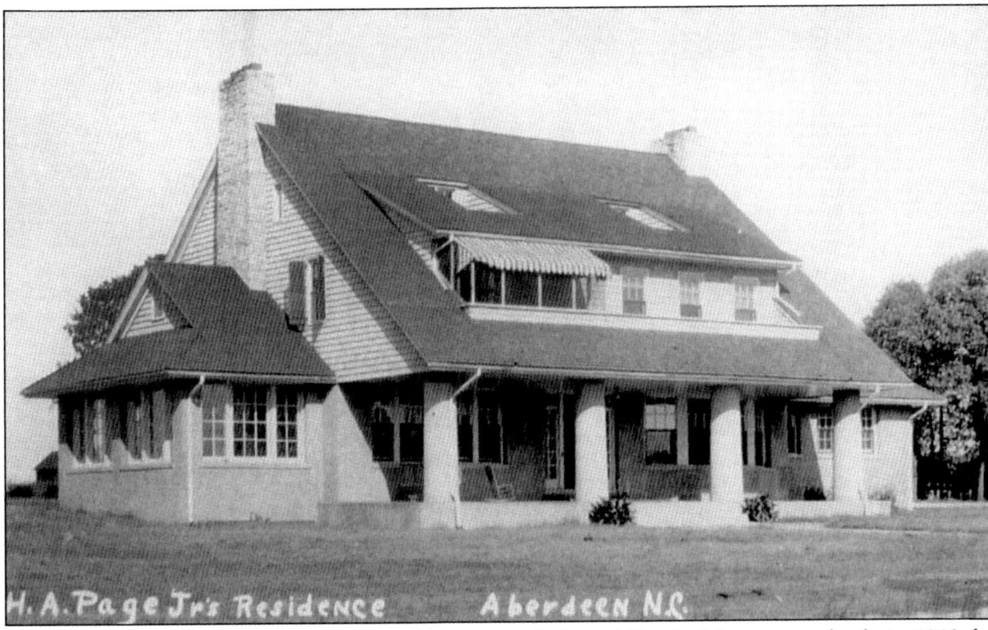

Designed by architect Arthur Keene, this unique Colonial Revival home was built in 1912 for the H.A. Page Jr. family. Page was a businessman who owned the Ford automobile dealership in Aberdeen. The house was operated as a bed-and-breakfast after being sold by the Page family. Today, this fine example of an early Aberdeen home is restored and is a private residence located on Page Street. (Author's collection.)

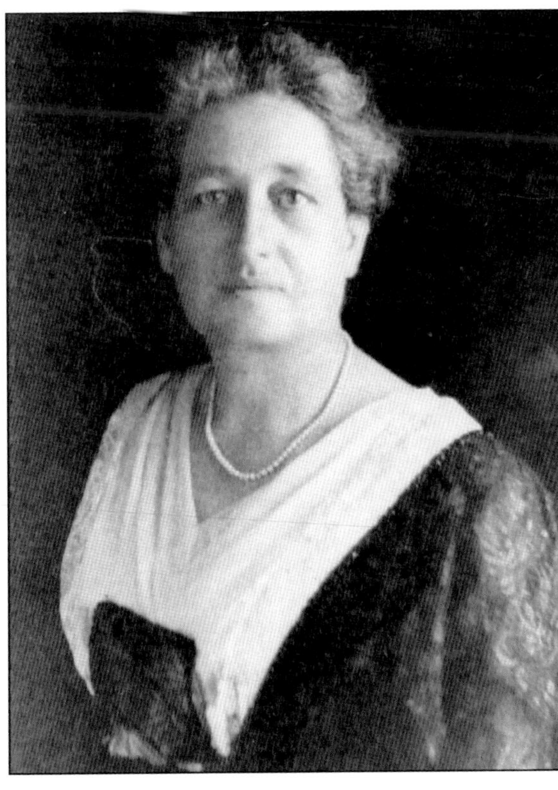
One of eight children born to Allison Francis and Catherine Robeteau Page, Mary E. Page (1869–1961) was a historian and philanthropist. She and her family moved to present-day Aberdeen from Cary, North Carolina, in 1891. Shortly after arrival, she wrote an essay chronicling her trip and her new surroundings in what would become Aberdeen. She donated funds for the construction of Page Memorial Library in honor of her parents; in 1952, she wrote a history of Page Memorial Methodist Church. (Courtesy of Aberdeen Centennial Committee.)

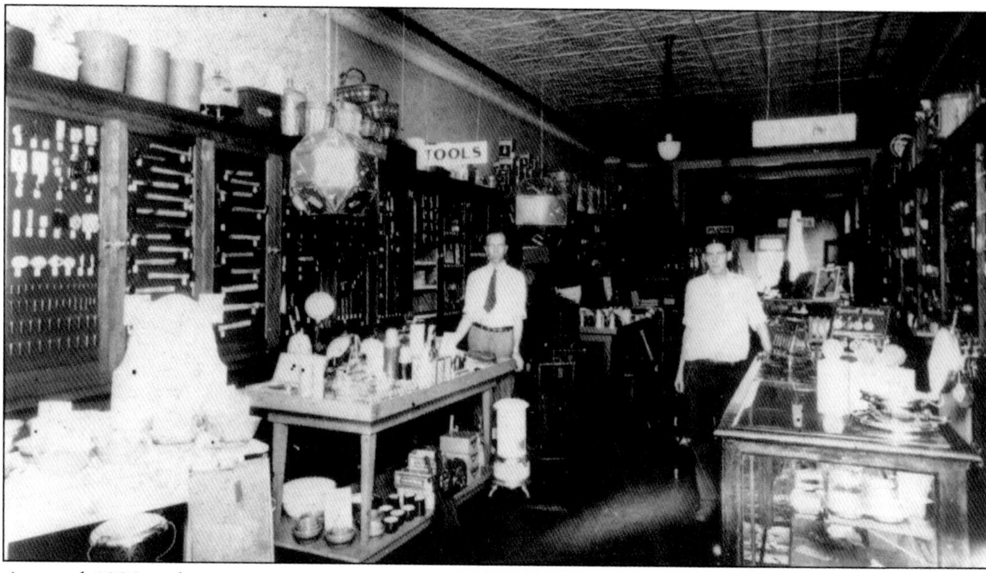

Around 1920, salesmen await customers in Aberdeen Hardware, located at 111 Main Street. Originally named North Carolina Hardware when it opened in 1912, it was later called Aberdeen Hardware and managed by John Dunk McLean, who was a major stockholder for many years. Today, the interior looks virtually unchanged and is home to an upscale home furnishings and gift store named for the store address. (Courtesy of Aberdeen Centennial Committee.)

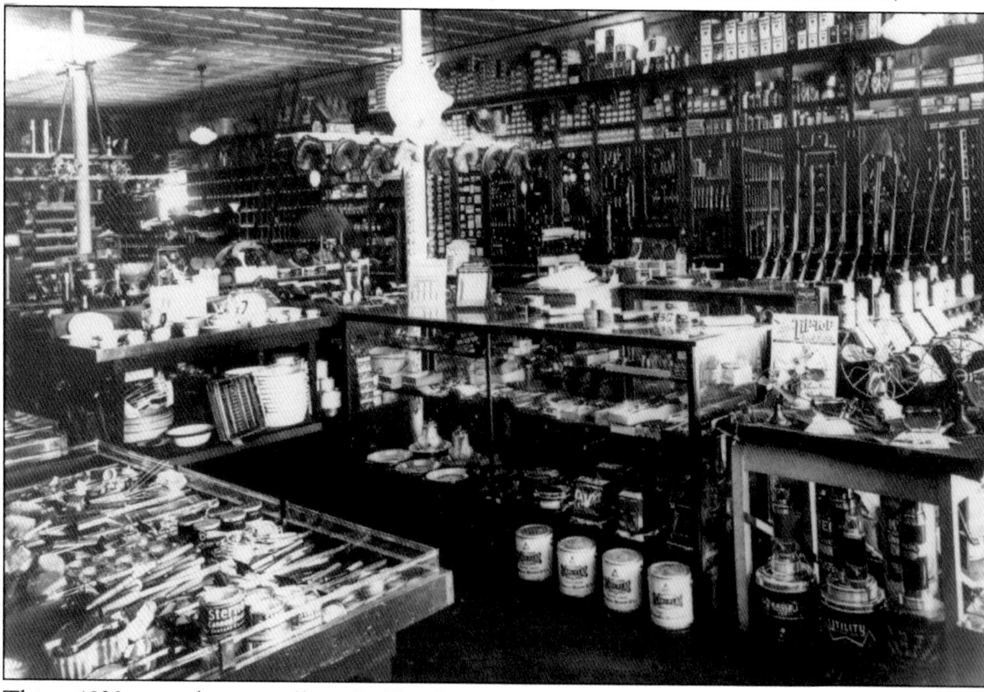
This c. 1930 scene shows a well-stocked hardware store. Burney Hardware, located on South Street, was built by A.L. Burney in 1925 and was the second hardware store to open in Aberdeen. The hardware store was later owned by J.C. Robbins who successfully ran the business for many years before selling it to the S.R. Ransdale family. In 1989, the business was moved to a new location south of town. (Courtesy of Aberdeen Centennial Committee.)

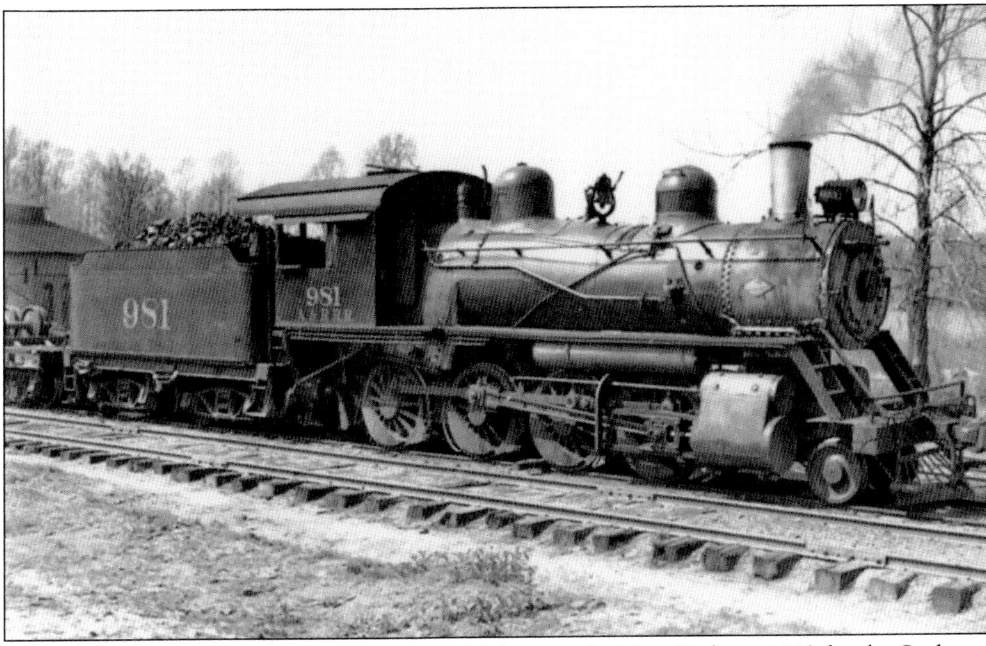

Built by American Locomotive Company of Schenectady, New York, in 1903 for the Seaboard Air Line Railway and numbered 981, this engine was sold to the Aberdeen & Rockfish Railroad in 1941 and renumbered 45. It is seen near the engine workshops with the original Seaboard Air Line Railway numbers and the Aberdeen & Rockfish Railroad logo painted on the cab of the locomotive. (Author's collection.)

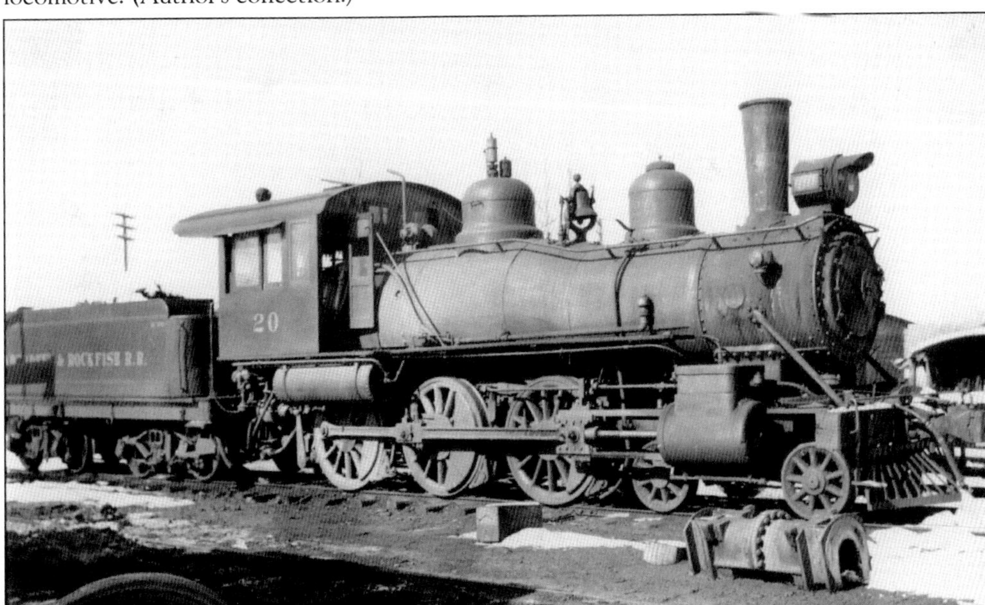

Aberdeen & Rockfish Railroad No. 20 is stopped in front of the railroad workshops. Baldwin Locomotive Works of Philadelphia, Pennsylvania, built this engine in 1913. It operated with the Aberdeen & Rockfish Railroad until it was sold in 1937. The railroad continued operating steam locomotives between Aberdeen, Raeford, and Fayetteville, North Carolina, until the late 1940s. (Author's collection.)

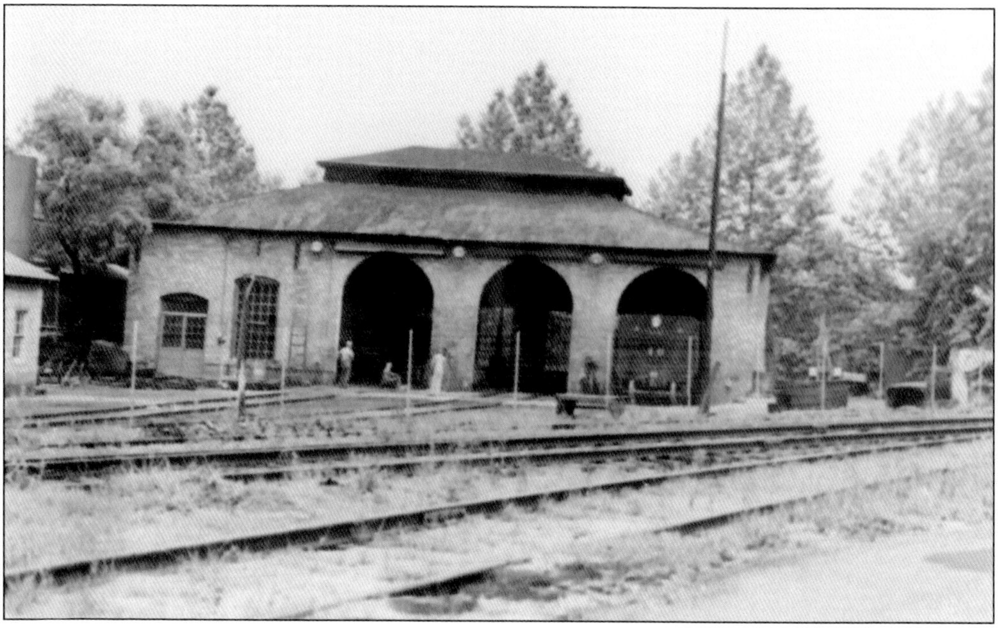

The Aberdeen & Rockfish Railroad engine house and workshops on Fayetteville Street were built in 1913 to service the steam engines of the era. The change to diesel locomotives beginning in 1947 required converting the facility to diesel maintenance. The shop is in continuous use today. (Courtesy of Aberdeen Centennial Committee.)

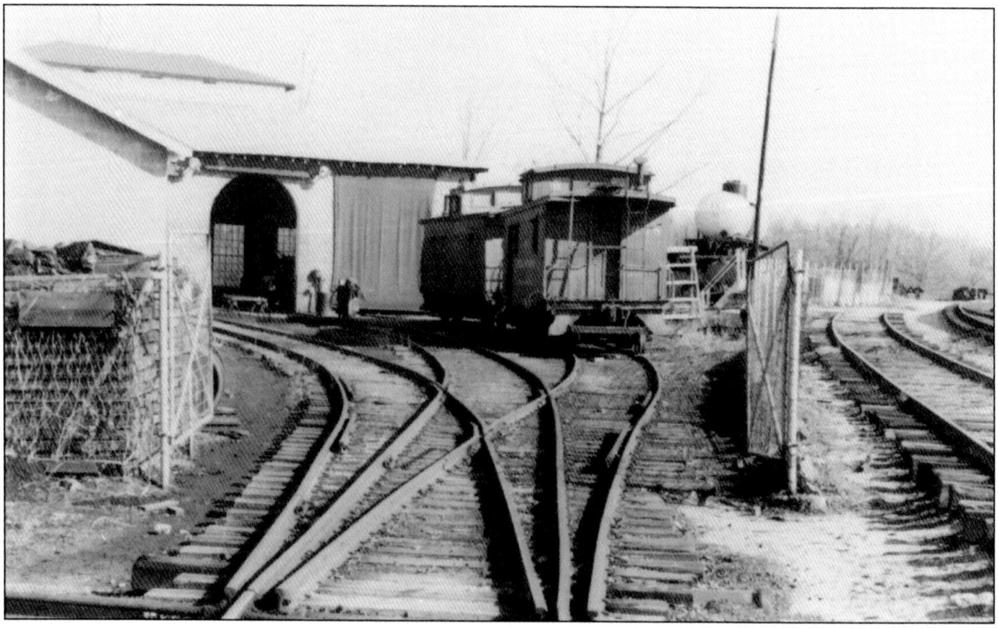

In the foreground is the famous triple switch leading to the maintenance bays of the Aberdeen & Rockfish Railroad engine house. Looking east, the track on the right is the main line between Aberdeen and Fayetteville, North Carolina. Known as the Bethesda grade, the track climbs a 2.5-percent gradient, the steepest on the line, before descending to a gradual leveling of the tracks to Raeford, North Carolina. Wooden cabooses can be seen parked on a siding next to the building. (Courtesy of Aberdeen Centennial Committee.)

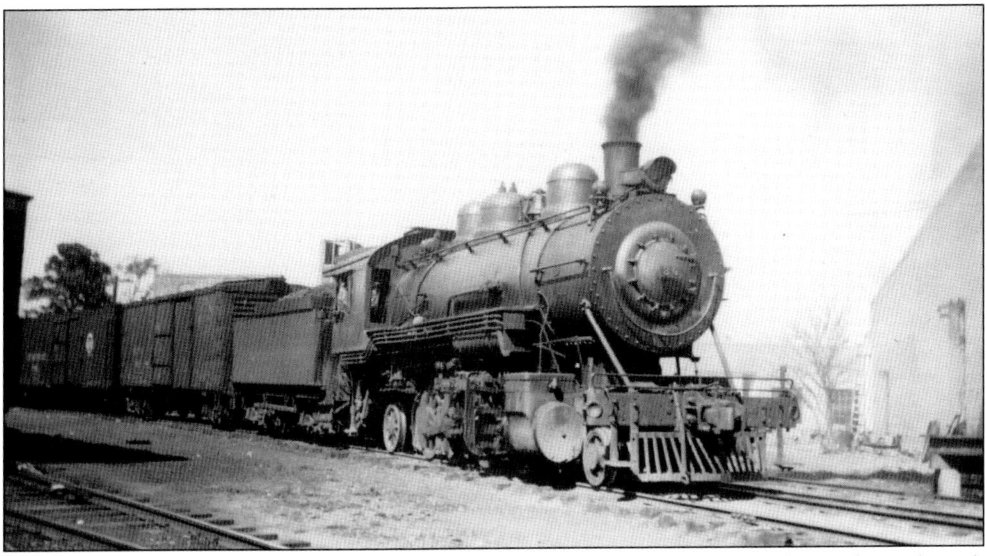

Aberdeen & Rockfish Railroad No. 30, with a mixed train, prepares to leave the rail yard. Built by the Baldwin Locomotive Works of Philadelphia, Pennsylvania, in 1929, it pulled freight to and from Fayetteville, North Carolina, until it was sold in 1948. By 1950, the last of the steam engines operated by the railroad were phased out in favor of more efficient diesel locomotives. (Author's collection.)

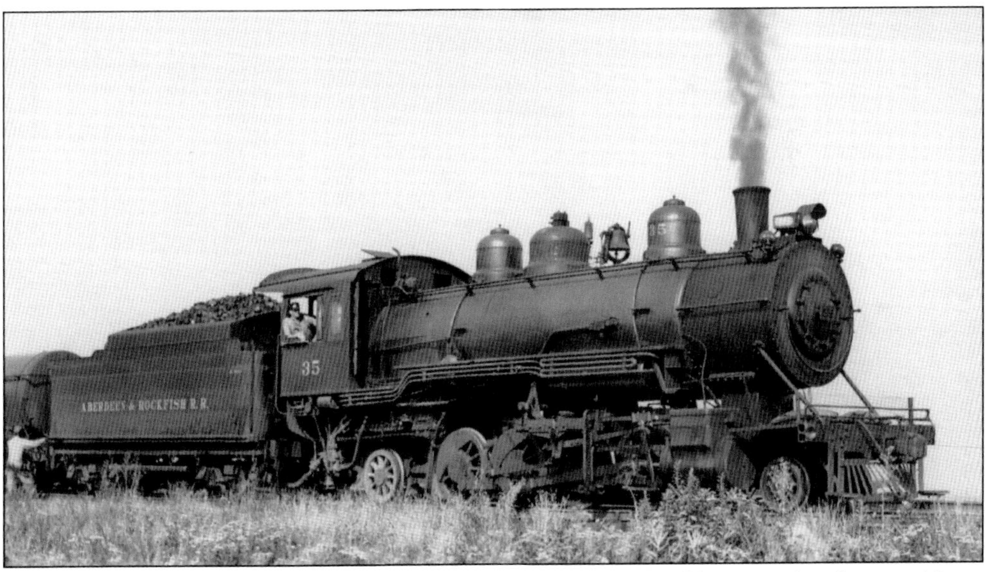

Built by Baldwin Locomotive Works of Philadelphia in 1922, No. 35 operated with several lines before being acquired by Aberdeen & Rockfish Railroad in 1929. Engineer Joe Marks alternated between this engine and No. 30 on daily runs to Raeford and Fayetteville, North Carolina. It was sold in 1948 as the railroad was entering the diesel locomotive age. (Author's collection.)

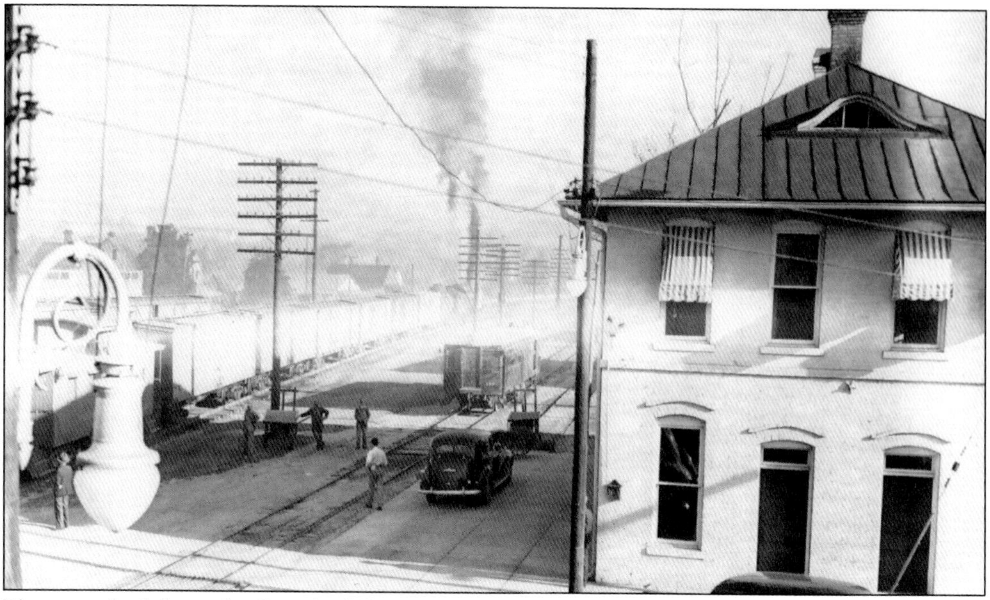

Photographed from the Standard Store across Main Street around 1935, a northbound steam engine begins the hard pull of a freight train up the steep gradient from Aberdeen to Southern Pines, North Carolina. This change in elevation between the neighboring towns was the greatest encountered on the entire length of the Seaboard Air Line Railway. A pusher engine would often be added to the rear to assist getting the trains up the hill. Parked on tracks in front of the Aberdeen & Rockfish Railroad offices is a jitney awaiting passengers and mail. (Courtesy of John Blue.)

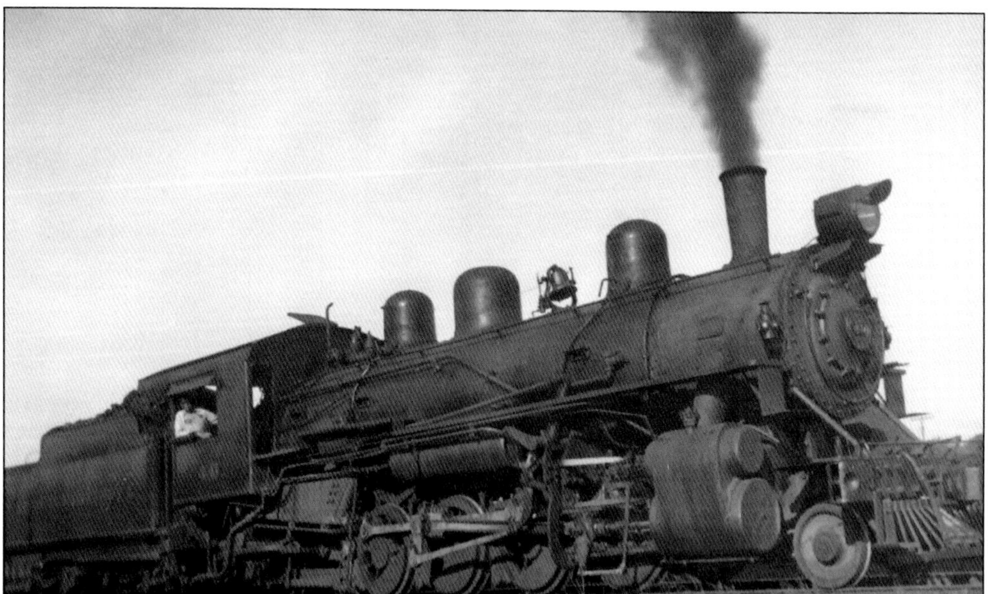

Aberdeen & Rockfish Railroad No. 40 was built by the American Locomotive Company of Schenectady, New York, in 1920 and acquired in 1935. It operated with the railroad until 1950. After years in storage, it was sold in 1974 to Valley Railroad in Connecticut. After a restoration by the new owners, it operates as an excursion train on the railroad. (Author's collection.)

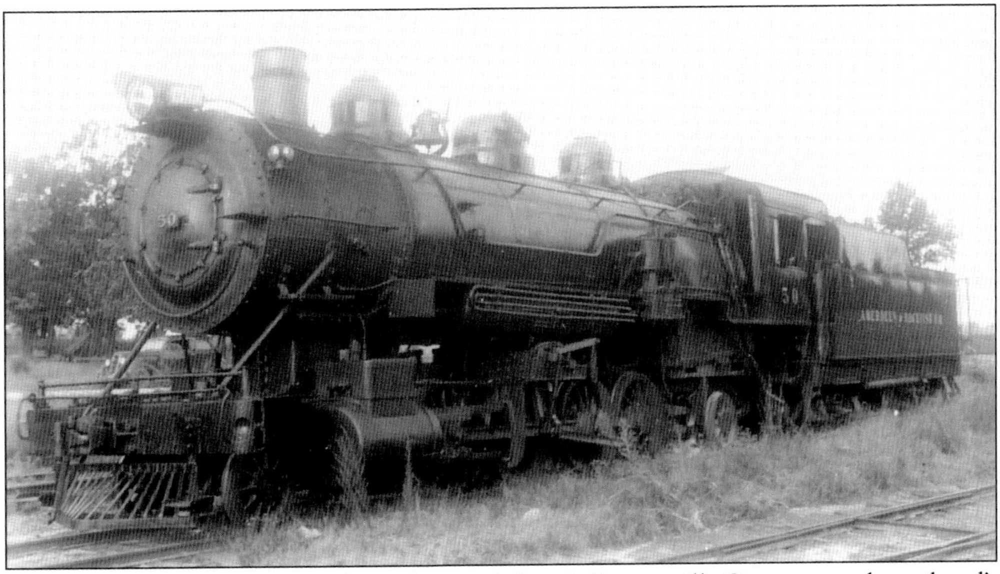

Aberdeen & Rockfish Railroad No. 50 stands beside Fayetteville Street near the railroad's workshops. Built by Baldwin Locomotive Works of Philadelphia, Pennsylvania, in 1917, it was on the roster from 1941 to 1960. It was used to transfer freight from the main line of the Seaboard Air Line Railway in Aberdeen to the main line of the Atlantic Coast Line Railroad in Fayetteville, North Carolina. No. 50 was the last operational steam engine used by the Aberdeen & Rockfish Railroad before the railroad converted to diesel engines. (Author's collection.)

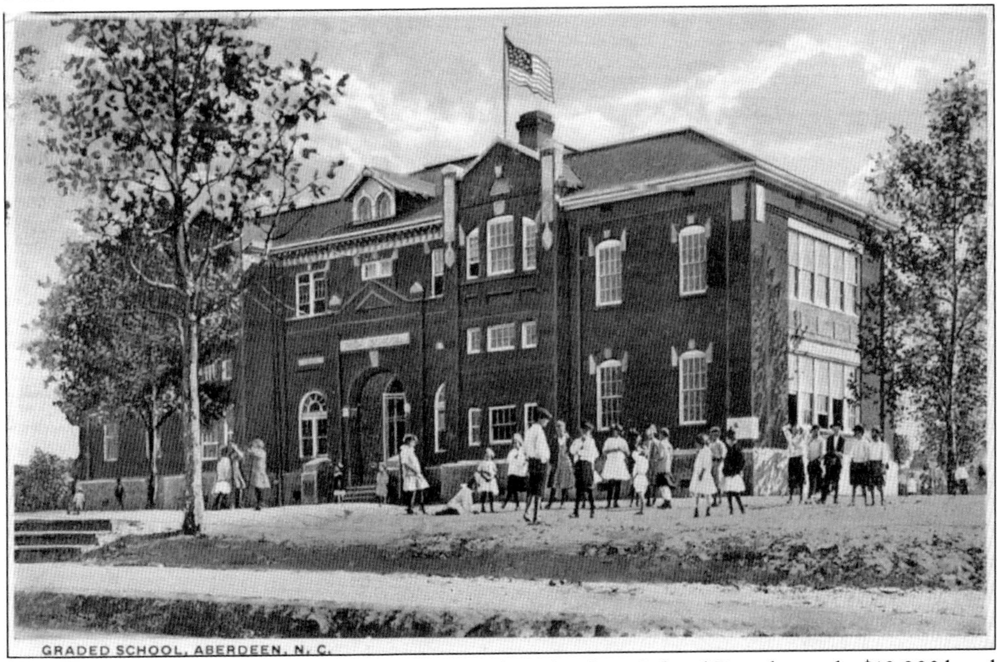

In 1913, to accommodate a growing population, the Aberdeen School Board issued a $12,000 bond for construction of a new two-story brick graded school to replace a wooden school on the corner of Pine and High Streets. It later served as Aberdeen High School and was an elementary school when destroyed by fire in 1949. The school was not rebuilt, and a new elementary school was constructed between West Elm and Montford Streets. (Courtesy of Aberdeen Centennial Committee.)

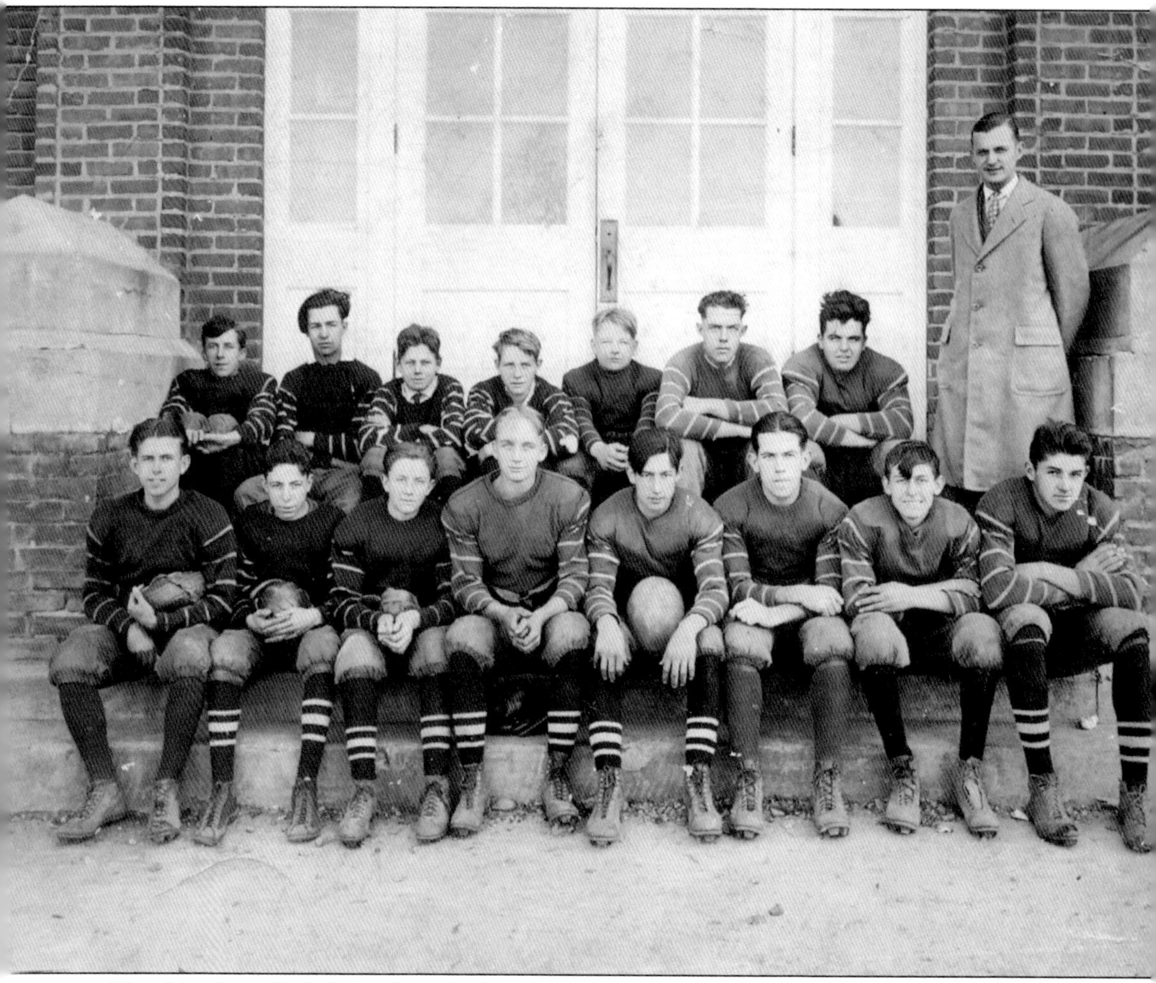

The Aberdeen High School football team poses in preparation for the 1925 season. The team was led by coach Dennis Cooke, and the players' positions were as follows: quarterback, Tom Johnston; center, John Melvin; fullback, Buck Tarlton; halfbacks, Robert Farrell and Ralph Gibson; tackles, Preston Stancil and Carl Gibson; guards, Clyde Cameron, Nicholas Ogelsby, Watson Thomas, and Leroy Johnson; and ends, Purvis Ferree, Ralph Caldwell, and Dannie Matthews. (Author's collection.)

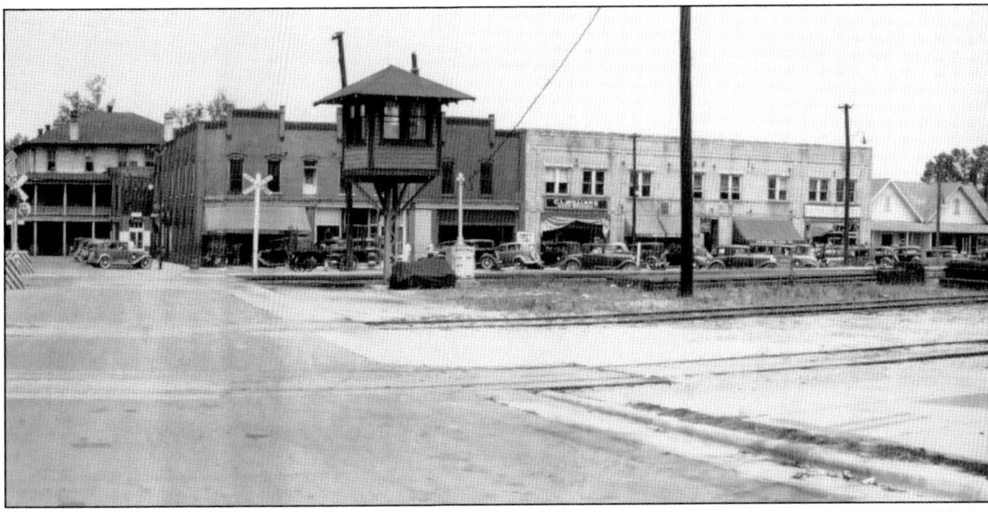

Sycamore Street is viewed from East Main Street on a sunny July day in 1936. The buildings in view are, from left to right, the Aberdeen Hotel, the Farrell Building, the Gichner-Johnson Building, and two wooden structures that would be torn down the following year and replaced with two single-story brick buildings. In the foreground is a switch and signal tower between the Seaboard Air Line Railway and the Norfolk & Southern Railroad tracks. The tower was manned daily to signal approaching trains and provide switching information in the rail yard. The wooden tower was removed in the 1950s and remote signaling poles were installed. (Courtesy of Forrest Lockey.)

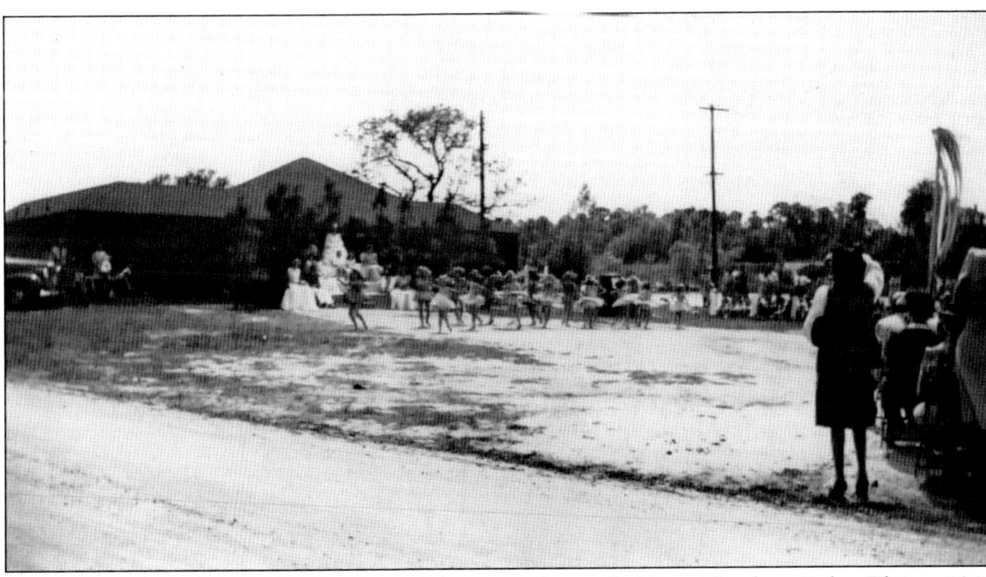

On the first day of May, the winding of the maypole was held at Aberdeen Lake. This c. 1940 maypole scene celebrates the welcome arrival of spring and would attract local residents and the parents of the young performers. A stage was erected beside the lake bathhouse with thrones for the May Day king and queen, selected from local schoolchildren. A group of boys would wind the streamers walking to the right, and a group of girls would walk to the left and intertwine the ribbons until they met at the pole. This event was held for more the three decades, ending in the 1950s. (Courtesy of John Blue.)

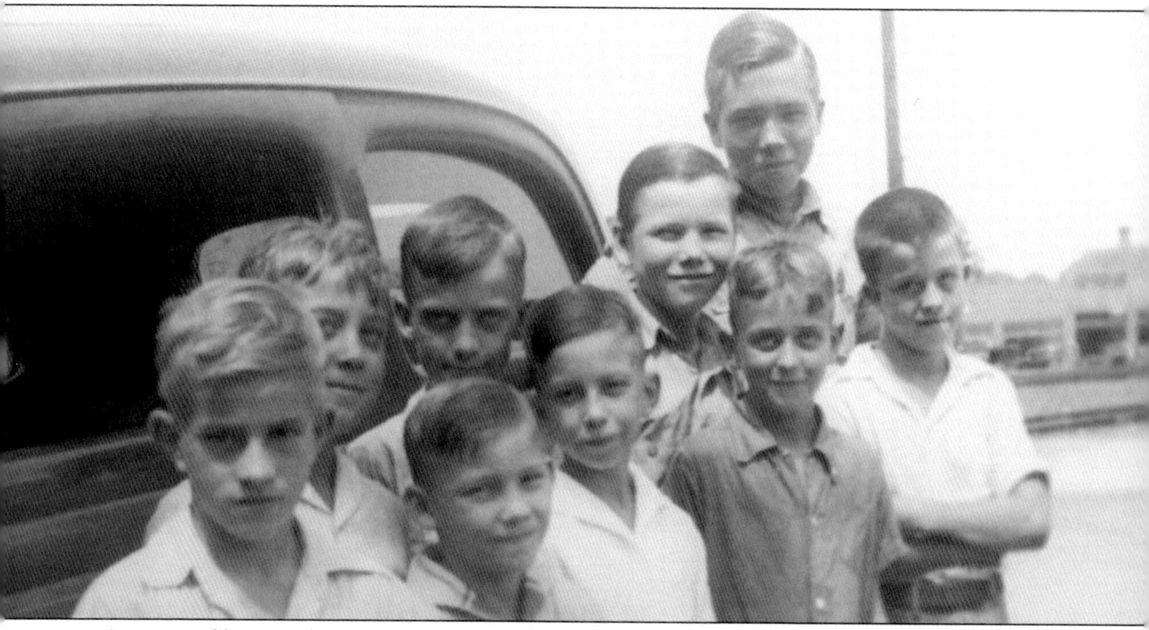

A group of boys gather for a picture in this c. 1937 summertime scene standing outside of the *Sandhill Citizen* newspaper office on Main Street. From left to right are (first row) Miller Cameron, Walter Wright, George Wright, Ed Wicker, and Hughie Cameron; (second row) Mack Wicker, Thad Marks, Curtis McInnis, and Jack McInnis. The editor of the newspaper, H. Clifton Blue, took the photograph. Buildings on Sycamore Street can be seen in the background. (Courtesy of John Blue.)

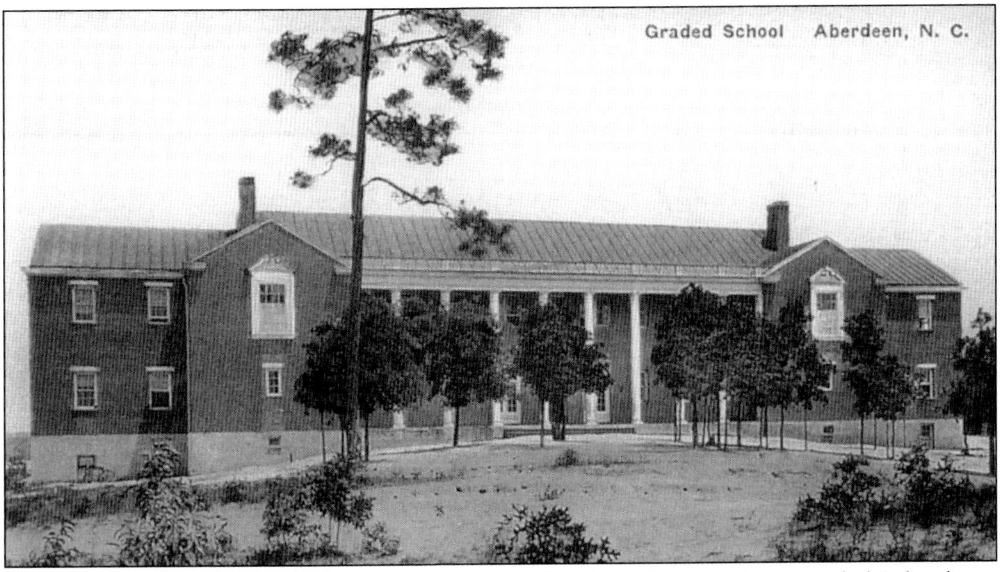

Built in 1922 from funds received from the sale of local bonds, Aberdeen Graded School was located on land known as the wolf pit on the northwest side of town. Originally built for grades one through seven, it became the high school when the high school on Pine Street became the elementary school. In 1941, a "gymnatorium" was added to the north side of the building. A new grammar school, cafeteria, and gymnasium were constructed adjacent to the building in 1951 with an auditorium being erected in 1957. Aberdeen High School was integrated in 1965 and closed and demolished in 1969 upon completion of a county consolidated high school. The Red Devils boasted of state championships in football in 1956 and 1965 and girls' state basketball in 1953. (Courtesy of Aberdeen High School Museum.)

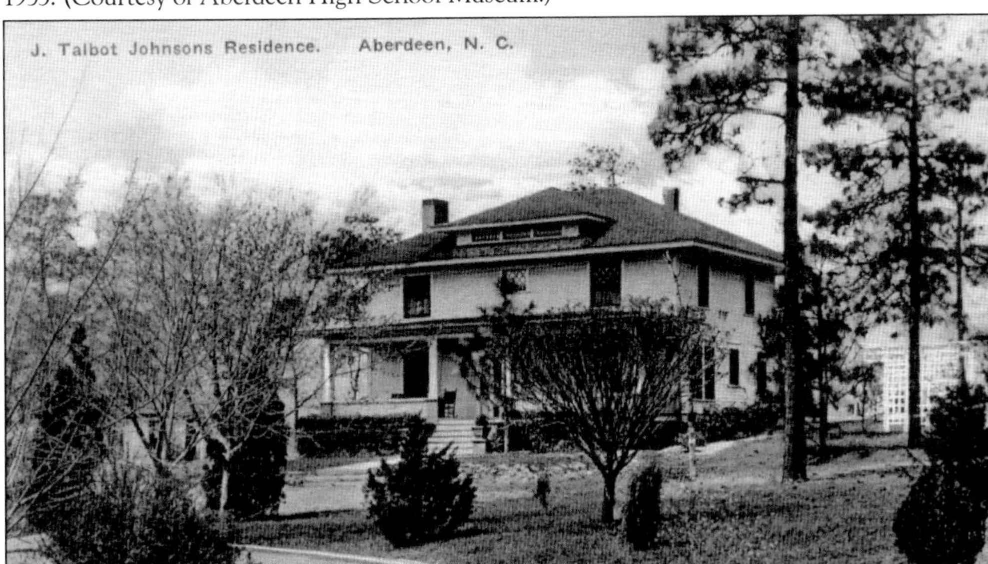

Pictured on a penny postcard is the home of the James Talbot Johnson family. Located on a rise above Poplar Street, this traditional two-story frame house has a one-story covered porch on the front elevation with a curved driveway leading from the street. James was a civil attorney practicing law with the Johnson and Johnson law firm in Aberdeen. The front portion of the yard abutting Poplar Street was later sold to create a church parking lot. (Author's collection.)

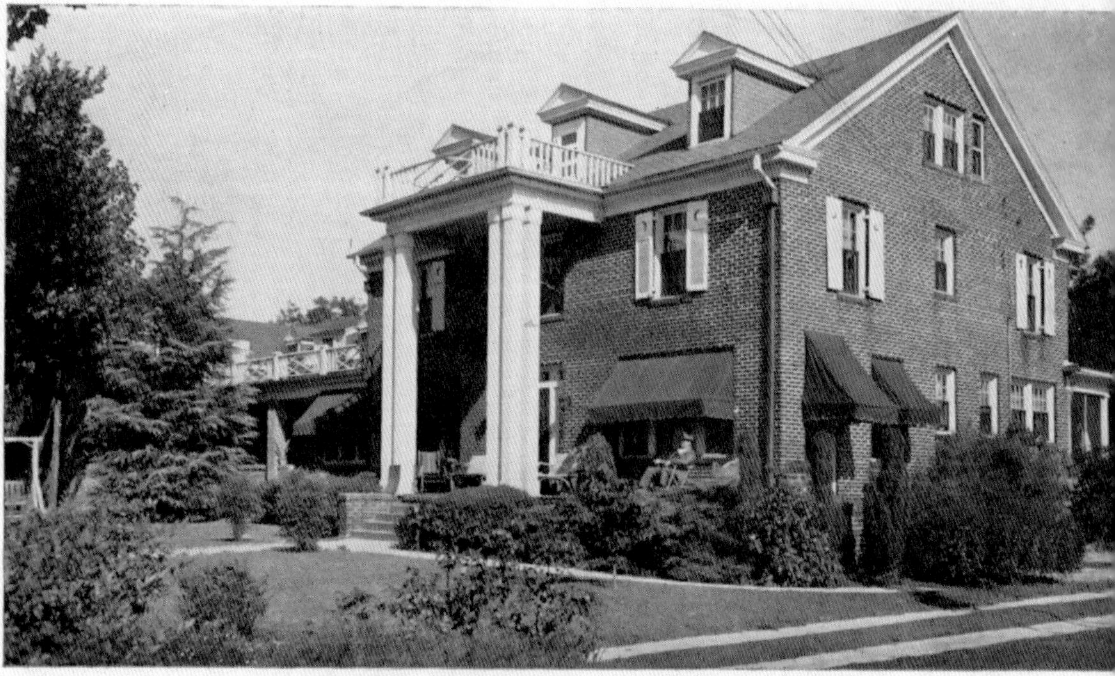

LLOYD HALL INN, ABERDEEN, NORTH CAROLINA
A completely fireproof, modern Inn of 22 rooms, located on U. S. Highway No. 1, convenient to Pinehurs
Golfing and other winter sports. Rates reasonable. Dial 9201
Mrs. R. G. Farrell, Box 43, Aberdeen, North Carolina.

Minnie Lloyd Farrell built this handsome brick-veneered Colonial Revival house in 1922. Located on North Poplar Street, formerly Highway 1, and known as Lloyd Hall, it was operated as a 22-room tourist home for travelers passing through town. After the highway was relocated in the 1940s, it was sold and used as rental property. Acquired in 1989 by Dr. Aziz and Sarah Ahmad, the building was extensively restored and the rooms were converted to condominiums. Today, it looks much as it did when built. (Author's collection.)

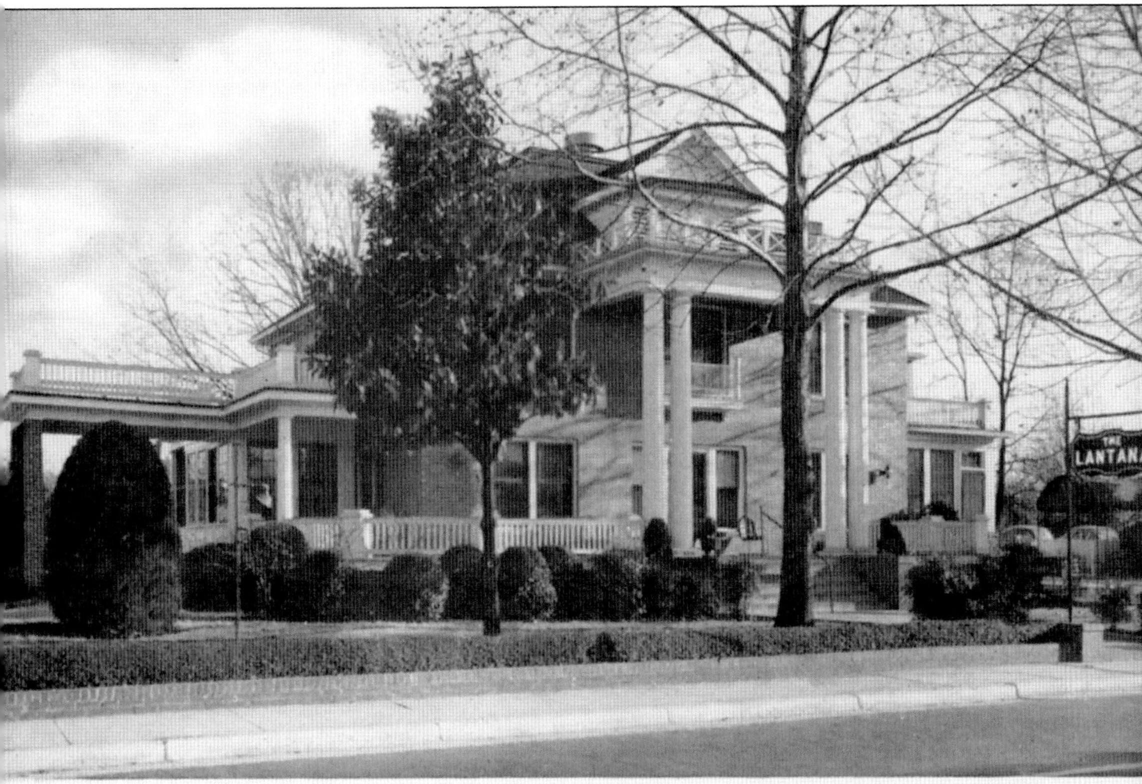

The Lantana, U. S. 1—15—501, Aberdeen, North Carolina

The Neoclassical Revival Julia Thagard Bryant house on North Poplar Street (formerly Highway 1) was built in 1900 as a private home. Originally of frame construction, it was converted to a tourist home in 1913 and later brick-veneered. Known as the Lantana, it was operated by J.A. and Julia Bryant and later sold when the highway was relocated after World War II. It became a private residence and later a bed-and-breakfast inn, closing in 2011. Today, the Bryant House is in need of restoration. (Author's collection.)

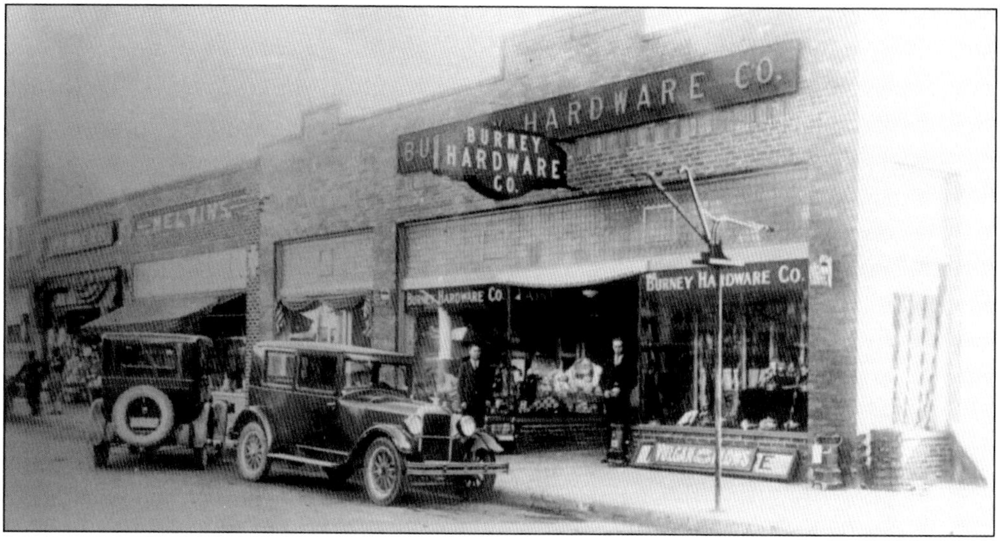

In 1925, A.L. Burney built Burney Hardware Company on the corner of what would be known as South Street and Tarbell Street. To the left of the hardware was a grocery operated by Knox Matthews. To the left of the grocery are Melvin's clothing store and Pender's store. In 1926, T.D. McLean constructed the two-story brick building for his furniture business. He built the two adjacent structures on the east elevation, with the A&P Company operating a grocery in one and Mack's Five and Ten renting the other. The former Burney Hardware Company was destroyed by fire in 2004, and the lot was cleared for a parking lot. Of note is a hand plow on a pole outside the hardware store. (Courtesy of John Blue.)

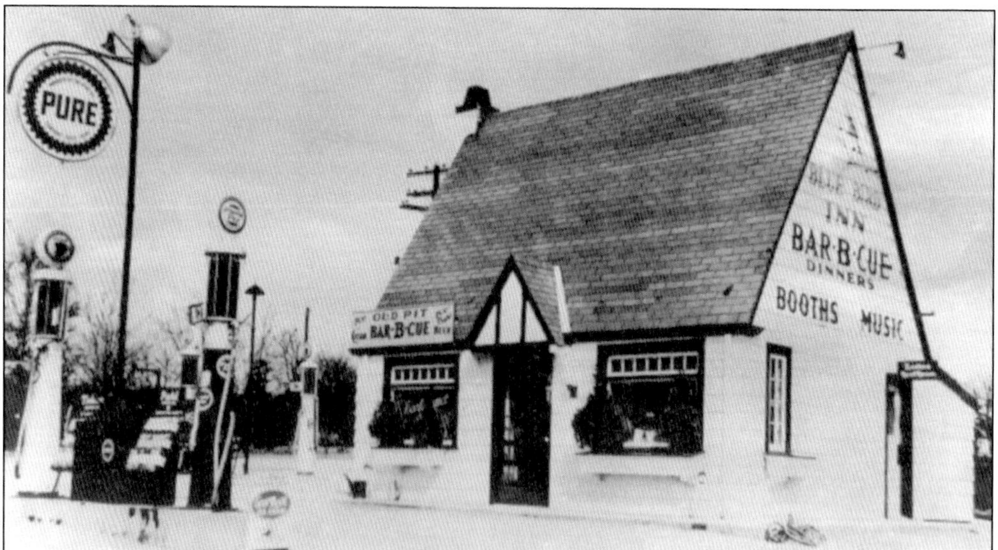

This is a c. 1940 photograph of the Pure Oil Station on the corner of Highways 70 and 501. It was a popular stop for food and nightlife. Known as the Blue Bird Inn because of its blue tiled roof, it served barbecue cooked on a grill and had a jukebox for entertainment. Ed Bert from Biscoe, North Carolina, built it on land owned by the Gertrude Campbell family. C.D. and Rachel Westbrook operated the store for many years before closing in the 1950s when Highway 501 was rerouted and the station became unprofitable. After the gas pumps were removed, it was converted to a residential rental property before being torn down in the 1980s. (Courtesy of John Blue.)

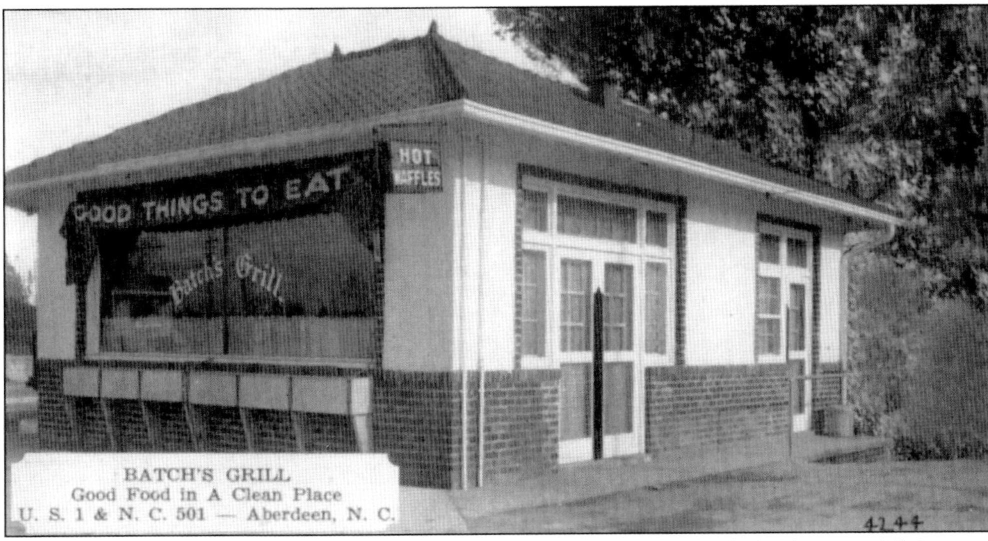

Known as Batch's Grill, this popular restaurant was operated by W.L. Batchelor (1890–1976). Located on old Highway 1 west of town on what is now Pinehurst Avenue, it opened in the late 1930s and it became a popular stop for travelers as well as local patrons for many years. Soldiers traveling to and from Camp Mackall during World War II made it a frequent stop. In-season oysters were steamed behind the grill and served outside on wooden tables. After the grill closed, Batchelor later became a successful real estate and insurance agent. The booths, stools, and lunch counter are gone today, and the building stands empty after being used as a bus station, a gasoline station, and a tire recapping company. (Above, author's collection; below, courtesy of John Blue.)

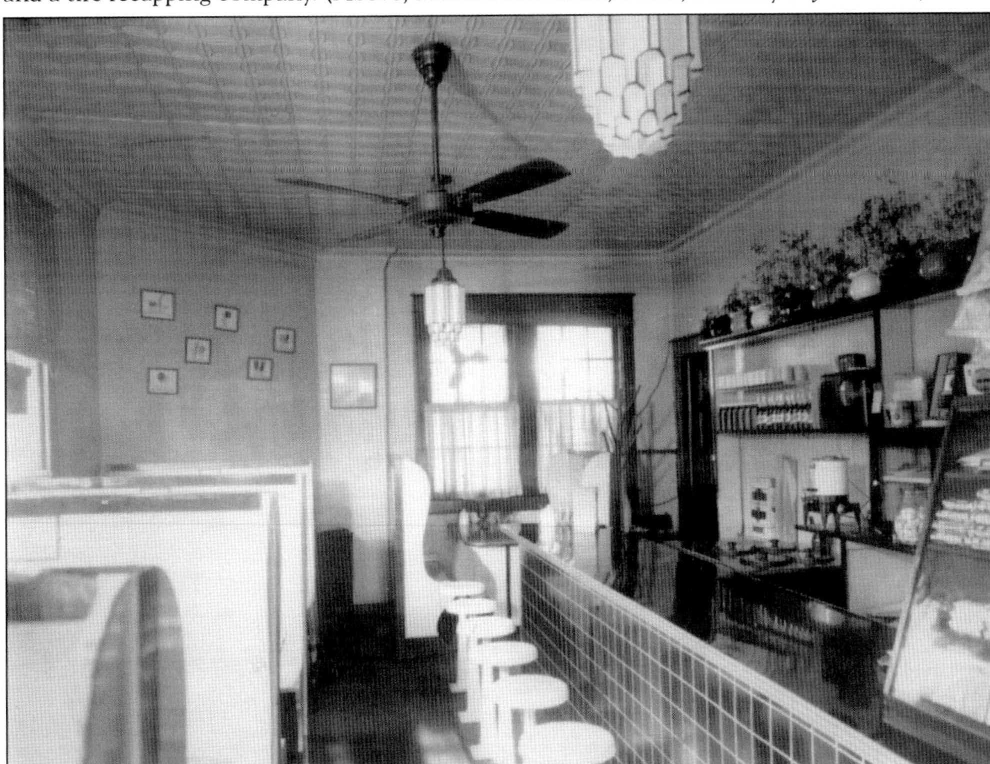

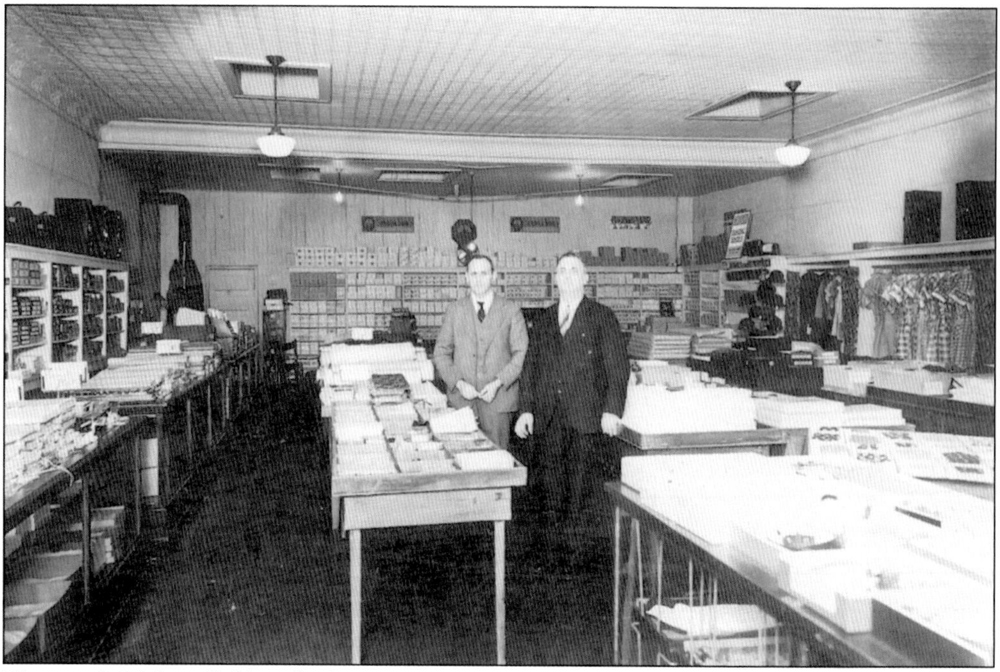

Thomas S. Melvin (left) and John K. Melvin Sr. await customers in their new Melvin Brothers store. They operated a men's clothing store on South Street prior to moving the business to Sycamore Street in 1938 to accommodate a growing clientele of Aberdeen shoppers. The store moved a third time to the corner of Main and Poplar Streets where it was in business for a number of years. (Courtesy of Kay Crissman.)

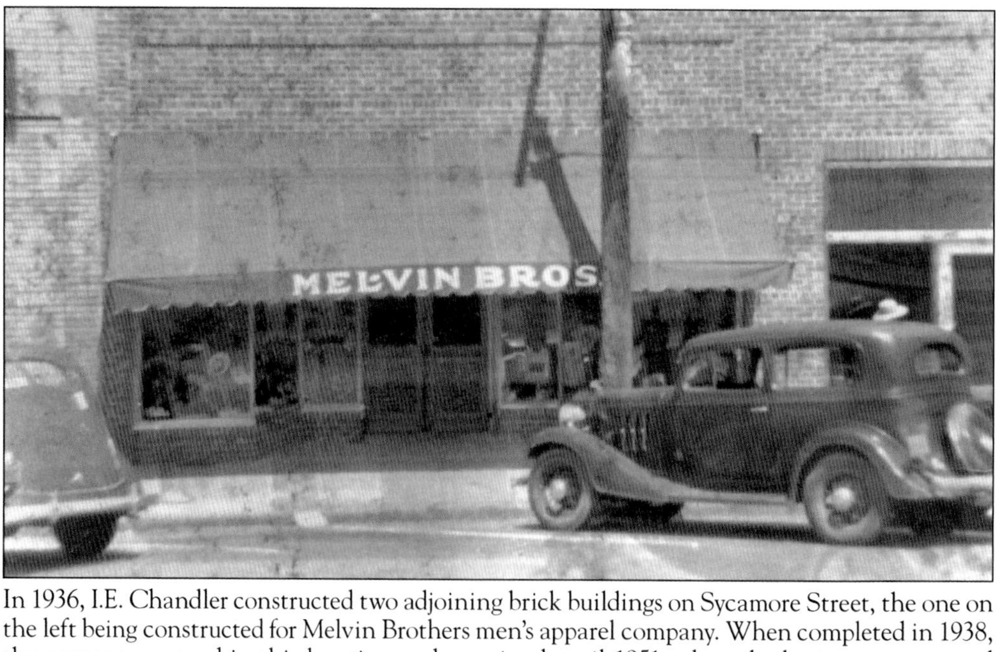

In 1936, I.E. Chandler constructed two adjoining brick buildings on Sycamore Street, the one on the left being constructed for Melvin Brothers men's apparel company. When completed in 1938, the company opened in this location and remained until 1951, when the business was moved to a larger building on Poplar Street. Today, the buildings are owned by an evangelistic society. (Courtesy of Kay Crissman.)

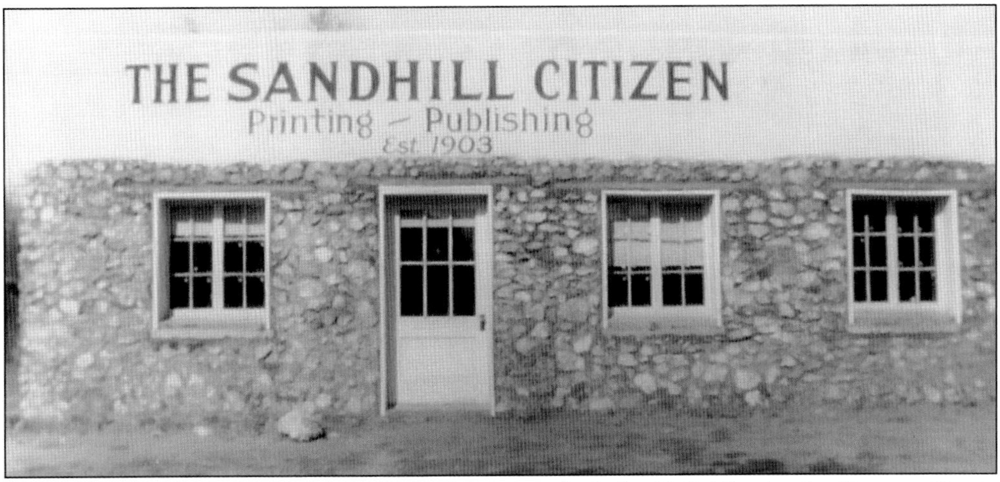

The Sandhill Citizen Building on Knight Street was built for H.C. Blue by the Duncan Currie construction crew under supervision from a Mr. Wiseman and a Mr. McKeithen. The rocks in the building were hauled down from upper Moore County. The newspaper was printed on letterpress for years before going to the offset process in the 1960s. Some of the employees in this building were Malcolm Blue, Ed Cox, Cad Benedict, Tom Wicker, Jack Barron, Jerry Thompson, Frances Marks, Catherine Burns, Ray Barber, Charles Merrill, Charles Swaringen, Curtis McInnis, Dana Kirk, and Robbie Monroe. W.L. Batchelor had an insurance office that later became Garner's Insurance, which is presently run by his son. An addition was built on the left side for the Carolina Beauty Shop, operated by Janette Farrell with Ann Lane, Catherine Blue Robeson, and Jo Ann Styers Galyean among the employees. Carolina Beauty Shop's location has now become the Interfaith Food Pantry, an interdenominational endeavor initiated by members of Page Memorial Methodist Church. The Barn Door, located beside Aberdeen Supply, a horse tack consignment shop owned by Debbie Mastrangelo and Suzie Jacobson, is on the right side of the building. H. Clifton Blue Jr. and John L. Blue currently own the building in partnership. (Courtesy of Herbert Clifton Blue.)

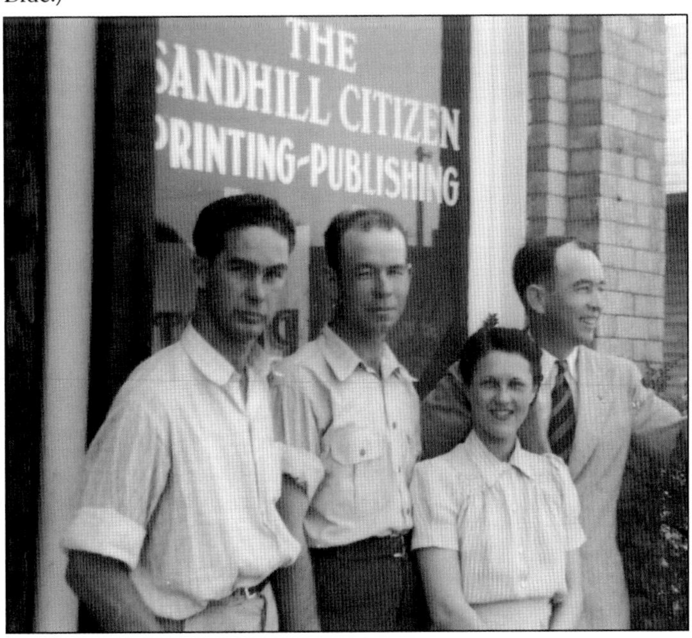

Sandhill Citizen newspaper employees stand in front of their new office in the former Carter's Pharmacy Building on East Main Street. In 1936, the newspaper moved from Vass, North Carolina, to Aberdeen, where it continued publishing for the next five decades. Standing are, from left to right, Atlas Eastwood, Marshall Blue, Lib Troutman, and Clifton Blue, owner and editor. (Courtesy of John Blue.)

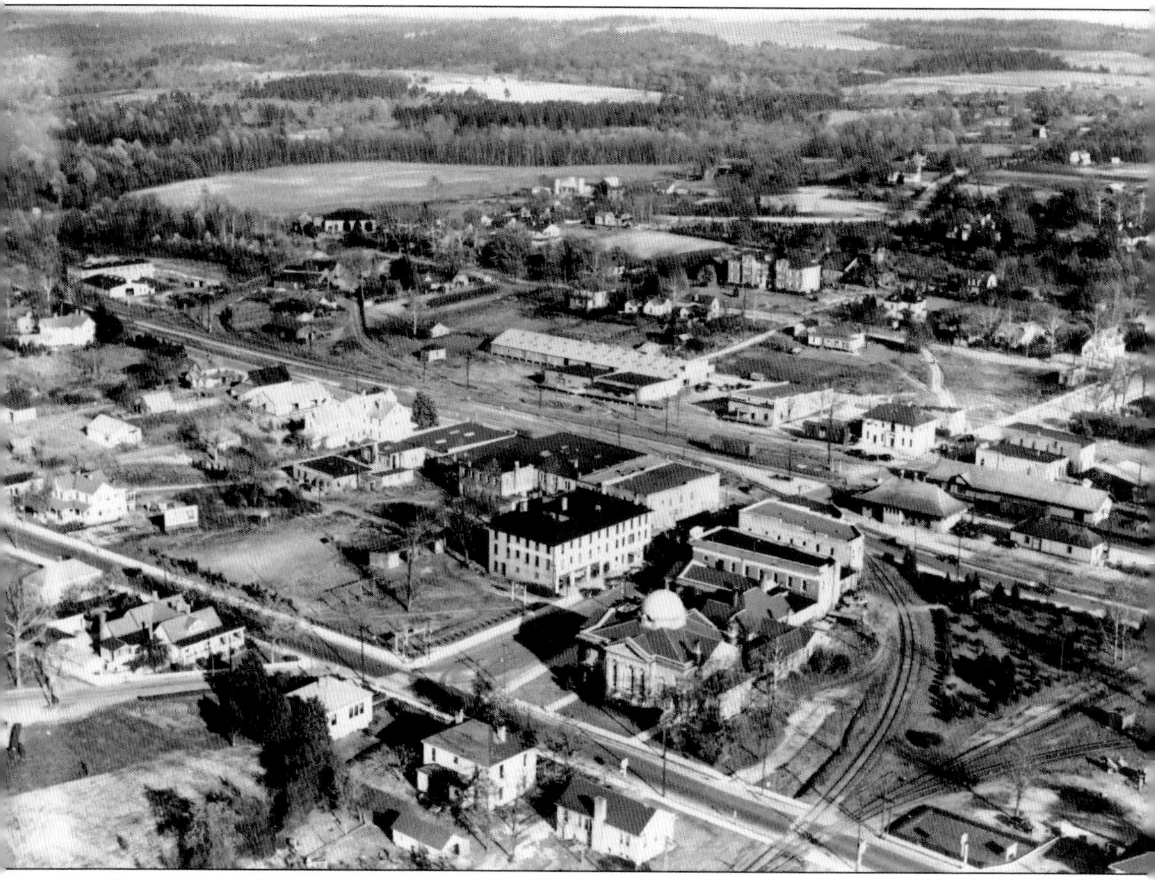

A c. 1941 aerial view looking east creates an image of a prosperous commercial, industrial, and railroad town. Prominent are the large Sandhill Hotel and Page Memorial Methodist Church with its Neoclassical dome. The Sandhill Hotel would burn shortly after this picture was taken. Of note are the many tracks that bisect the town and the railroad wye behind the buildings on Main Street. Highway 1, seen at the bottom of the photograph, was a major highway artery for travelers between New York and Florida. After World War II, a new three-lane highway was built a short distance to the west and ran parallel with the old road through town. (Courtesy of Aberdeen Centennial Committee.)

Three

Coming of Age

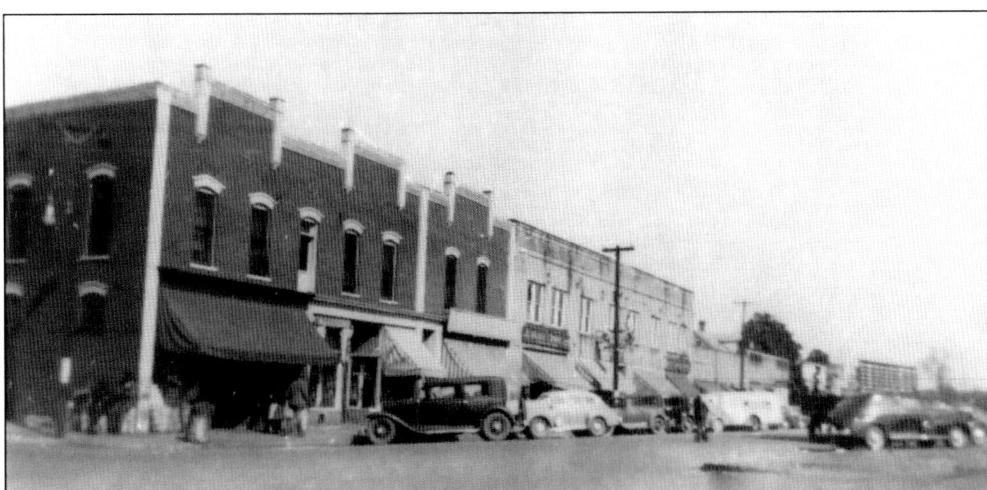

Photographed in 1942, Sycamore Street is filled with shoppers and automobiles. The Farrell Building (1900) and Annex (1912) were built by T.B. Creel. M.W. Dew constructed the Gichner-Johnson Building in 1920. This structure once housed offices and businesses, including a Ford garage. They are all in use today in the town's historic district. (Courtesy of Aberdeen Centennial Committee.)

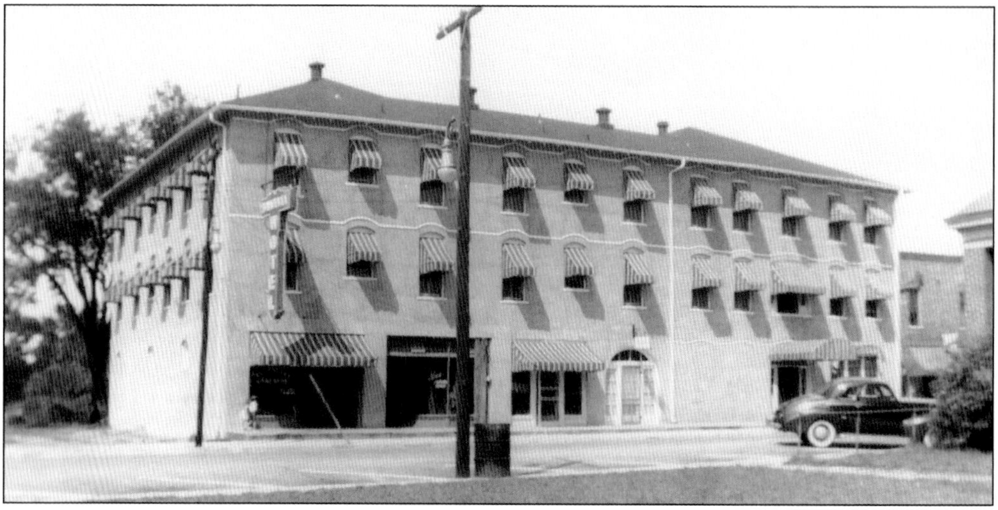

Opened in 1941, the Sandhill Hotel was located on North Main Street on the site of the Aberdeen Hotel, which partially burned the same year. After extensive renovations, the remodeled brick hotel boasting 44 rooms was destroyed by fire less than a year after its opening. The lot remained vacant for many years until a one-story brick commercial building was constructed for the Collins Department Store. The department store later moved to Town and Country Shopping Center in the 1970s, and today, a lighting fixture store occupies the building. (Courtesy of John Blue.)

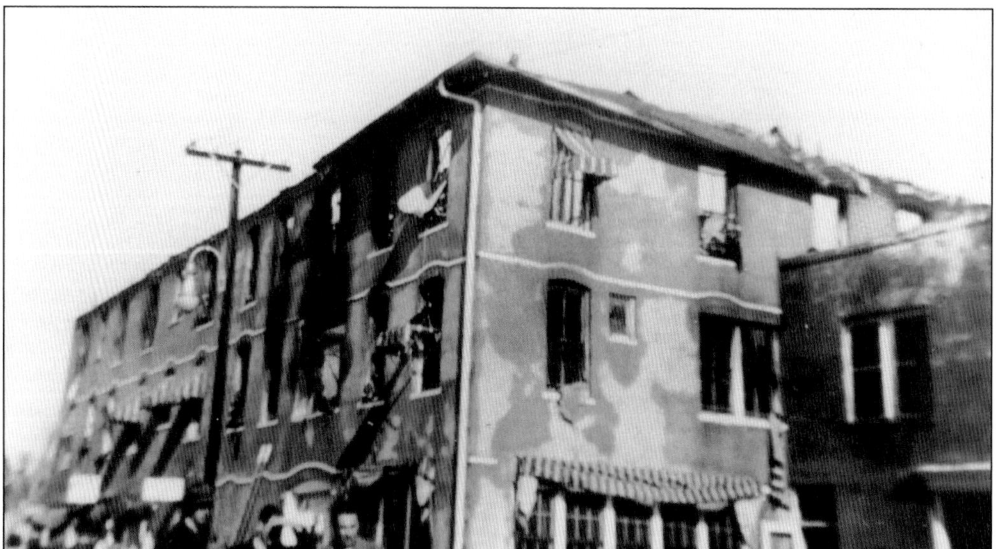

A winter's day in February 1942 reveals the charred remains of the Sandhill Hotel, which had burned the night before. The hotel was the second one built at this location, replacing the Aberdeen Hotel, which had burned the previous year. Photographed looking west from Main Street, the extent of damage to the structure is apparent and necessitated razing the remaining walls. The loss of life and destruction of the hotel was a major blow to the area. After the lot was cleared, it remained empty for a number of years, leaving a vacant spot in the central business district. The property was later sold, and a department store building was constructed on the site. (Courtesy of Aberdeen Centennial Committee.)

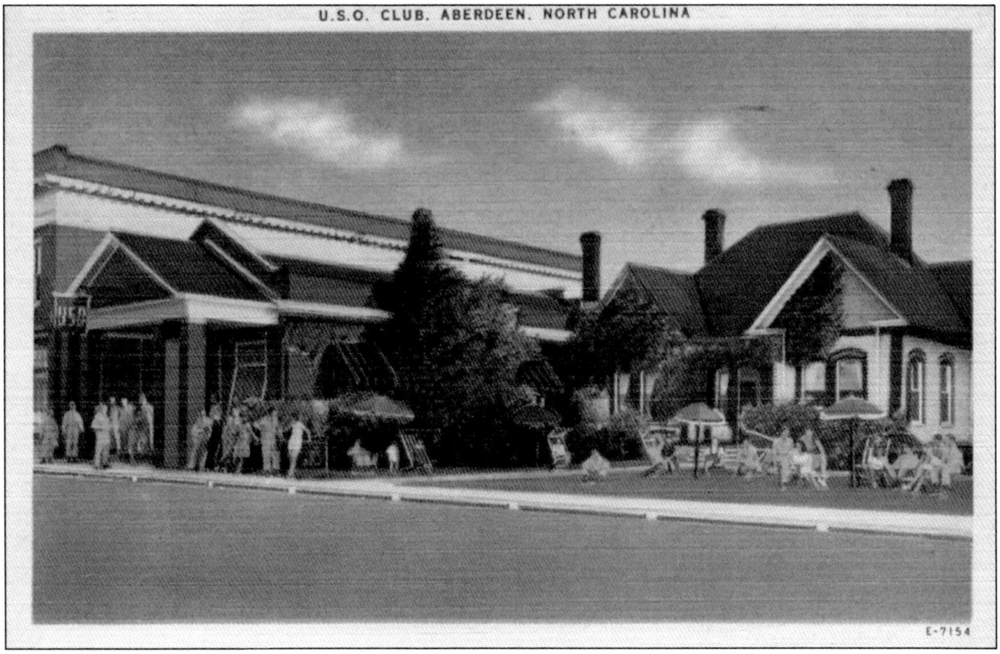

World War II came to Aberdeen when a large paratrooper and glider training center opened a few miles south of town in 1942. This United Service Organizations (USO) club in the former Page Trust Company Building on Main Street offered rest and relaxation to soldiers stationed at Fort Bragg and nearby Camp Mackall. A second USO club was opened at Aberdeen Lake. (Author's collection.)

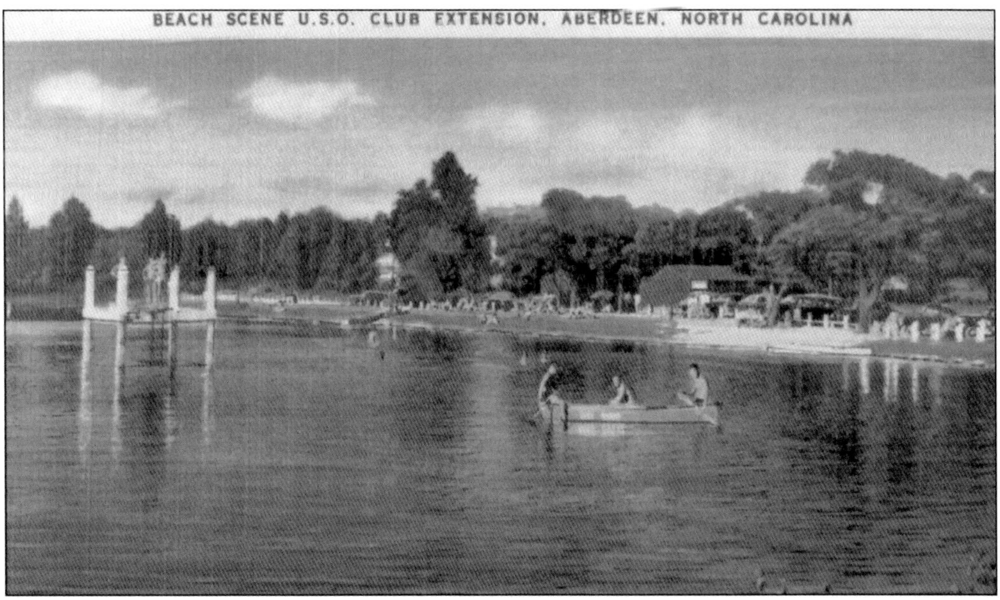

Off-duty soldiers from nearby Camp Mackall are enjoying a swim in Aberdeen Lake during World War II. The image is from a postcard sold at the USO on Main Street in the former Page Trust Building. A second USO was located at the bathhouse and concession stand at the lake. At its peak, over 32,000 men were stationed at Camp Mackall. At the camp, they undertook paratrooper and glider training prior to overseas deployment. (Author's collection.)

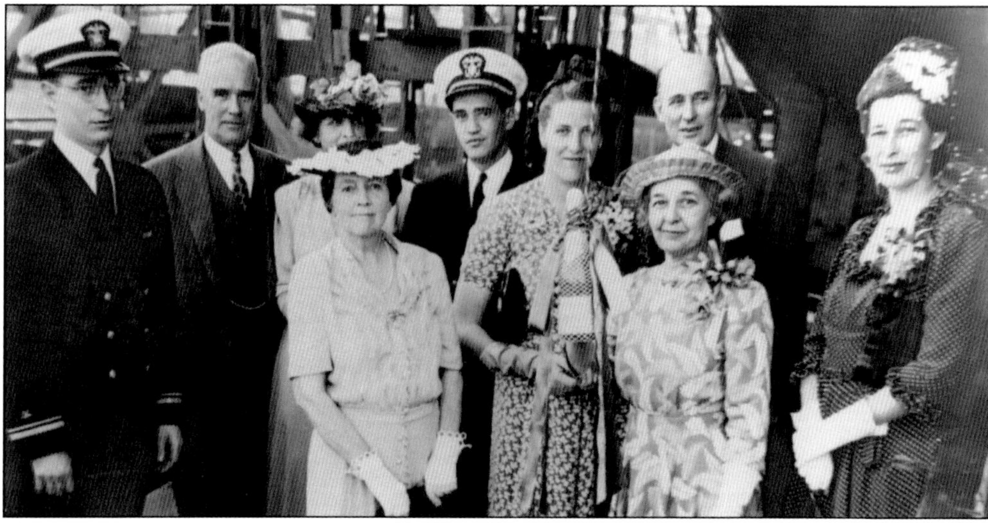

Christening day for a C-2 class Liberty ship, the *Walter Hines Page*, is seen in this April 1943 photograph. Named for the US ambassador to the United Kingdom during World War I, members of the Page family from Aberdeen attended the launching ceremonies. Built for the war effort by the North Carolina Shipbuilding Company in Wilmington, North Carolina, it had a long career. The ship was scuttled as an artificial reef in 1975 off the coast of Virginia. (Courtesy of Aberdeen Centennial Committee.)

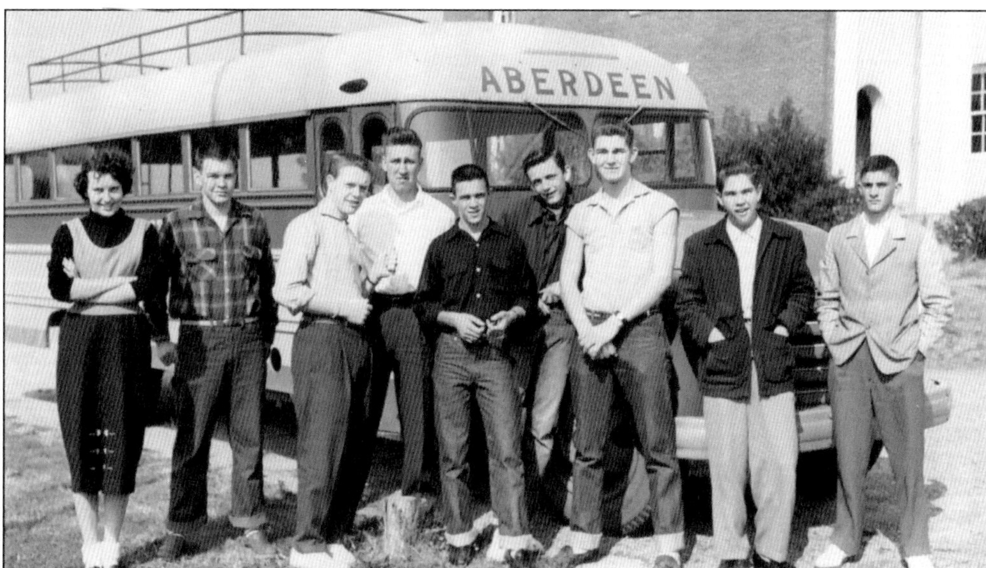

The 1954 Aberdeen High School bus drivers pose for a group picture in front of the school activity bus. For many years, local school districts employed high school students as bus drivers until passage of the Commercial Motor Vehicle Safety Act of 1986, which effectively ended students as drivers. Standing from left to right are Sybil Newton, Adrian Allred, Bill Tulloch, Robert Barber, H. D. Madison, Al Cruce, Joe Layton, Jerry Adams, and Bill Price. The Chevrolet activity bus was purchased in 1948 and was used to transport athletic teams and marching band members to away games and used for class field trips. County school consolidation in 1969 closed the high school and ended a 21-year career of continuous service by the activity bus. (Courtesy of Aberdeen High School Museum.)

COURTEOUS and RELIABLE SERVICE

HUGH'S TAXI

PHONE - 9061 **ABERDEEN, N. C.**

Owned by Hugh Styers, Hugh's Taxi operated from the Glory Hole service station on Sycamore Street. He began the service during World War II, transporting soldiers at nearby Camp Mackall to and from the Aberdeen USO. Two of Hugh's brothers, Fred and Ordell, drove the taxicabs until Ordell was involved in a fatal accident. After Hugh's death in 1990, Fred took over the business and continued driving taxicabs until his failing health forced the closure in 1992. The company business card has a schedule of destinations and prices and a disclaimer that those who did not behave would be refused service. Of note are the four digit phone number and the segregated white and colored sanatoriums. (Both, author's collection.)

HUGH'S TAXI SERVICE

Telephone - 9061 Aberdeen, N. C.

These Prices Direct From Taxi Stand Shortest Way

Addor	$2.00
Ashley Heights	1.50
Berkley	.50
Broadway	.50
Camp Mackall	2.50
Carthage	5.50
Colored Sanatorium	2.50
Midway	1.00
Hoffman R. R. Station	3.25
Jackson Hamlet	1.25
Lakeview Service Station	3.00
Laurinburg	8.50
Montrose	2.75
Moore County Hospital	2.25
Niagara	2.50
Pinebluff Post Office	1.00
Pinebluff Sanitarium	1.25
Pinehurst	2.00
St. Joseph's Hospital	2.00
Raeford	5.50
Resort Airline Airport	2.75
Rockingham	3.50
Southern Pines	1.25
Taylor Town, Pinehurst	2.25
White Sanatorium	2.25

The above prices do not include waiting time and extra stops. We reserve right to refuse to carry passengers who do not behave. Bundles and baggage 25 extra. Extra stops not to exceed 25 cents per stop. Waiting time extra at rate of $3.00 per hour. Places not mentioned above not less than 30 cents per mile.

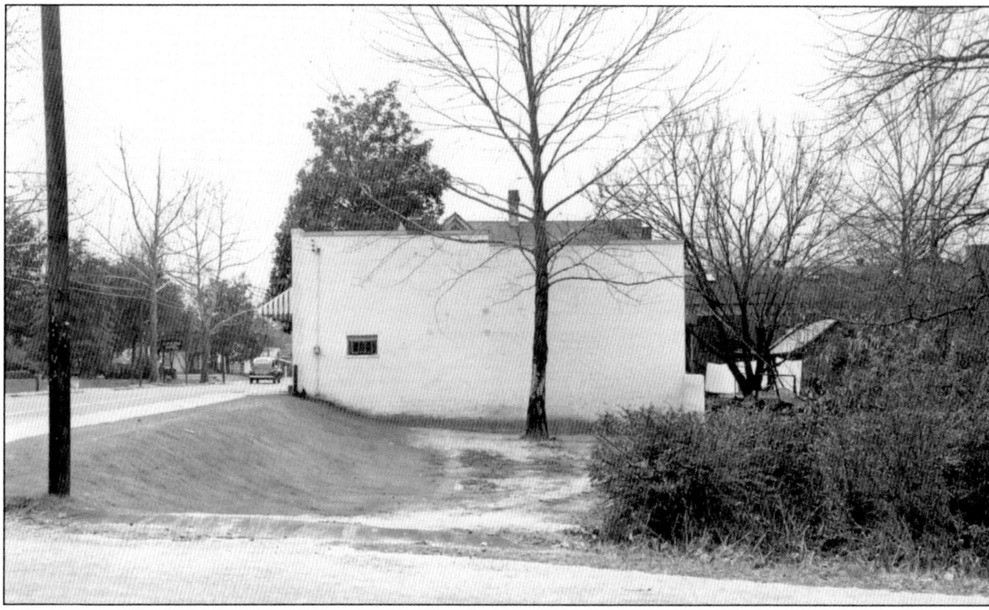

E.P. Freeman and E.O. Freeman purchased the Aberdeen magneto telephone exchange from Bernard Leavitt in 1928 under the name of Piedmont Telephone Company. A new building was constructed on Poplar Street in 1929, and the company initially had 154 subscribers. The first telephone operators were Bertha Herring, Mattie Wilson, and Edna Yow, with Eunice Creel as a substitute. Curtis Freeman, a cousin of E.O. Freeman, was the installer and repairman. An all-relay dial switchboard was installed in 1940 and served until 1956, when a newer system to handle the growing number of subscribers was added. The name was changed to Sandhill Telephone Company in 1937 and was later merged in the 1970s with a regional telephone system. (Courtesy of Page Memorial Library.)

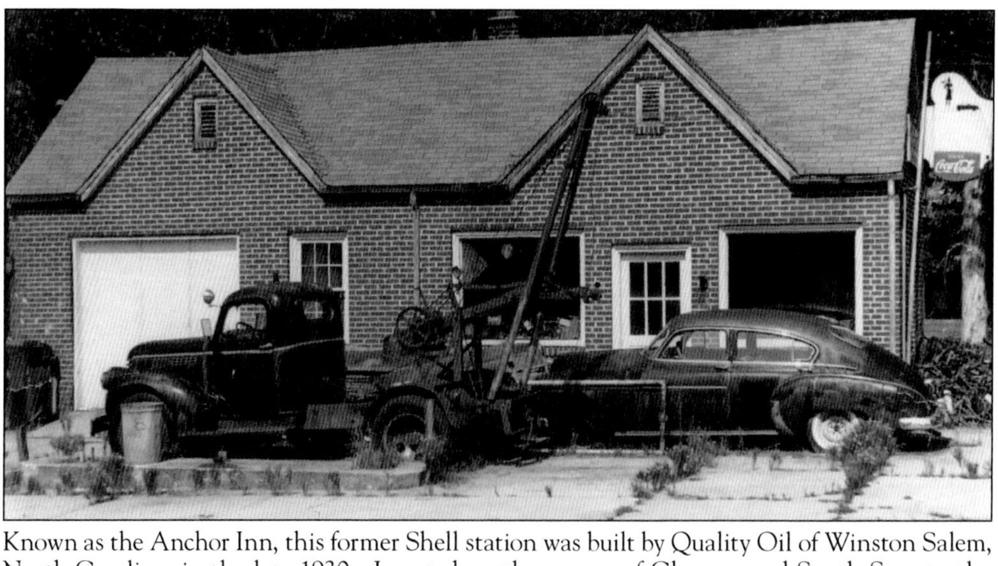

Known as the Anchor Inn, this former Shell station was built by Quality Oil of Winston Salem, North Carolina, in the late 1930s. Located on the corner of Glasgow and South Streets, the business offered auto servicing, gas, and a café. The rerouting of Highway 501 forced the closure as a service station. Mack Wallace operated an auto repair shop in the building for a number of years. Today, it stands empty and boarded up. (Courtesy of John Blue.)

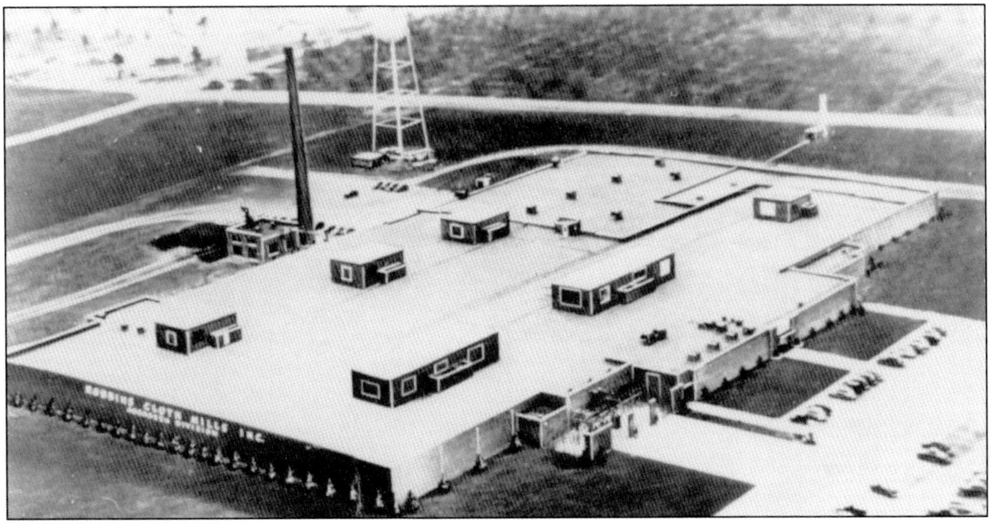

Photographed shortly after construction in 1946, Robbins Mills became the town's largest employer when it opened. Built by Karl Robbins, who would later become a prominent philanthropist in North Carolina, and W.P. Saunders, president of Robbins Mills, it produced a variety of unfinished cloth that was sold to finishers and eventually made into clothing. Over the years, the plant has been expanded and modernized and has produced a variety of textile products under different ownerships. Located on Highway 5, it currently is a privately owned company producing residential and commercial carpets. In the top left corner is Colonial Heights, a planned residential development. It was built on a former peach orchard to house mill workers and their families when the plant opened. Today, Colonial Heights is a neighborhood of well-kept homes in what was once a mill village. (Courtesy of John Blue.)

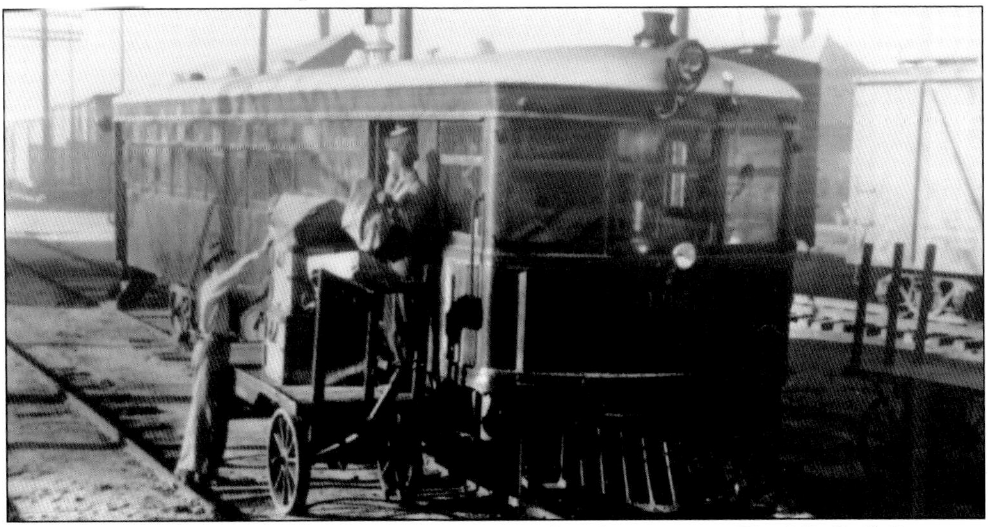

Aberdeen & Rockfish Railcar No. 103 is taking mail and passengers. The J.G. Brill Company of Philadelphia, Pennsylvania, built this railcar in 1933. The Brill Company was the largest manufacturer of streetcars and interurban railcars in America and ceased production in 1954. The Aberdeen & Rockfish Railroad operated several railcars between Aberdeen and Fayetteville, North Carolina, prior to World War II. Passengers rode the railcars, known as jitneys, to Fayetteville in the morning and returned in the afternoon. No. 103 was wrecked in 1945 and rebuilt as No. 107, ceasing operations in 1950. (Courtesy of Aberdeen Centennial Committee.)

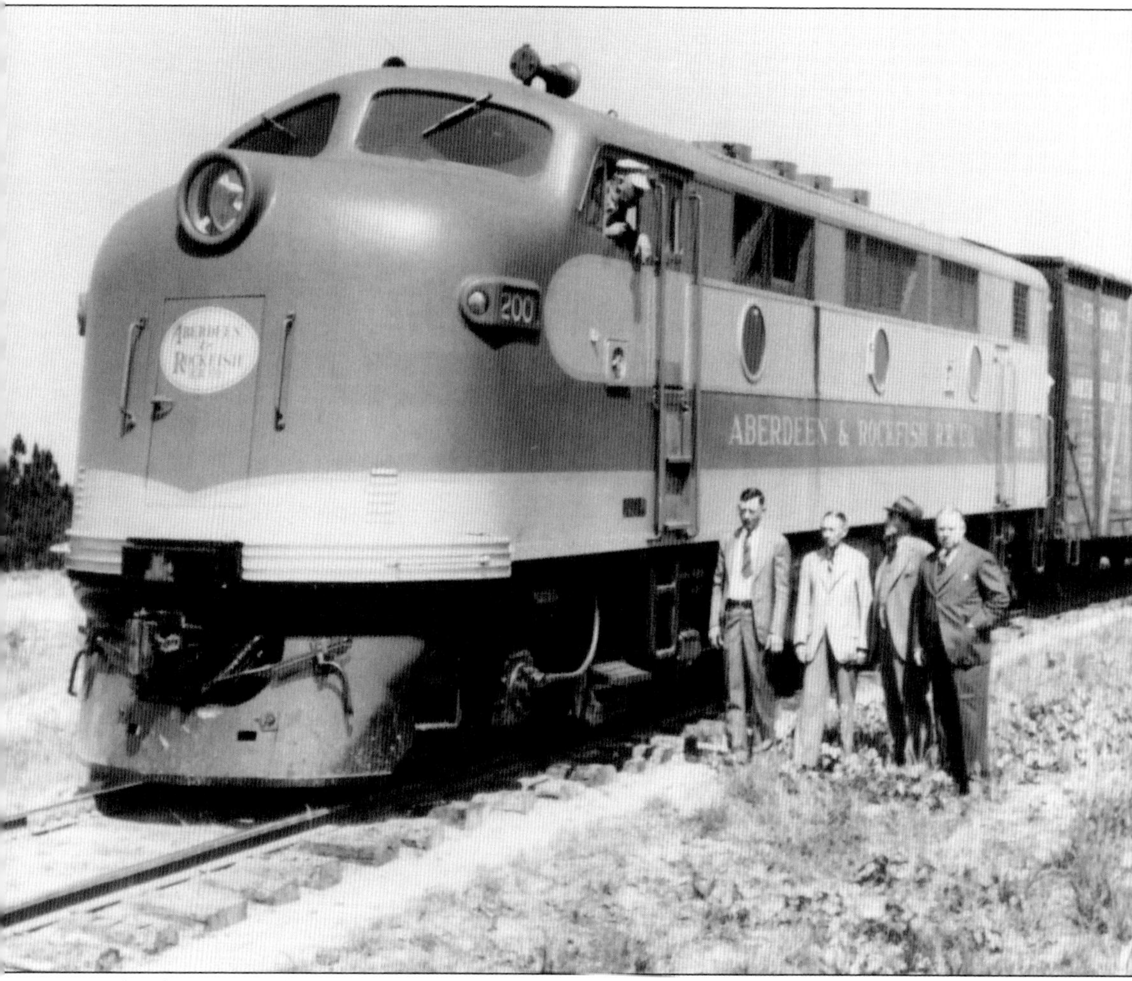

Aberdeen & Rockfish Railroad entered the diesel era with the 1947 purchase of a new F-3A unit built by Electro-Motive Division of General Motors in LaGrange, Illinois. Here, engineer Joe Marks looks down from the cab on company owners and managers Curtis Lawhon, Halbert Blue, Henry Blue, and Forrest Lockey Sr. Used for general freight service, it was sold in 1963. (Author's collection.)

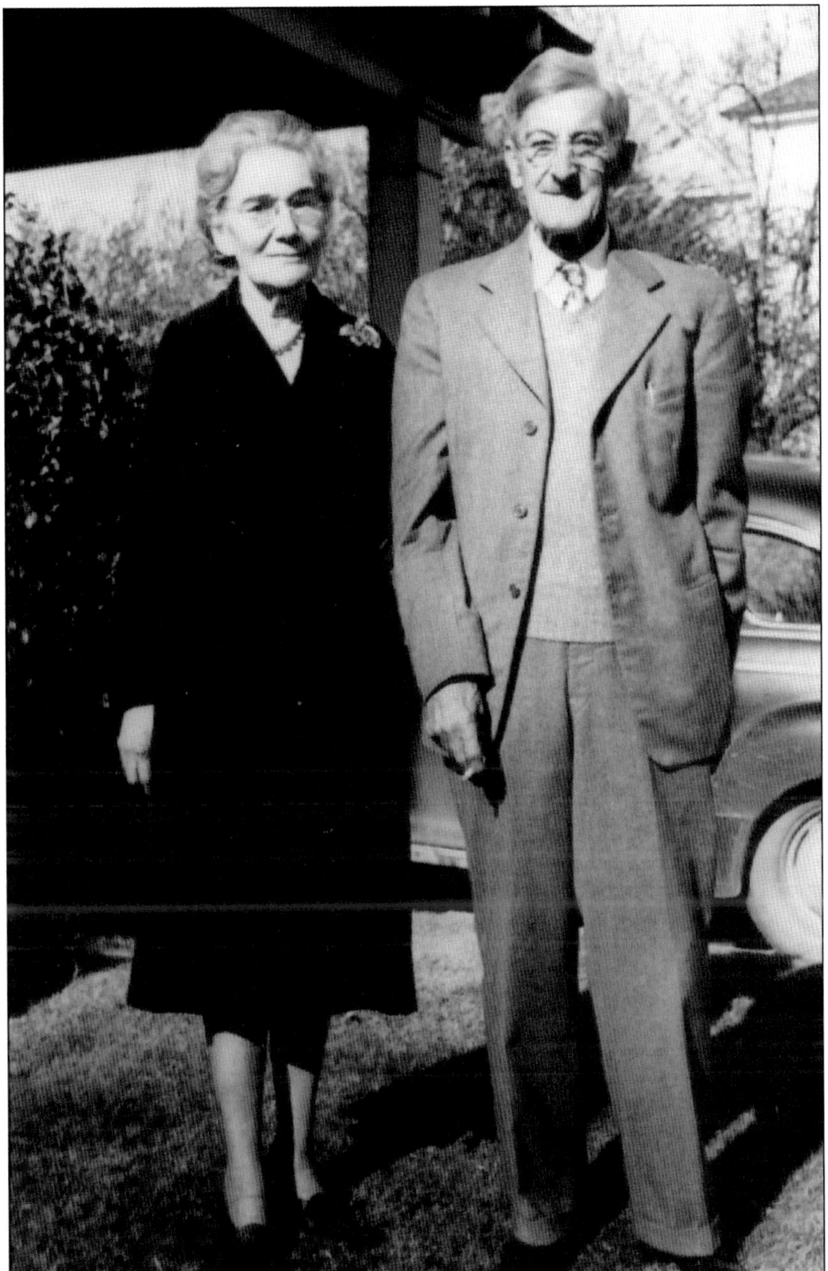

Bertha O. Bowman and Dr. Hugh E. Bowman (1870–1950) are standing in the front yard of their home on North Poplar Street in this 1940s photograph. Dr. Bowman was born in Virginia and graduated from Emory and Henry College. He moved to Oklahoma and acquired land through the Homestead Act of 1862; however, he found farming unsatisfactory and moved to North Carolina where he worked on a newspaper and taught school. Enrolling in Davidson College, he obtained a medical degree and was recruited from medical school by the Page family to provide services for railroad and sawmill workers on the western terminus of the Aberdeen & Asheboro Railroad. He and his family moved to Aberdeen about 1911, and he practiced medicine from an office in his home until his death. (Courtesy of Beverly Warren-Leigh.)

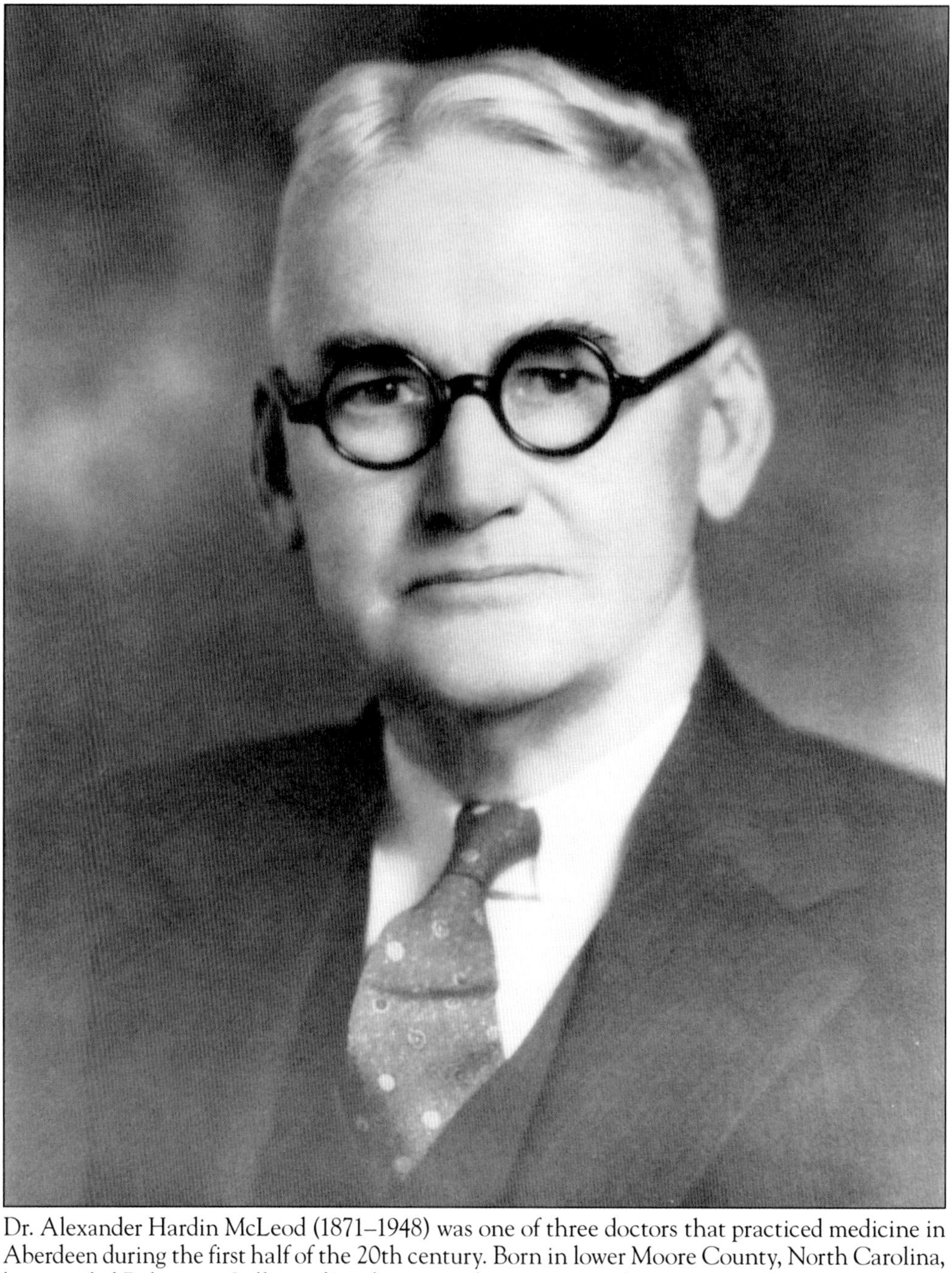

Dr. Alexander Hardin McLeod (1871–1948) was one of three doctors that practiced medicine in Aberdeen during the first half of the 20th century. Born in lower Moore County, North Carolina, he attended Baltimore College of Medicine, graduating in April 1896. He returned to Aberdeen and opened his practice at 204 East Main Street. His former office is in the Aberdeen Historic District. Before his death, he was always seen about town with his Airedale dog named Chief. He was buried in Bethesda Cemetery, where an inscription on his tombstone proclaims he practiced medicine for 52 years. (Courtesy of Lee Buchan.)

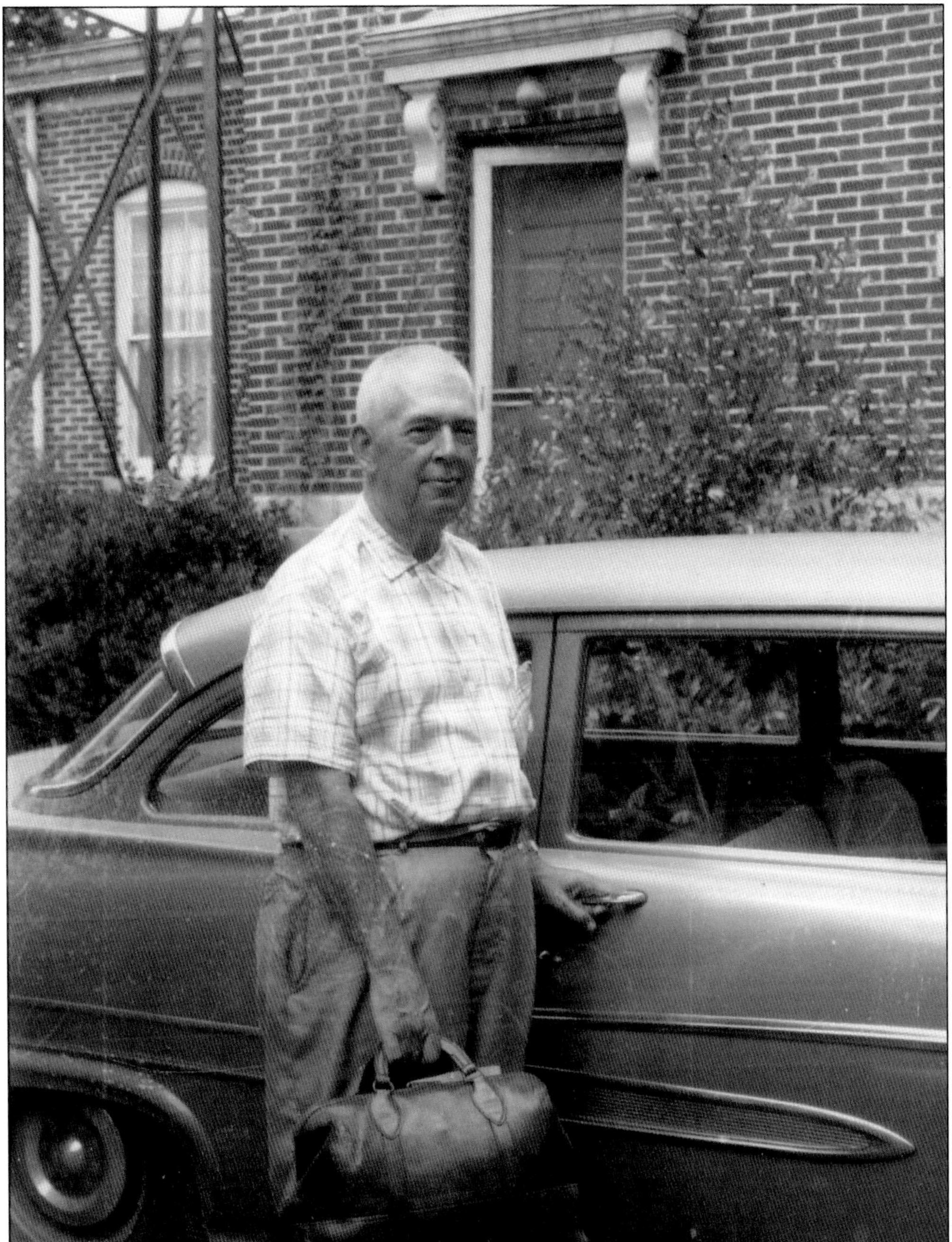

Preparing to go on a house call, Dr. J.P. Bowen stands outside his office in this 1950s photograph. Dr. Bowen was born in Belton, South Carolina, and graduated from the University of South Carolina Premedical School and the Maryland School of Medicine. He interned at St. Joseph's Hospital in Baltimore, Maryland, and moved to Aberdeen in 1930. Practicing in Aberdeen for many years, he was one of the last physicians in town to make house calls. Many remember him for his two-room doctor's office, which was located in the former Aberdeen & Asheboro Railroad offices on Main Street. (Courtesy of Herbert Clifton Blue.)

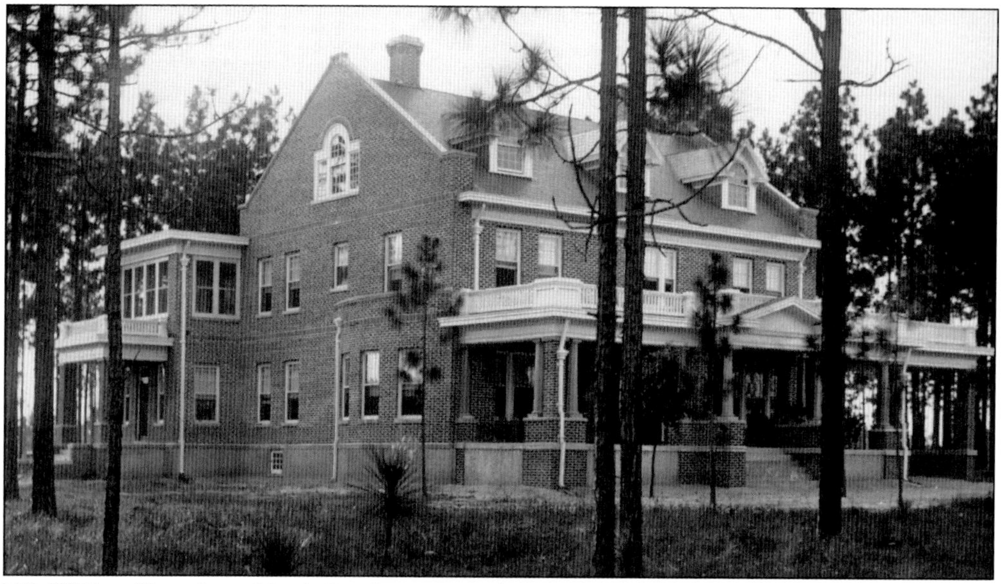

T.B. Wilder of Louisburg, North Carolina, married Frances Page, daughter of Allison and Catherine Francis Page, who were prominent in the development of Aberdeen. Wilder built this home, located on Allison Page Road on a large tract of land, in 1913. Seen shortly after completion, this large brick home, as well as others owned by the Page family, is located on the west side of town, known as Page Hill. Wilder was a lawyer and in the insurance business for a number of years. In 1936, he, along with others from Moore County, was instrumental in influencing the North Carolina Department of Transportation in routing Federal Highway 15 through Aberdeen. The Wilder family sold the house in the 1950s. (Author's collection.)

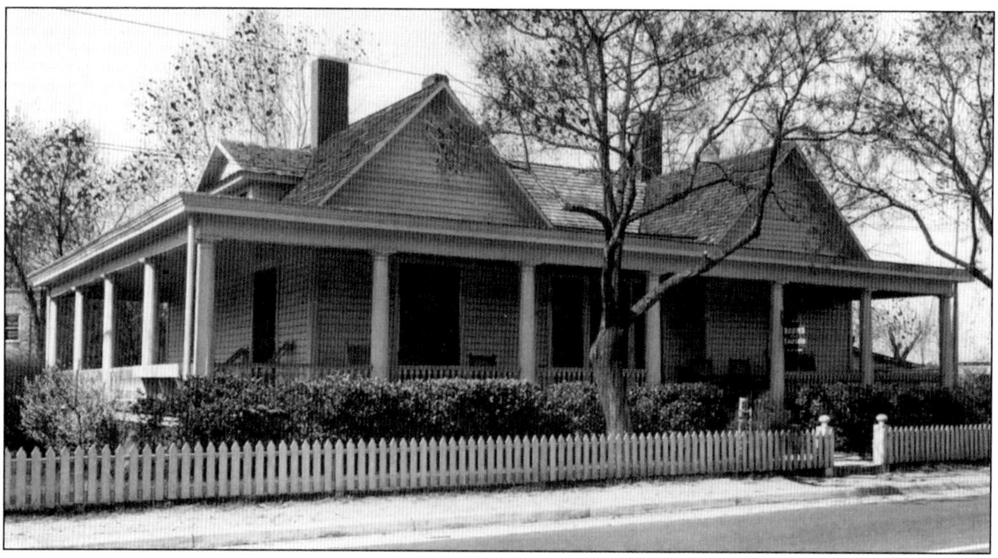

The home of J.J. Heckart (1876–1918) and his wife, Ella (1877–1947), stood on the corner of Poplar and Main Streets. Heckart operated a real estate company and served on the board of aldermen in 1907 with W.A. Blue, H.A. Page, W.W. Maurer, and T.B. Creel. It was known that Ella had a talking parrot that would call out to passersby on the sidewalk in front of the home. The house was demolished in 1950, and Melvin Men's Store was built on the site. (Courtesy of Aberdeen Centennial Committee.)

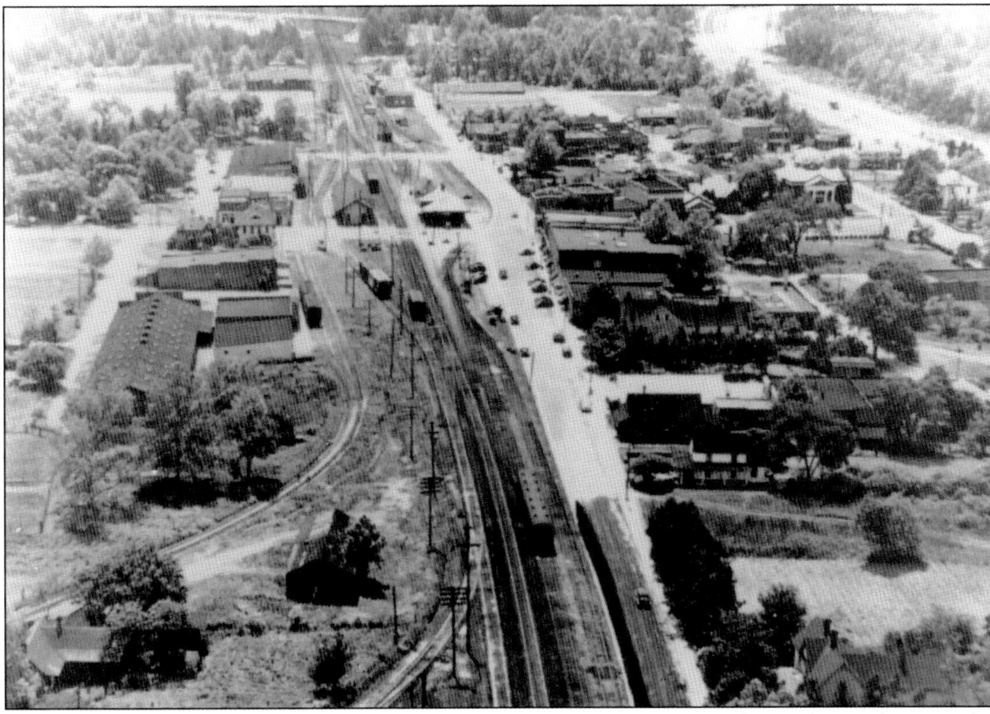

The extensive rail network in Aberdeen is evident in this 1950s north-south aerial view. The main line of the Seaboard Air Line Railway bisects the downtown with warehouses on the left and commercial buildings on the right. Union Station is seen facing the tracks. Newly constructed Highway 1 is seen at the top of the photograph. (Courtesy of Martha Swaringen.)

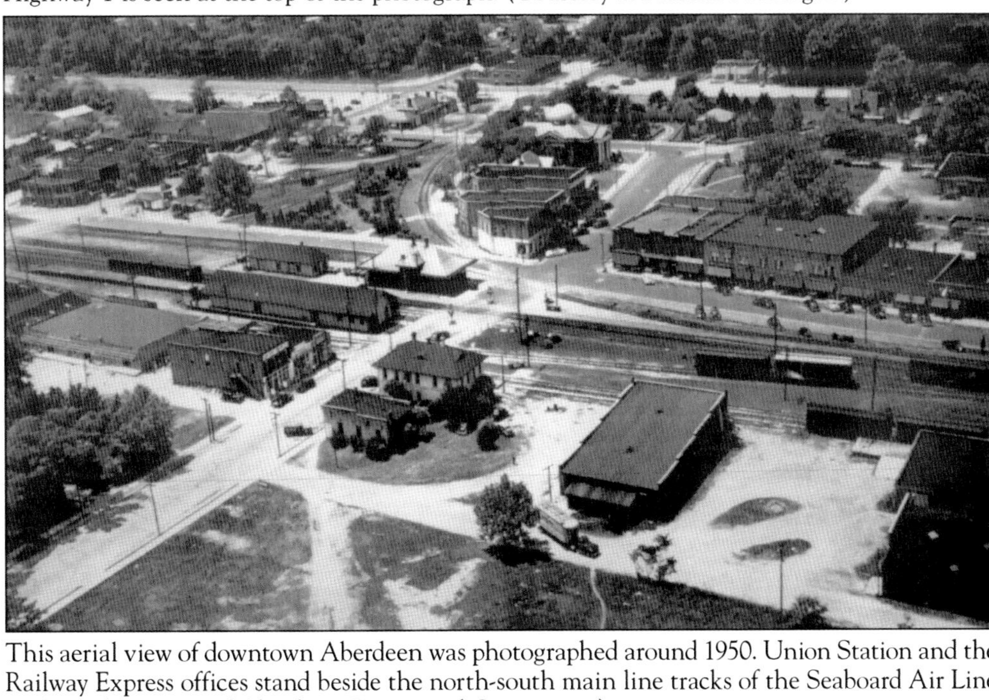

This aerial view of downtown Aberdeen was photographed around 1950. Union Station and the Railway Express offices stand beside the north-south main line tracks of the Seaboard Air Line Railway. (Courtesy of Aberdeen Centennial Committee.)

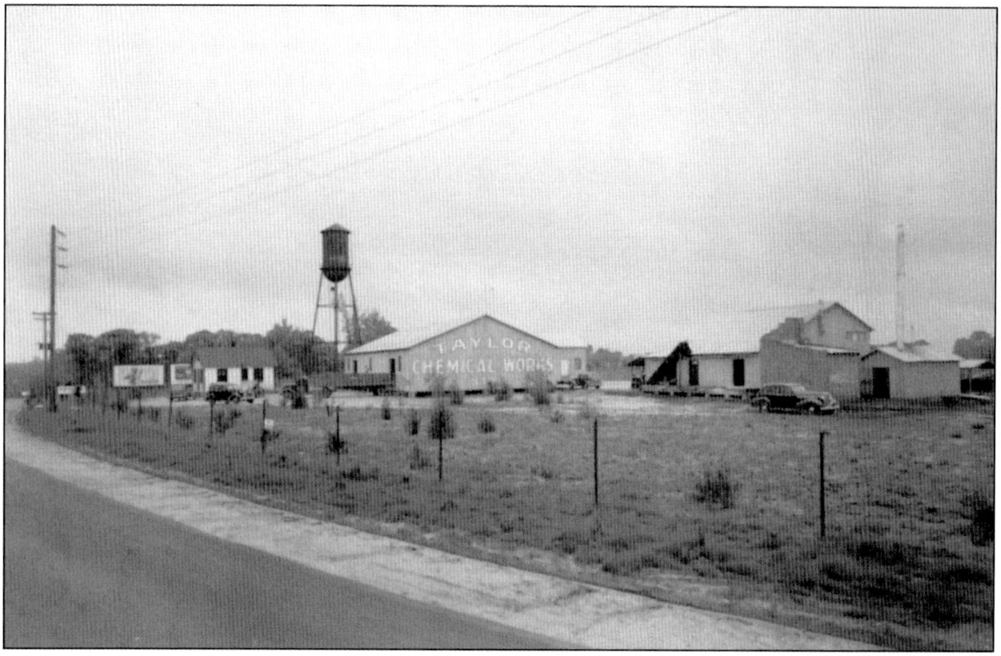

Established in the 1930s, Woolfolk Farm Chemical Company was acquired by Jack Taylor Sr. in 1940. Renamed Taylor Chemical Company, it continued to operate until it was sold to Farm Chemicals, Inc., in 1964. The site on Highway 5 was later demolished and is now an industrial park. (Courtesy of Aberdeen Centennial Committee.)

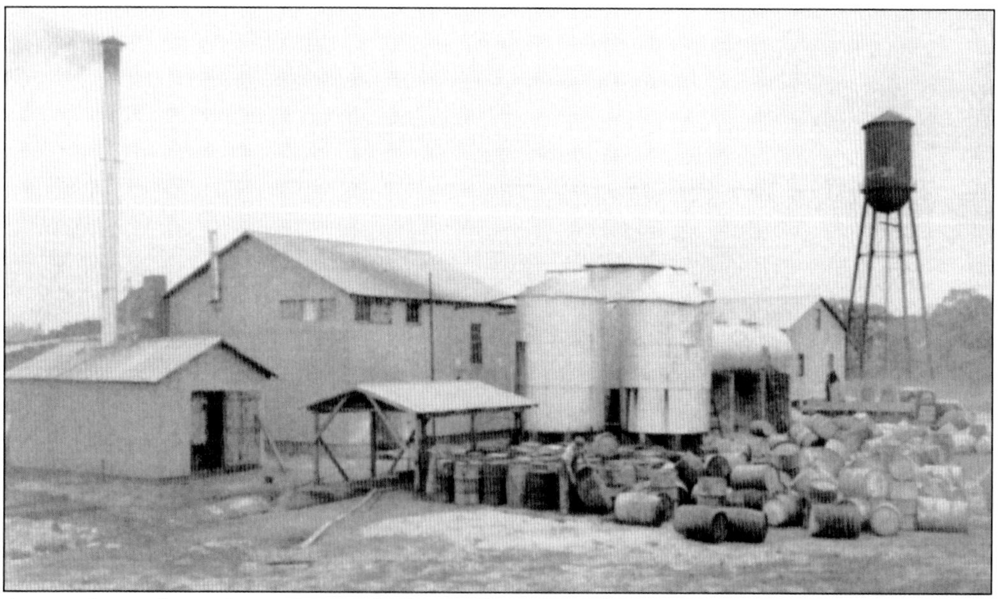

A second view shows the production facility and barrels used in transporting the finished products. The company manufactured pesticides for farming operations and shipped products nationwide. Located adjacent to the plant was a grass airstrip and metal hangar that housed the company airplane used for sales trips. The Environmental Protection Agency later deemed the property a Superfund site, and it would be cleared of any chemical residue from years of operations. (Courtesy of Aberdeen Centennial Committee.)

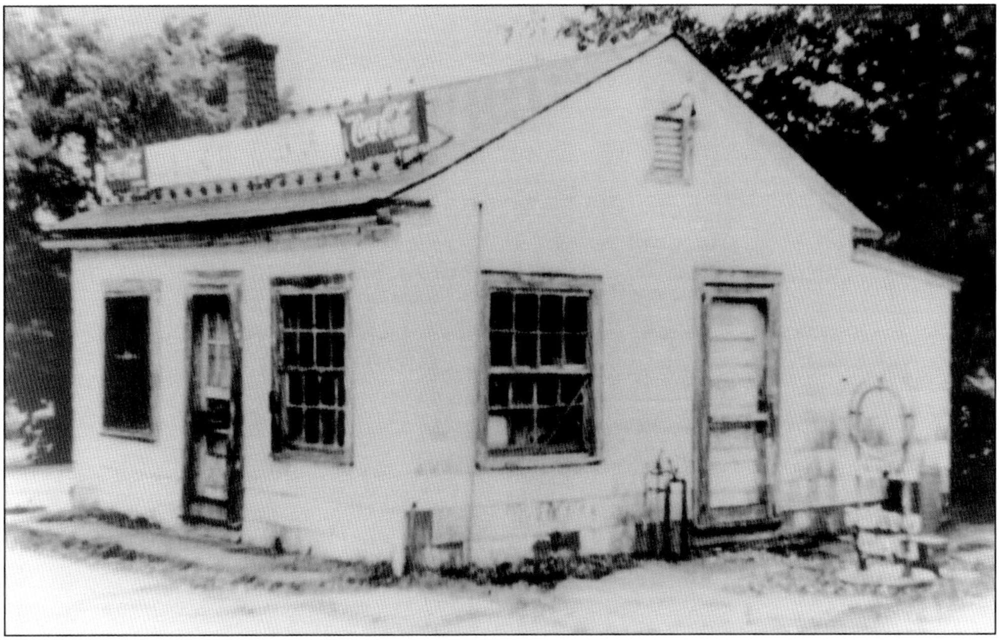

Paul Kellis's Esso Station was located on the corner of Lakeshore Drive and Highway 1. Built in the late 1940s after Highway 1 was realigned, it became a popular destination for cold sodas and snacks on the way to Aberdeen Lake. Kellis's home was next door, and he walked to work each morning. After Kellis retired, the building stood empty and was torn down in 1990. (Courtesy of Aberdeen Centennial Committee.)

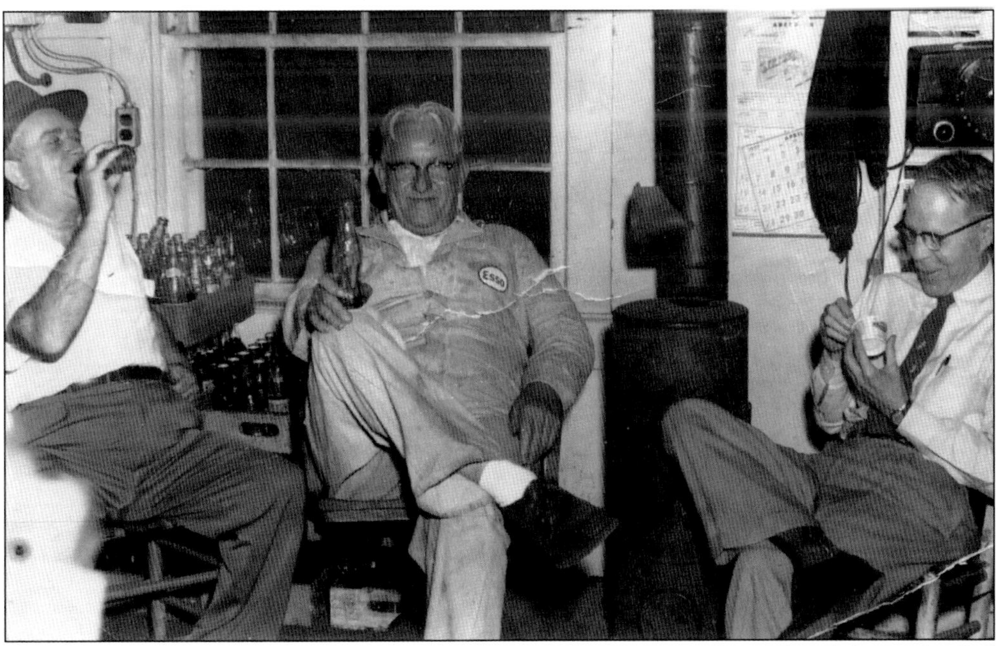

Sitting around the stove in Kellis's Esso Station in this 1957 photograph are, from left to right, Earl Freeman, owner of Sandhill Telephone Company; owner Paul Kellis; and John Sloan, personnel director of Robbins Mills. The store was a gathering place to enjoy a bottle of soda from the self-serve drink boxes, get a tire patched, and talk politics. (Courtesy of Herbert Clifton Blue.)

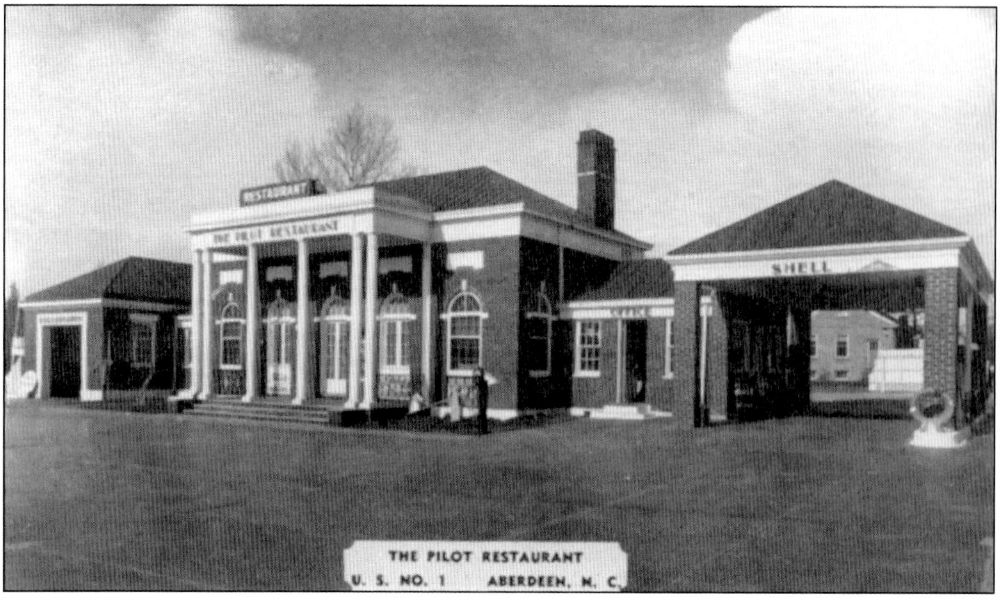

This Colonial Revival building was the Carolina Discount Company, owned by H.A. Page Jr. It would become the Fruit Growers Association offices in the 1920s. Situated on the corner of Poplar and South Streets, it later became the Pilot Restaurant and local bus stop. Morris Snell operated a Shell gas station from this building until it closed; it was demolished in the 1970s. One remaining wing was incorporated into a new office building on the site now owned by the Aberdeen Coca-Cola Bottling Company. (Author's collection.)

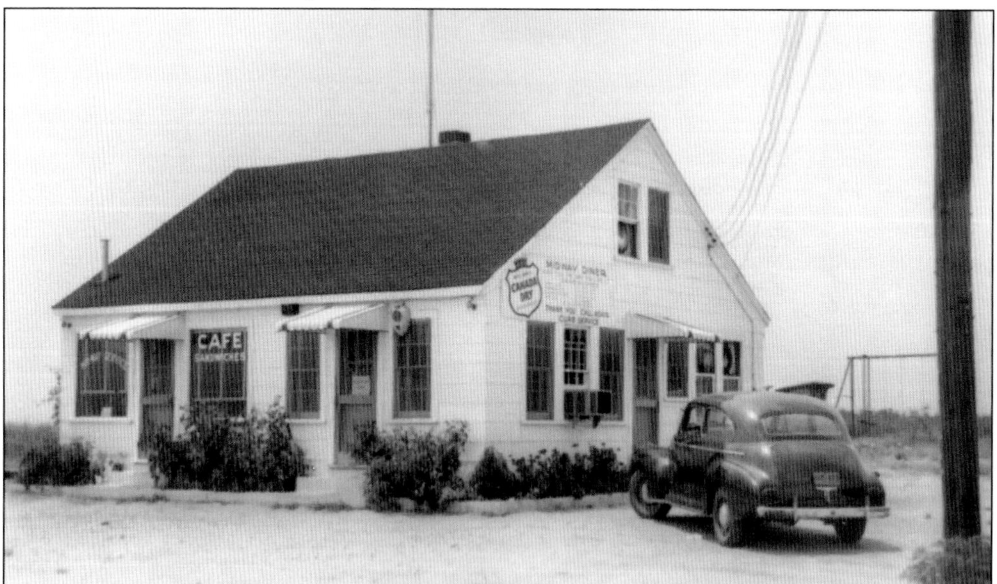

Originally a Gulf service station, Midway Diner was operated by John and Hannah Frye from 1951 to 1989. Locals often referred to it as Frye's Diner. For many years, the Frye family lived above the diner before they built a home nearby. It offered home cooking and was a popular eatery located on the corner of Highway 5 and Linden Road. Today, the building looks much as it did when photographed by H. Clifton Blue in the 1950s. (Courtesy of John Blue.)

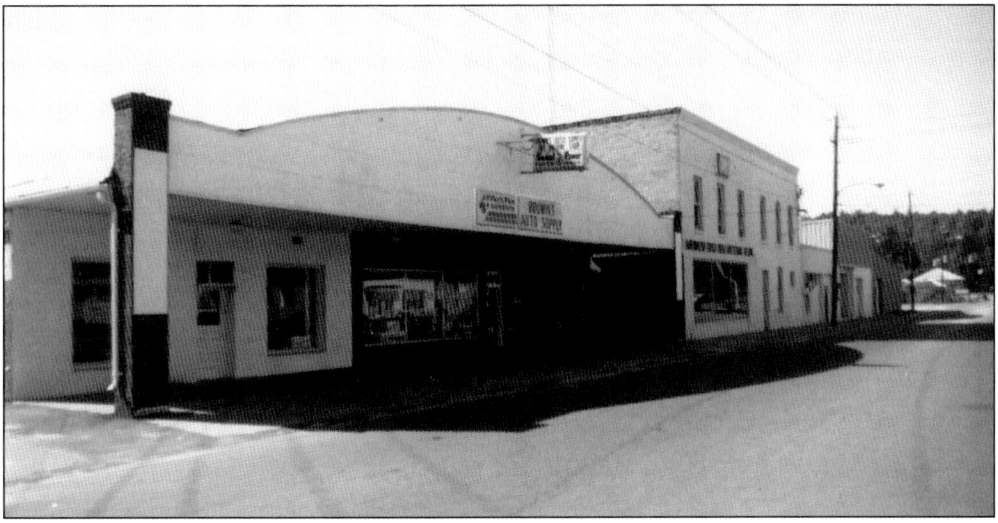

The building on the left was originally constructed around 1919 as a livery stable on South Street. The Allred Chevrolet Agency moved from Main Street into the building in the late 1920s. George Martin acquired the building and opened Martin Motors in 1930 as a Buick dealership. He added an arched canopy on the front for automobile display. The company was taken over by Robert Gwynn in the 1930s, and he operated the dealership until 1965. It later became Brown's Auto Supply for a number of years, and today is the home of Calvary Chapel of the Sandhills. On the right stands the Aberdeen Coca-Cola Bottling Company, opened by G.C. Seymour. After moving to Aberdeen in 1913, he began his career selling food and drinks on the daily north-south trains. When the building was completed in 1915, he began bottling Coca-Cola products, and today, the company he founded is one of the longest continuously operating businesses in town. He was a philanthropist and civil leader, serving as mayor of Aberdeen from 1925 to 1929. (Courtesy of the Town of Aberdeen.)

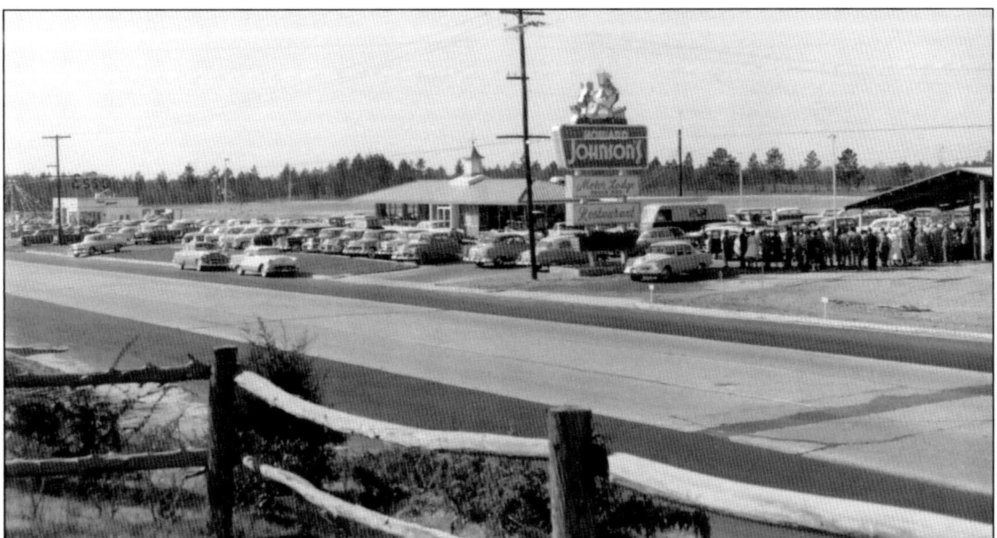

The 1958 grand opening day of Howard Johnson's Restaurant was attended by a large crowd of well-wishers and anxious patrons. Located on Highway 1 north of town, it served its famous 29 flavors of ice cream for more than 30 years. It closed in the 1990s, and the site was redeveloped. (Courtesy of Moore County Historical Society.)

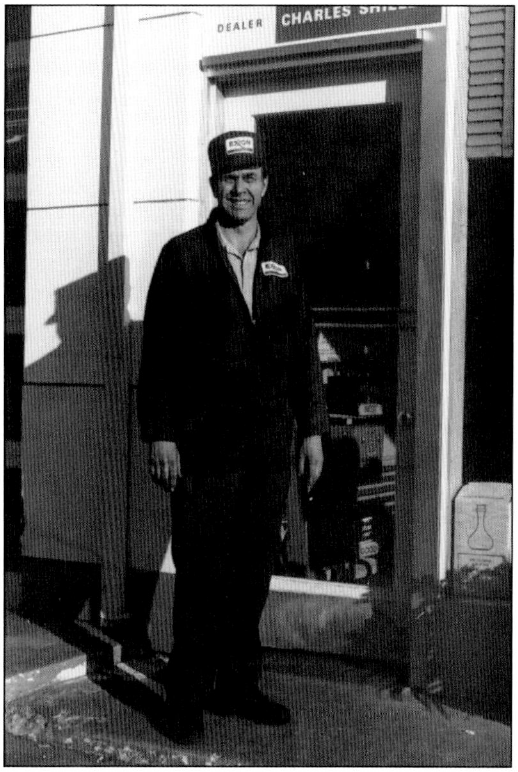

As traffic increased with the rerouting of Highway 1 after World War II, full-service automobile service stations began to appear along the highway in Aberdeen. Charles Shields owned and operated the Esso station on the corner of Highway 1 and Main Street, pumping gas and offering services such as washing windows and changing oil. His service station was located across Main Street from the volunteer fire department. When a fire call was received, he would cross the street to turn on a siren located on the roof and also drove one of the fire trucks. In retirement, Shields was active in his church and community. (Courtesy of Charles Shields.)

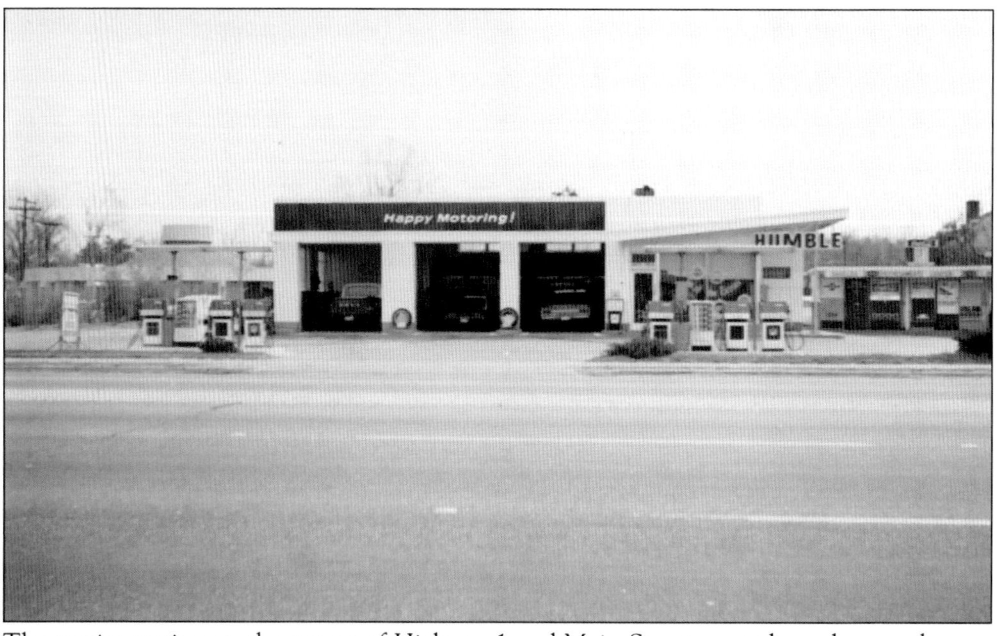

The service station on the corner of Highway 1 and Main Street went through several name changes during its lifetime. Built by Standard Oil in the 1950s after Highway 1 was completed, it operated as an Esso, Humble, and later an Exxon station. It offered full- and self-service gasoline pumps, oil changes, and engine tune-ups. Today, the gas pumps are gone, and an automobile repair garage operates in the building. (Courtesy of Charles Shields.)

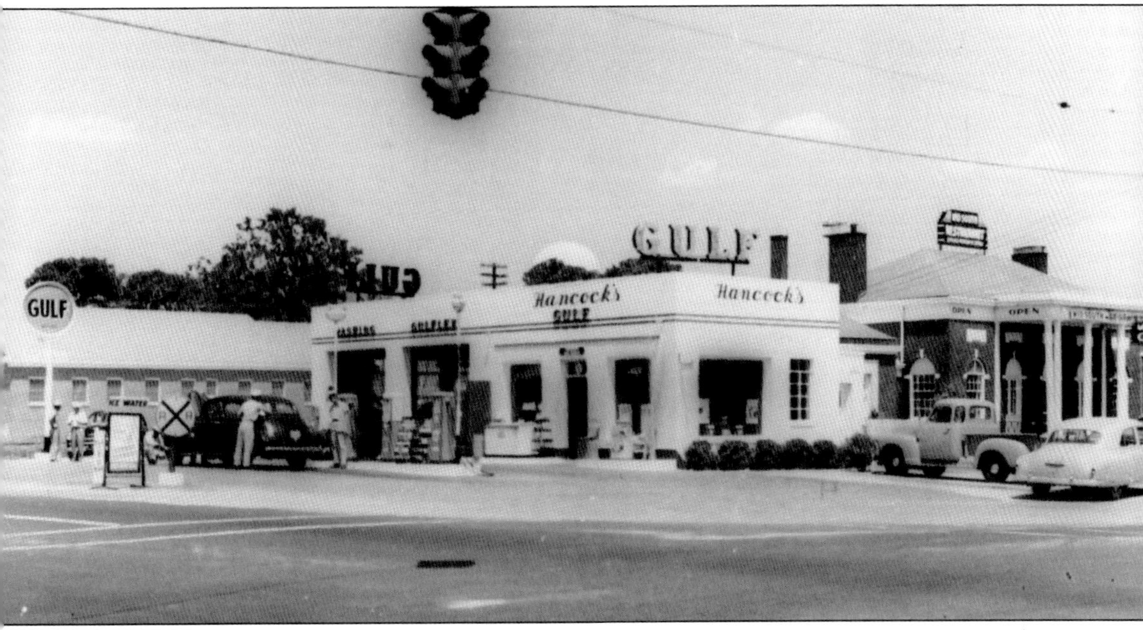

Located on Highway 1 and South Street, Edgar Hancock's full-service Gulf station is seen in this 1950s photograph. Built after Highway 1 was moved from Poplar Street, it provided full service to the motoring public for many years. Today, the gas pumps are gone, and it is used as a tire center. The dome of Page Memorial Methodist Church can be seen above the roof of the station, and the Pilot Restaurant is on the right. (Courtesy of John Blue.)

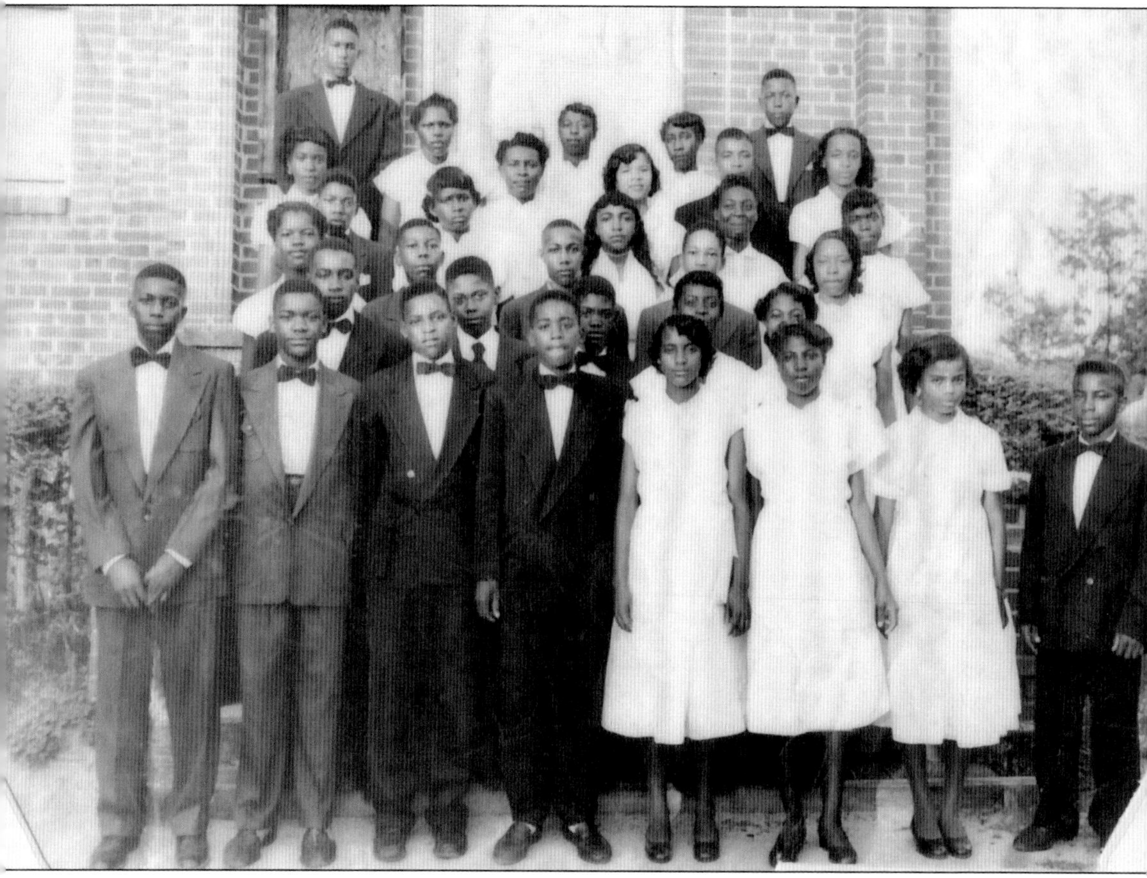

The Berkley School's eighth grade class poses in this 1953 photograph in front of St. Joseph's Church. C.C. Clark, Allen Kelly, Robert Moss, Sampson Kelly, and Henry Harris organized the school in 1939. The church was located across Keyser Street from the school. The school served as an elementary and high school until 1969, when countywide high school consolidation took place. (Courtesy of Earl Martin.)

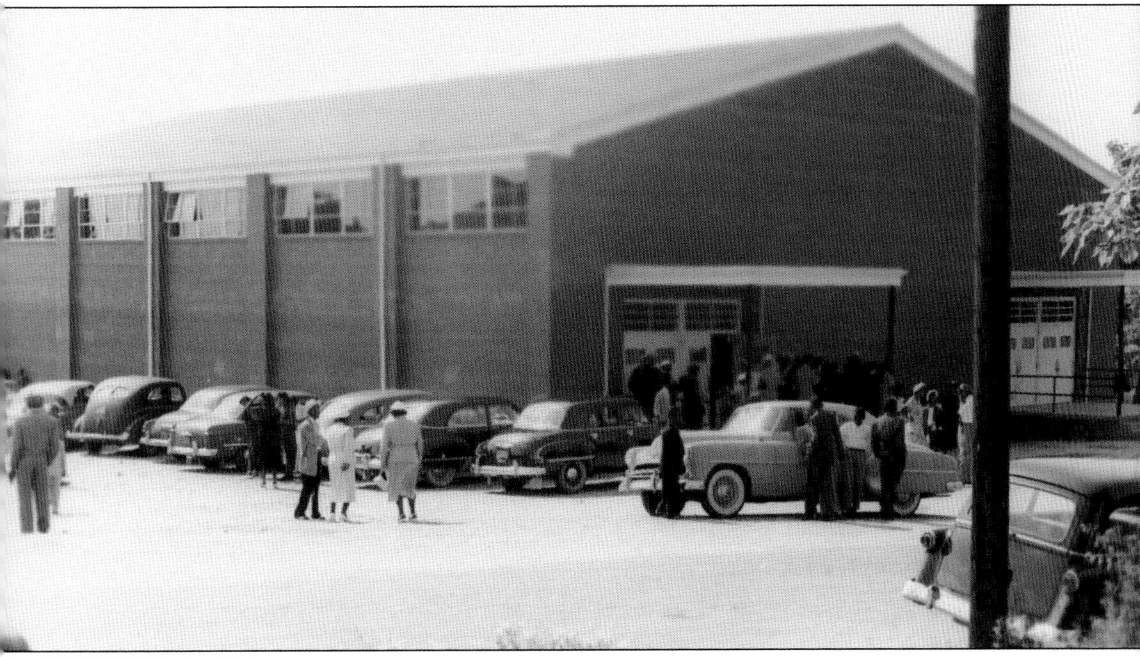

Dedication day of the newly constructed Berkeley High School gymnasium in 1954 was a highly anticipated event. The school served the Berkeley, Midway, and Broadway communities from 1935 to 1969. The basketball team mascot was the Tiger. The school, located on Keyser Street, is now Aberdeen Primary School, serving the southern end of Moore County. (Courtesy of John Blue.)

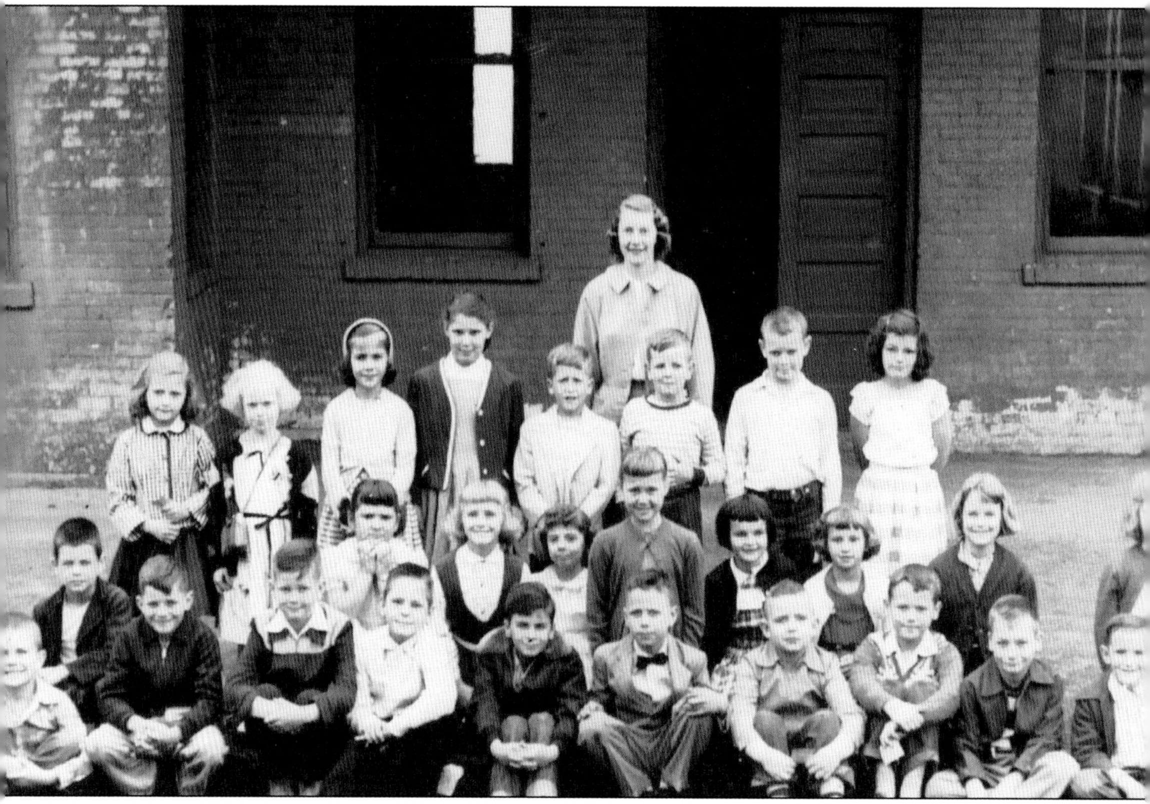

In this 1955 photograph, Daisy Watson's second grade class from Aberdeen Elementary School poses in front of Union Station prior to boarding a northbound train to the nearby town of Vass, North Carolina. This annual rail excursion was the highlight of the year for many of her students. At the end of the trip, her students returned to school, where many recounted their experience riding a passenger train. (Author's collection.)

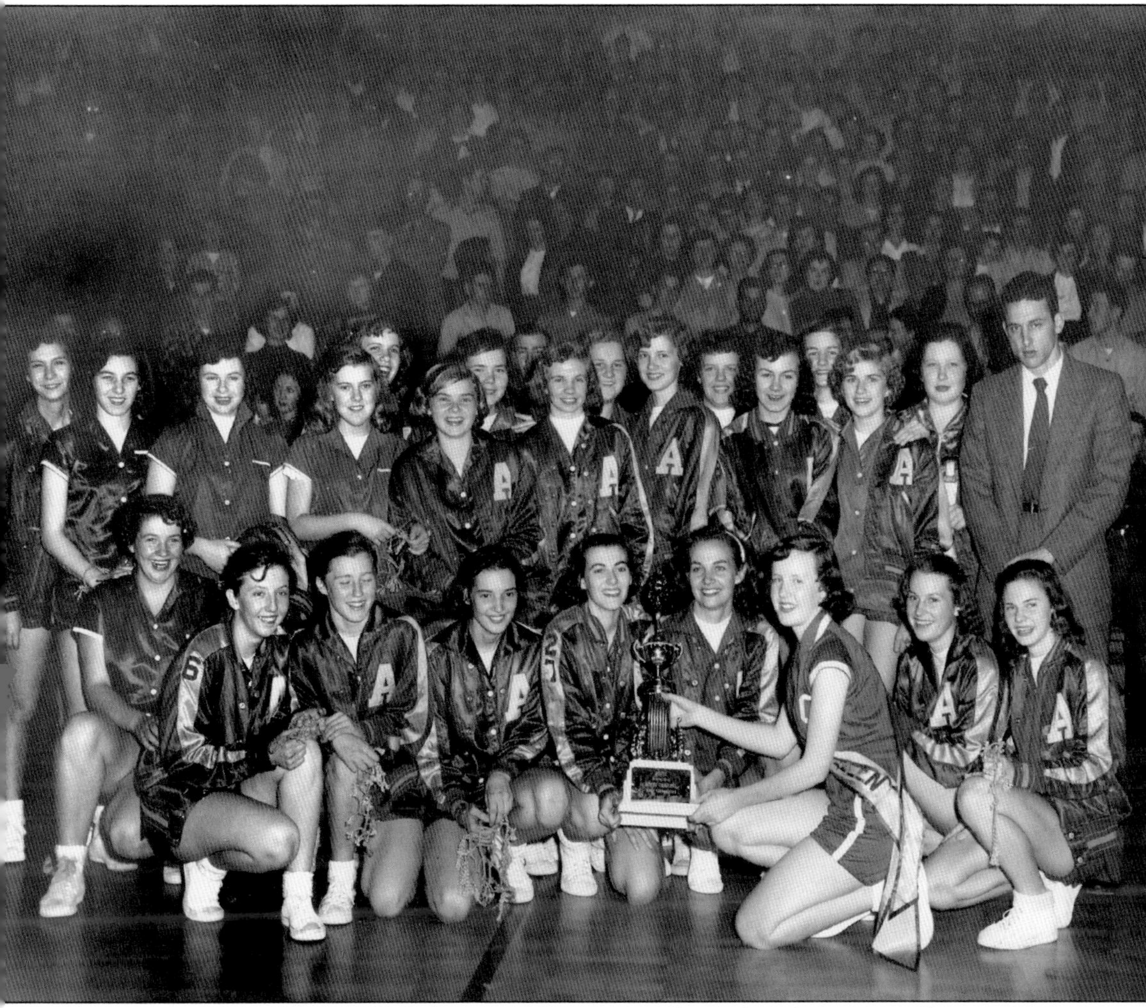

The Aberdeen High School girls' basketball team poses with coach Robert E. Lee after winning the 1953 state championship. Placing second in the 1950 championship game and finishing fourth in the 1952 final standings, the girls beat a fired-up Lincolnton High School team 59-54 before an overflow crowd of over 1,400 fans. From left to right are (first row) Elizabeth Dunn, Mary Jane Peele, Peggy Davis, Lorraine Morgan, Doris Troutman, Gladys Matthews, Ruth Currie, Dorothy Riley, and Barbara Myrick; (second row) Doley Creel, Pauline Lampley, Joan Henderson, Jackie Clippard, Ella Phillips, Phyllis Cook, Jean West, Jean Rice, Elizabeth Russell, Helen Hardister, Carol Wiley, Mary Jane Marts, Carol Baker, Carol Arey, Fay Matthews, and Lee. (Courtesy of Aberdeen High School Museum.)

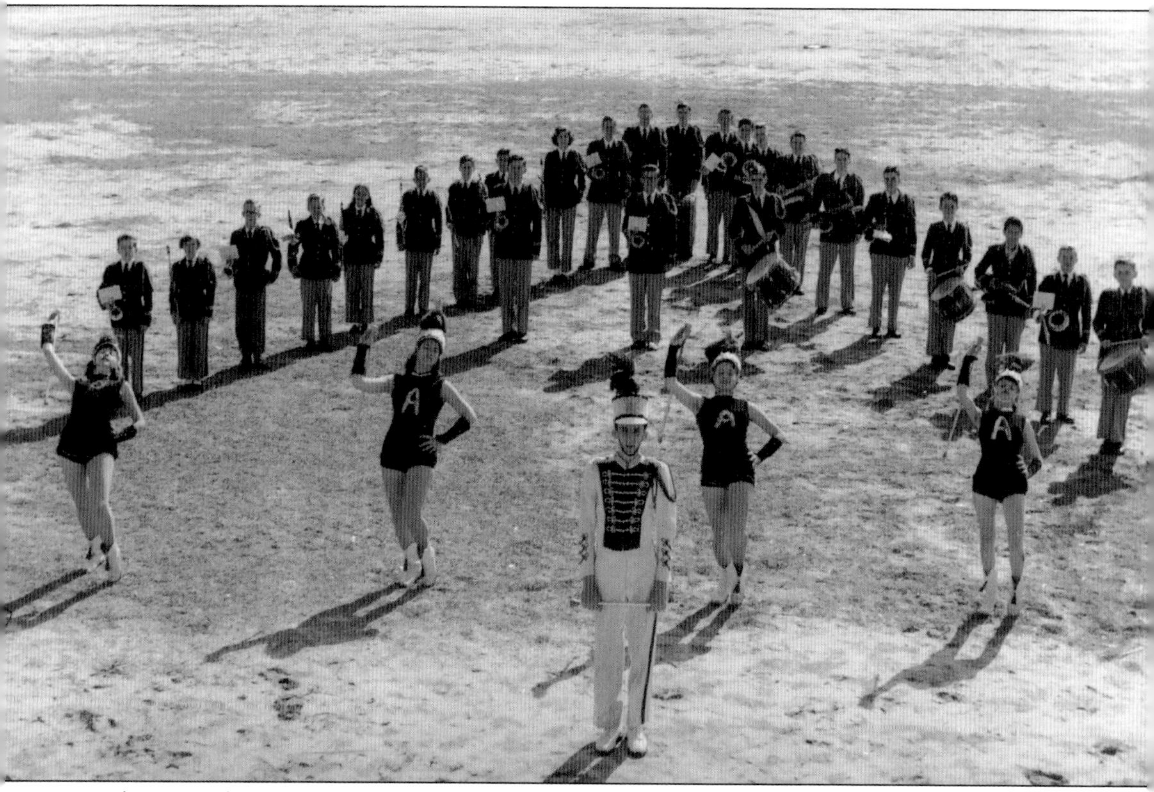

The 1956 Aberdeen High School Red Devils marching band and majorettes pose on the football field. The band director was E.H. Poole, and John Carpenter was drum major. Home team fans eagerly waited for their performances at halftime. The school had one activity bus, and the football team and band members would share seats going to away games. Due to budget constraints, the band program was phased out in the early 1960s. It was reinstated after county school consolidation in 1969. (Courtesy of Herbert Clifton Blue.)

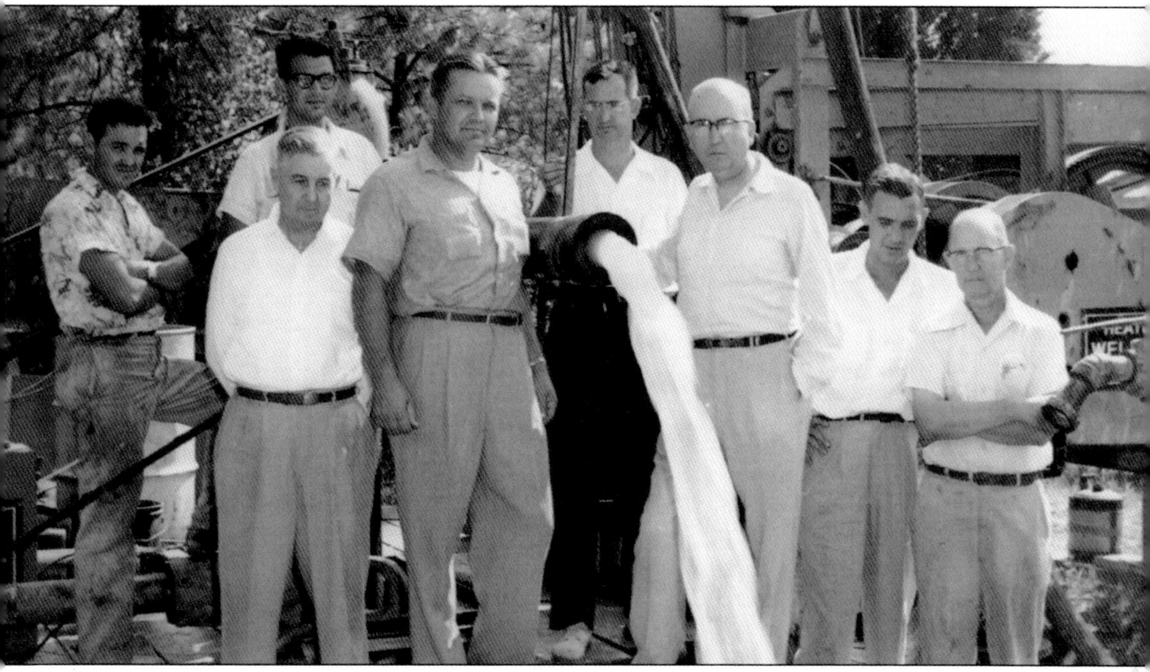

Aberdeen town officials attend the opening of a new town well in this 1950s photograph. Standing alongside a successful drilling are, from left to right, (first row) Make Pleasants, Sidney Taylor, Jere McKeithan, Mayor Erbie Medlin, Ralph Leach, and Murd Muse; (second row) employees Mario Salvador and a Mr. Jones. (Courtesy of Herbert Clifton Blue.)

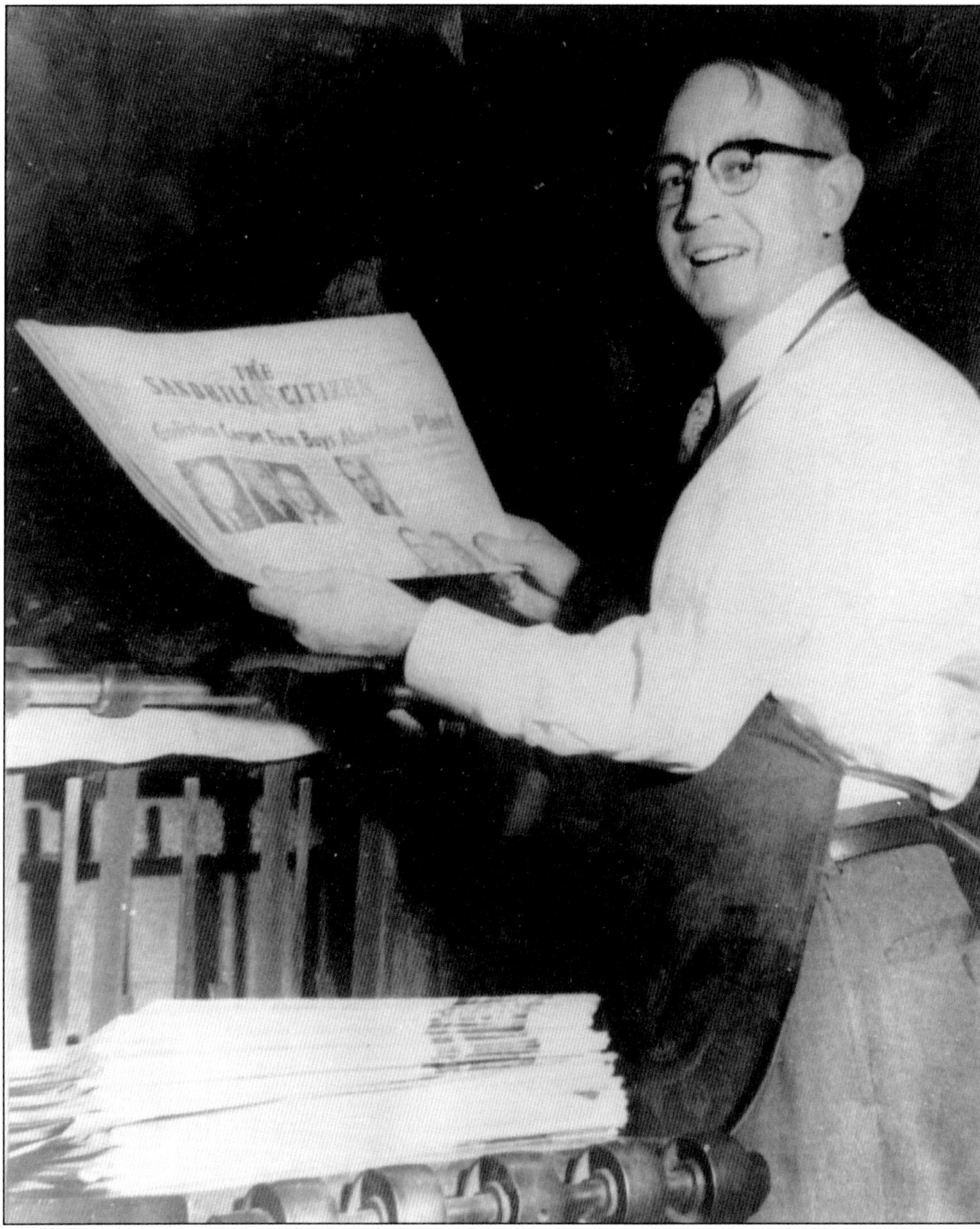

H. Clifton Blue was editor and publisher of the *Sandhill Citizen* newspaper. Blue also served nine terms in the state House of Representatives, from 1947 until 1963, when he was elected speaker of the House. In Aberdeen, he started the Fourth of July celebration in the 1960s and also established the 12:12 Club, where local business folks would meet for lunch at Horne's Restaurant on Highway 1. (Courtesy of Valerie Nicholson.)

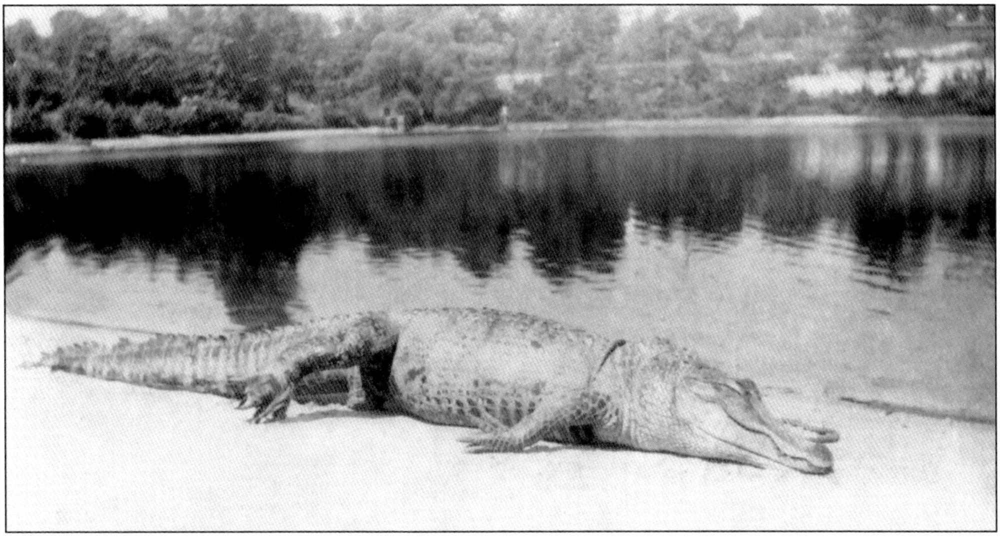

During a somewhat dull week during a summer in the 1950s, a rumor was started that a monster had been seen around Aberdeen Lake. Police chief Lamar Smith, along with men from town, investigated and solved the mystery. A very large dead alligator was pulled from the lake after gunfire was heard from the head of the lake the previous night. News editor Clifton Blue photographed the alligator and printed the story in the *Sandhill Citizen* newspaper, which caused much discussion in town as to how the alligator got into the lake. Decades later, the mystery of the monster in the lake is still a topic of conversation. Needless to say, swimming in the lake was not very popular for several summers after this incident. (Courtesy of Clifton Blue.)

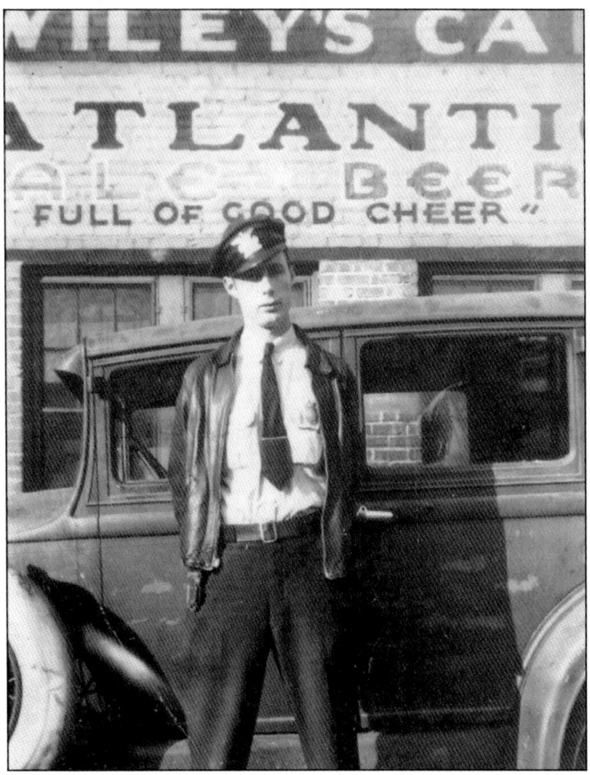

Lamar K. Smith stands outside Wiley's Café on South Street in this 1940s photograph. After graduating high school and playing college sports, Smith moved to Aberdeen from South Carolina and joined the police department. He was chief of police from 1943 to 1960 of a force that consisted of three officers, one for each eight-hour shift. Wiley's Café was a meeting and eating spot on South Street during the 1930s and 1940s. The building remains unchanged today, but the lunch and alcohol were replaced with a beauty salon. (Courtesy of Michael Conner.)

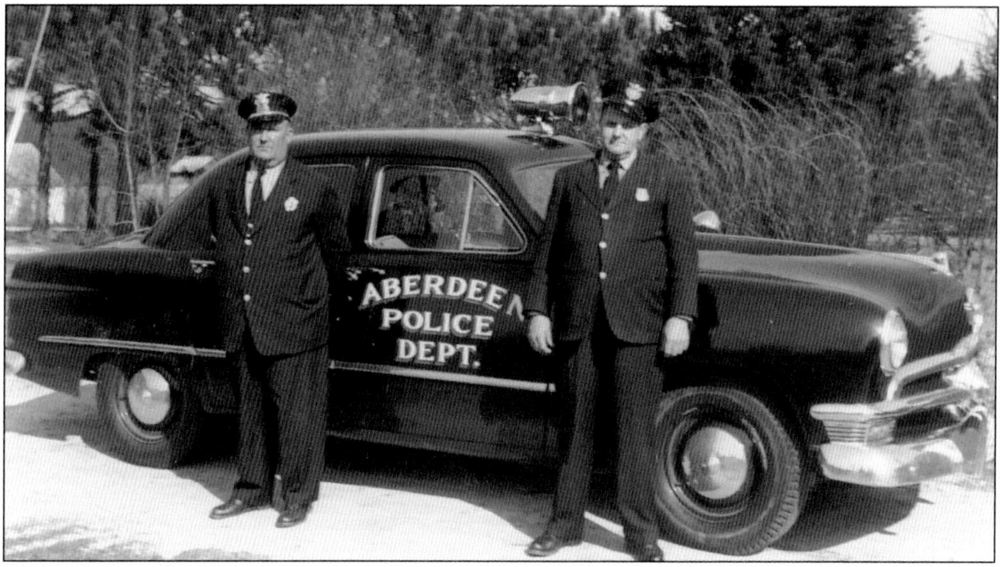

Two of Aberdeen's finest pose in this 1954 scene in front of the department's only patrol car. Policemen Archie Dees (left) and Archie Phillips were two of three full-time policemen on the force until the 1960s. When this photograph was taken, the police department consisted of a small one-room frame building on West Main Street. When a new municipal building and police department was opened in 1957, the wooden structure was torn down. The site of the one-room office is now a bank parking lot. (Courtesy of John Blue.)

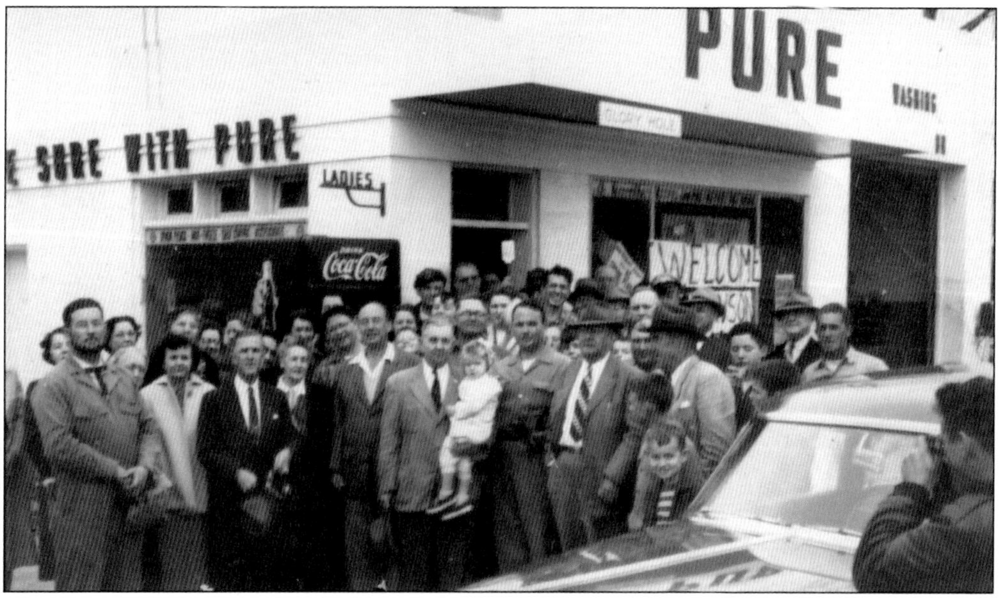

Presidential candidate Adlai Stevenson II (1900–1965) greets Aberdeen well-wishers at Hugh Styers's Pure Oil station on South Sycamore Street during the 1952 campaign. He lost to Dwight D. Eisenhower and was unsuccessful as a presidential candidate in the 1956 election. Pres. John F. Kennedy appointed him US ambassador to the United Nations, where he served from 1961 to 1965. Known as the Glory Hole, the gas station was a must stop for local, state, and national political candidates. Local men gathered at the station in the evenings, where lively discussions of sports and politics took place for several decades. (Courtesy of Herbert Clifton Blue.)

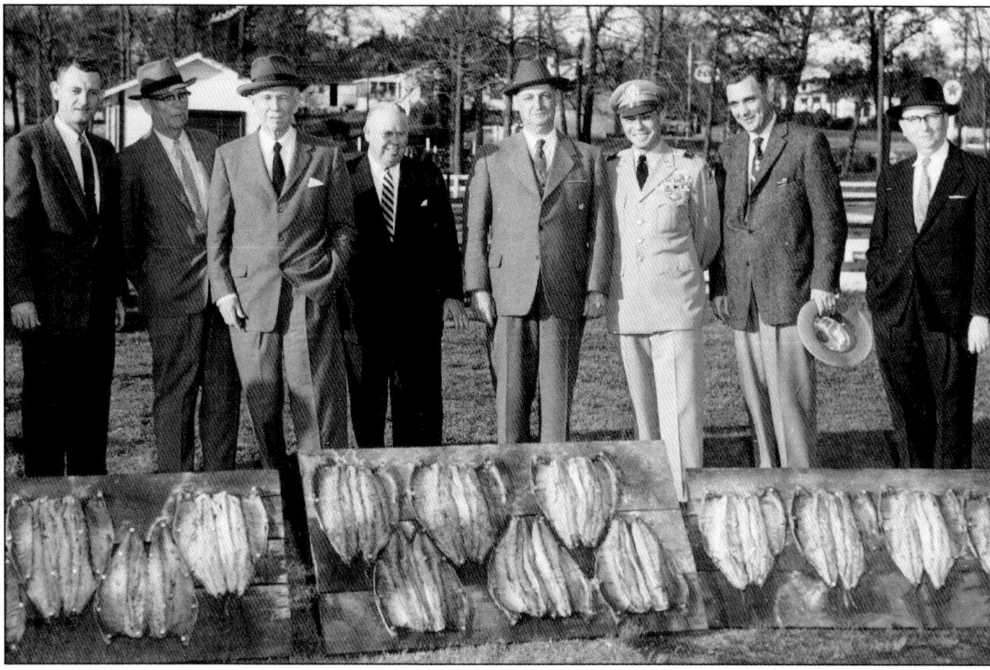

The annual shad bake began in the 1940s and continued until 1972 at Aberdeen Lake. It attracted local citizens along with politicians, members of the armed forces, regional figures, and state dignitaries. Organized by Forrest Lockey from the Aberdeen & Rockfish Railroad along with town officials, it was a popular gathering to discuss the issues of the day. The shad was brought from the coast by Curtis Lawhon and refrigerated by Aberdeen Packing Plant until prepared at the fireman's shed by local cooks. Seen in this c. 1955 photograph are, from left to right, Norfleet Pleasants, Sam Worsley, Gen. George C. Marshall (ret.), Forrest Lockey, Gen. John A. Lang, unidentified, Ralph Leach, and Dr. Erbie Medlin. (Both, courtesy of Forrest Lockey.)

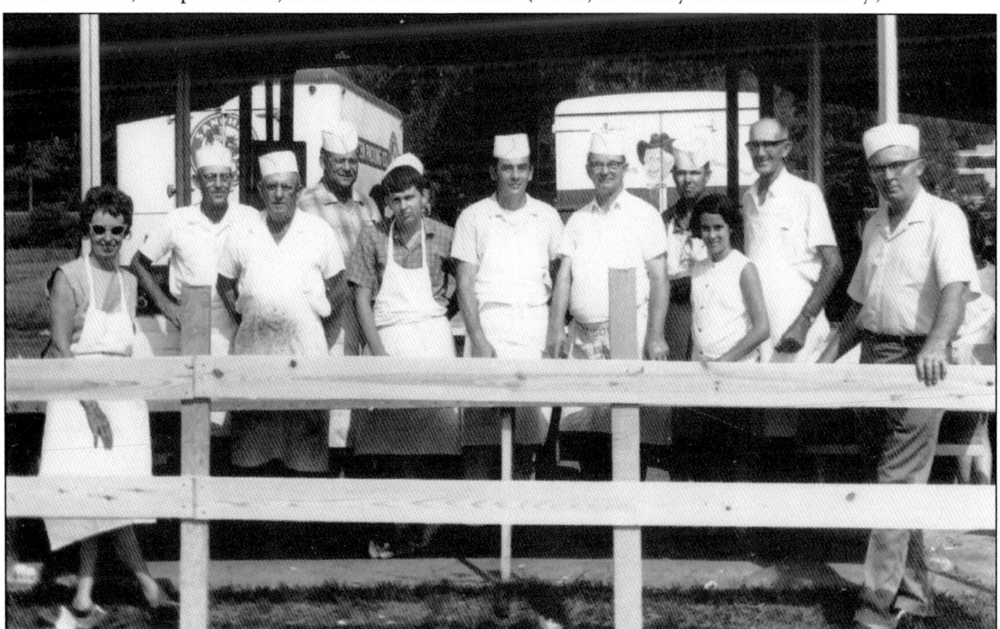

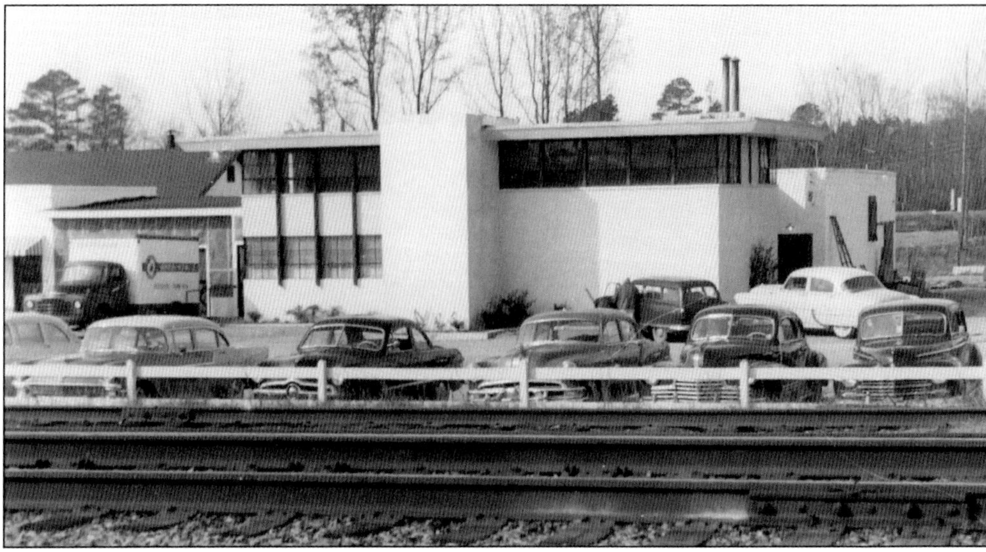

Opened in 1946, the Aberdeen Packing Plant on South Sycamore Street was an abattoir and supplier of fresh meat and meat products to local grocery stores. Started by Knox Matthews and Ernest Greene, it remained in operation slaughtering hogs and cattle into the 1970s. A wholesale distributor occupies the building today. (Courtesy of John Blue.)

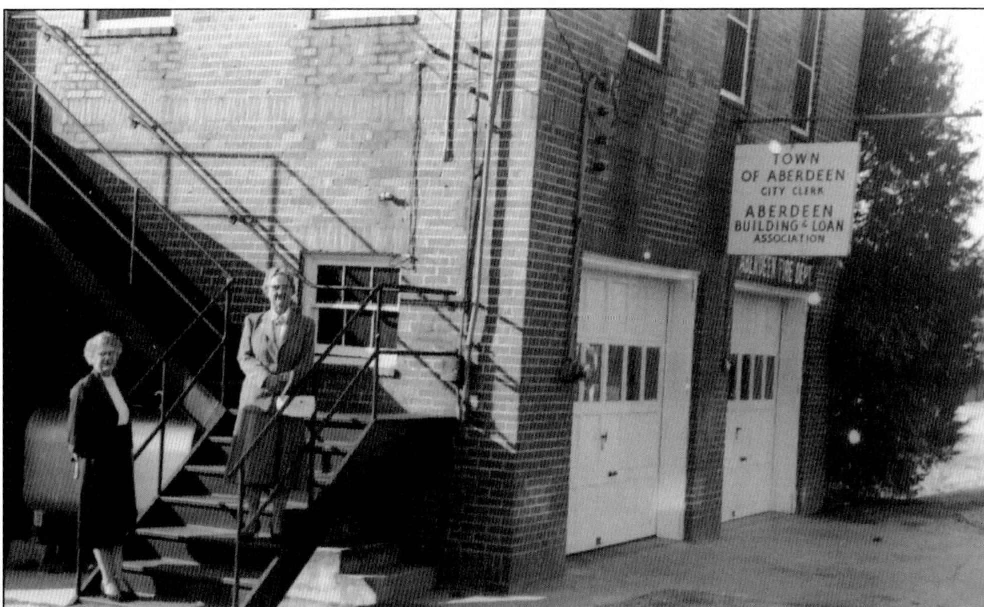

The first brick combination town hall and fire department was located on the corner of Main Street and Highway 1. In this 1954 photograph, town employees Bess Gunter (left) and Evelyn Pleasants stand on the steps that lead upstairs to the municipal offices. The two-bay volunteer Aberdeen Fire Department was located downstairs. In 1957, a new town administration building was constructed adjacent to this structure, and the administrative offices moved, leaving the entire building as the fire department. A modern fire department facility was constructed on Holly Street in 1984, and the old building, after sustaining a fire, was demolished in 1986. (Courtesy of John Blue.)

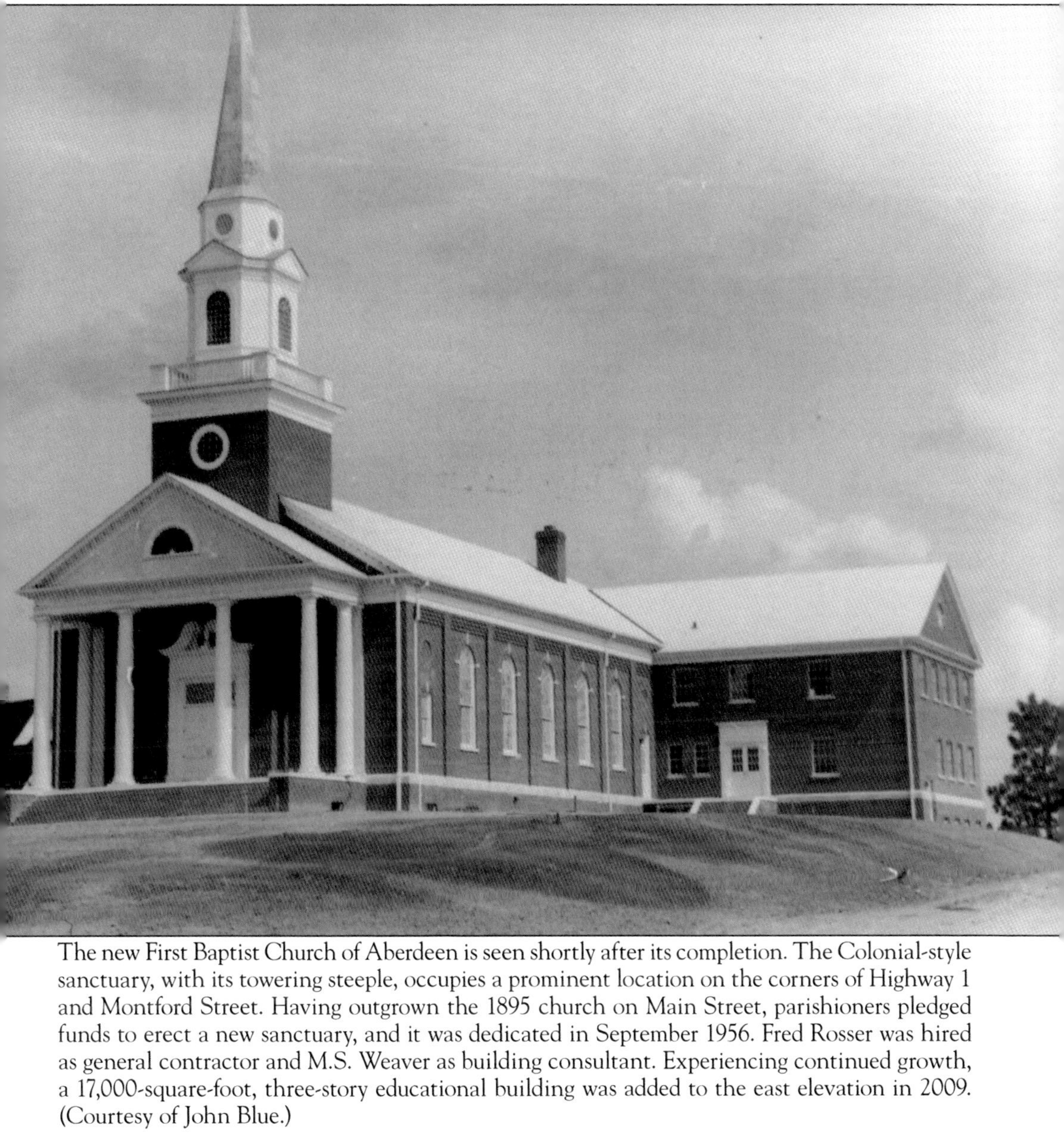

The new First Baptist Church of Aberdeen is seen shortly after its completion. The Colonial-style sanctuary, with its towering steeple, occupies a prominent location on the corners of Highway 1 and Montford Street. Having outgrown the 1895 church on Main Street, parishioners pledged funds to erect a new sanctuary, and it was dedicated in September 1956. Fred Rosser was hired as general contractor and M.S. Weaver as building consultant. Experiencing continued growth, a 17,000-square-foot, three-story educational building was added to the east elevation in 2009. (Courtesy of John Blue.)

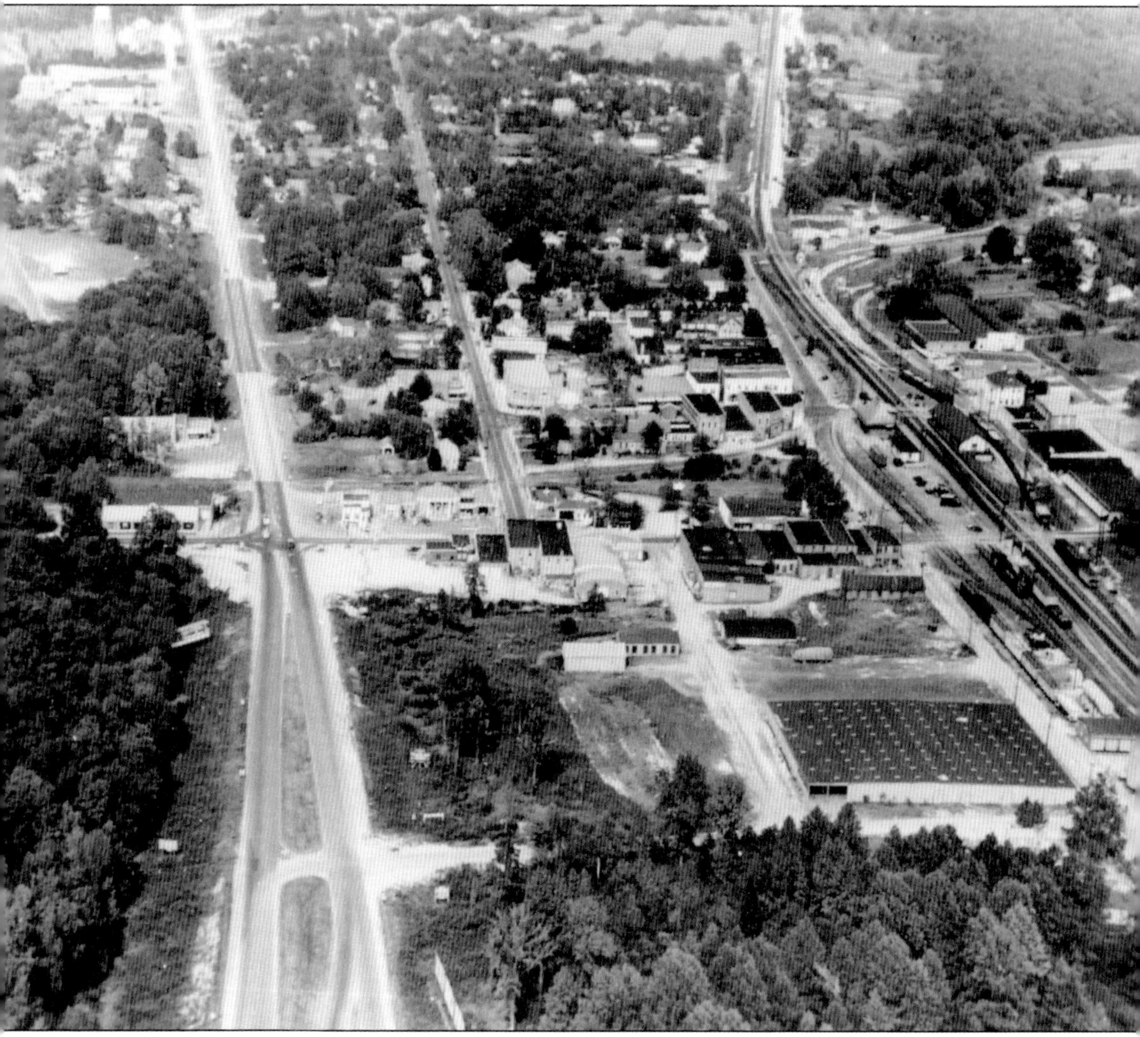

A 1950s aerial view looking north shows Highway 1 and the downtown section of Aberdeen. The large, metal roofed building seen on the right is one of the many tobacco warehouses in town that was important for local growers selling their tobacco crops. The process of growing, selling, and warehousing tobacco was a major industry in the area for many years. Only a few of the warehouses remain today and are occupied by other businesses. (Courtesy of Martha Swaringen.)

Four

A Century of Growth

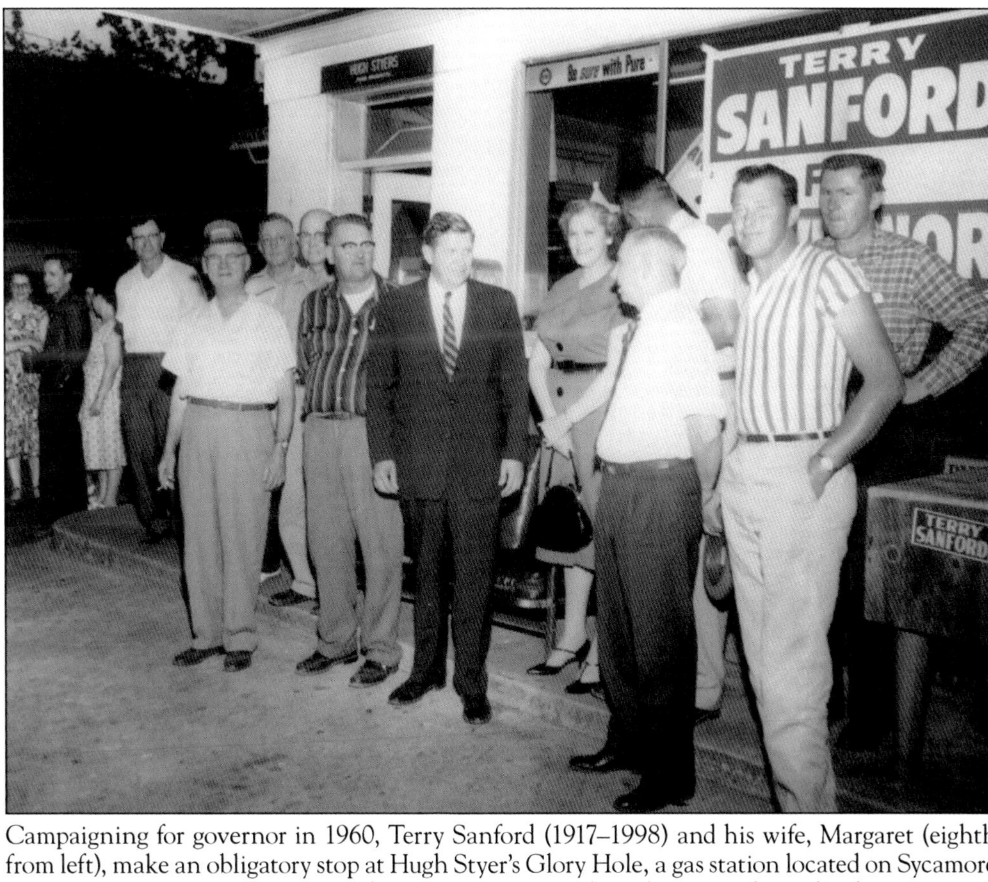

Campaigning for governor in 1960, Terry Sanford (1917–1998) and his wife, Margaret (eighth from left), make an obligatory stop at Hugh Styer's Glory Hole, a gas station located on Sycamore Street. Sanford served as governor from 1961 to 1965 and was later president of Duke University. The Glory Hole was a hotbed of local politics in Aberdeen for many years, and candidates running for public office often made it a campaign stop. (Courtesy of John Blue.)

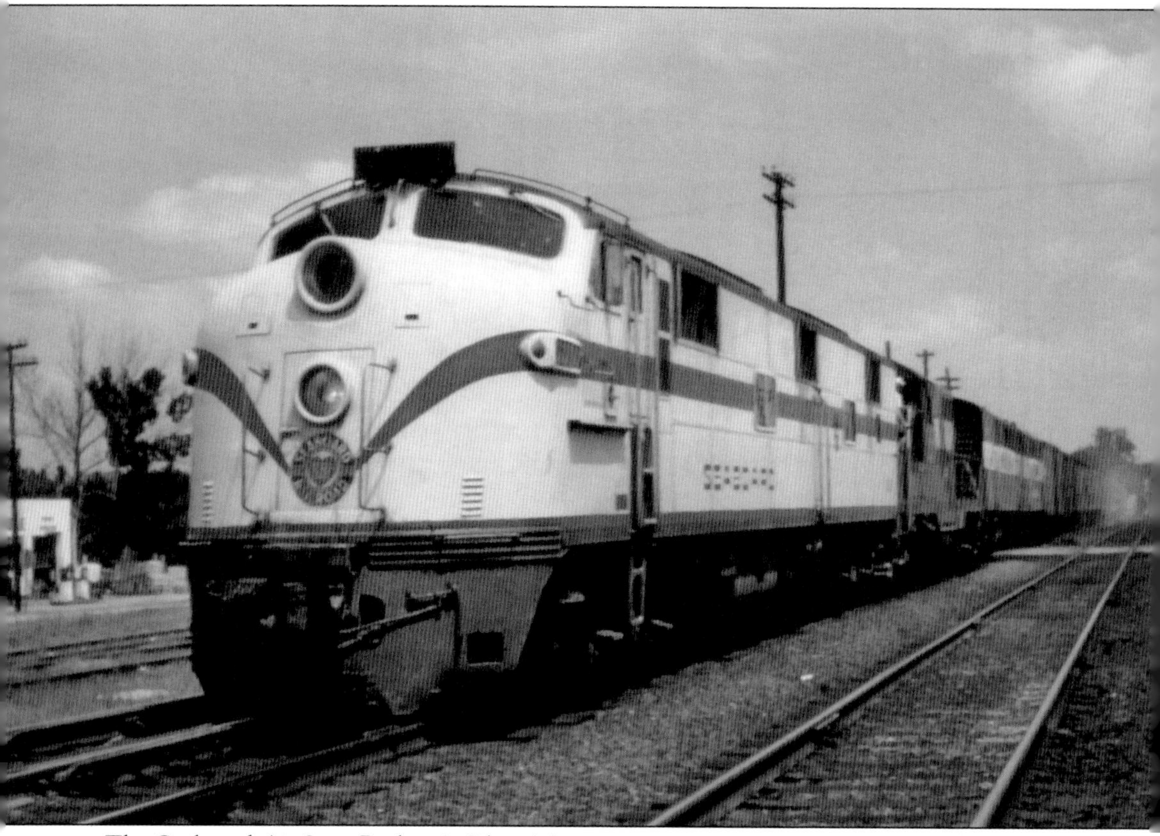

The Seaboard Air Line Railway's Silver Meteor passenger train is preparing to depart Union Station for points south in 1962. The train began service in 1939, transporting passengers between New York and Florida. Passenger service from Union Station ended in the 1970s. The building on the left is Hugh Styers's Pure Oil service station. (Author's collection.)

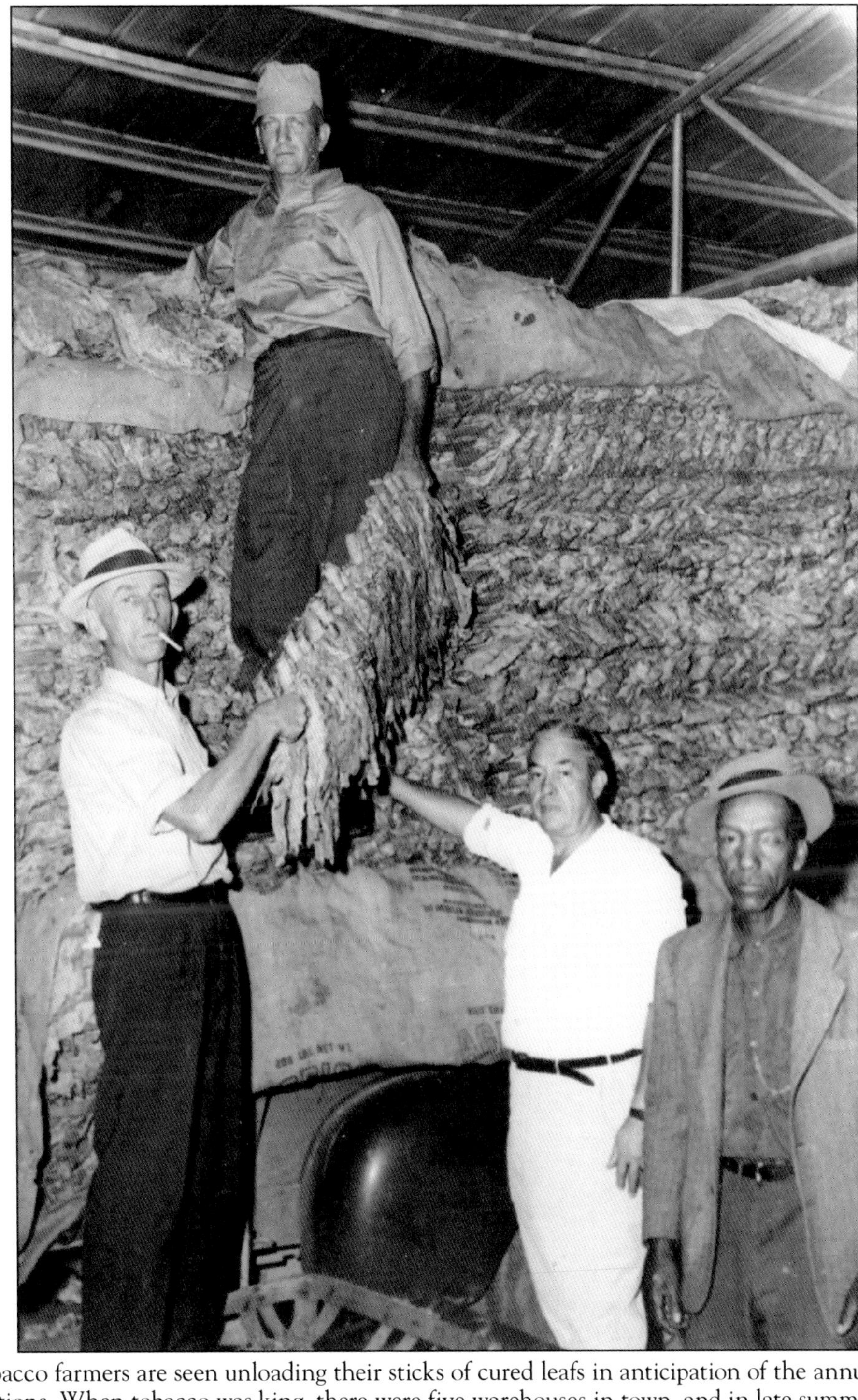

Tobacco farmers are seen unloading their sticks of cured leafs in anticipation of the annual fall auctions. When tobacco was king, there were five warehouses in town, and in late summer, the streets would be full of trucks and trailers bringing the crops in for sorting and grading. When the warehouses were full, the aroma of tobacco permeated the town. (Courtesy of Herbert Clifton Blue.)

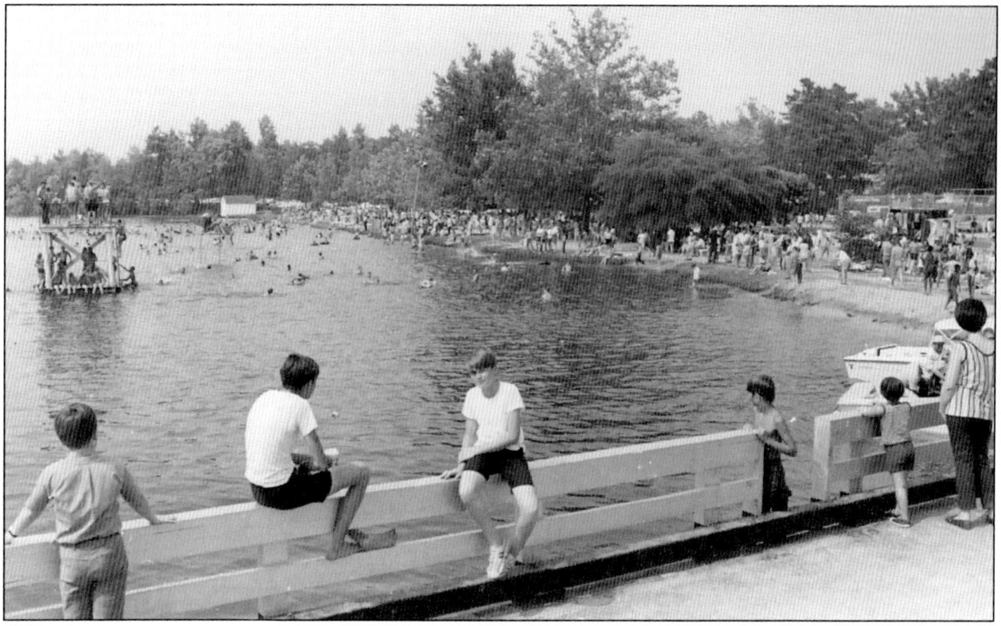

For more than five decades, Aberdeen Lake was the summer place to be. Originally dammed by Allison Francis Page for a sawmill, it evolved into a popular swimming, sunbathing, and recreation destination for miles around. A wooden bathhouse with a concession stand was built in the 1930s, and three platforms were erected on poles for diving into the lake. The distance from the shore to each platform varied by swimming abilities, the farthest one having two levels and a diving board. A concrete pad and jukebox provided music and a place to dance into the night. Locals and visitors from surrounding communities filled the lake from the first day of summer until Labor Day. A USO was opened during World War II and was a frequent stop for off-duty soldiers from Camp Mackall. The lake was closed for swimming in the 1990s, and the towers and bathhouse were torn down. Boating, fishing, and hiking are favorite pastimes for many who visit the lake today. (Both, author's collection.)

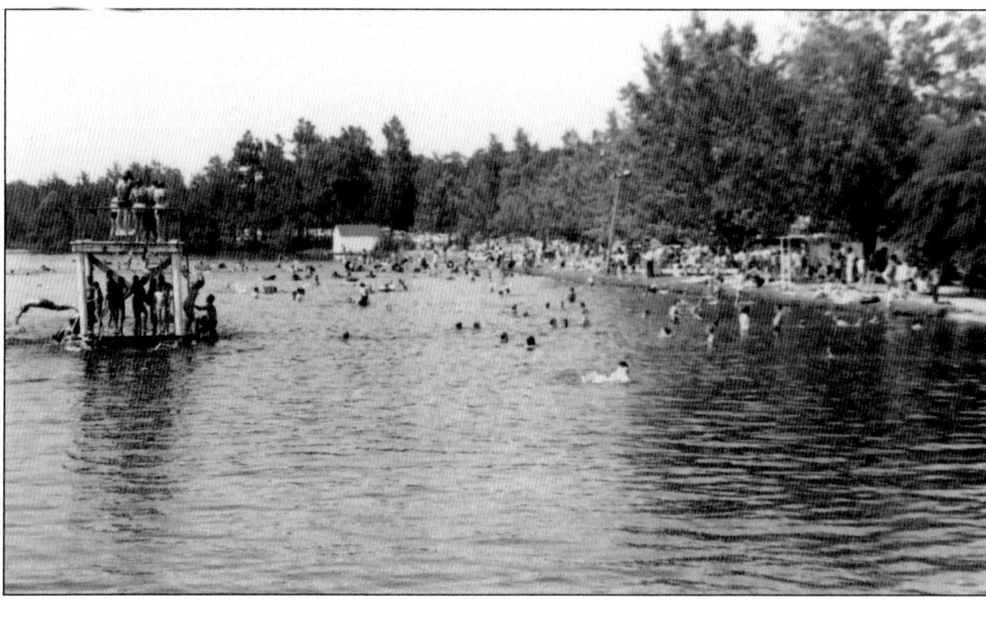

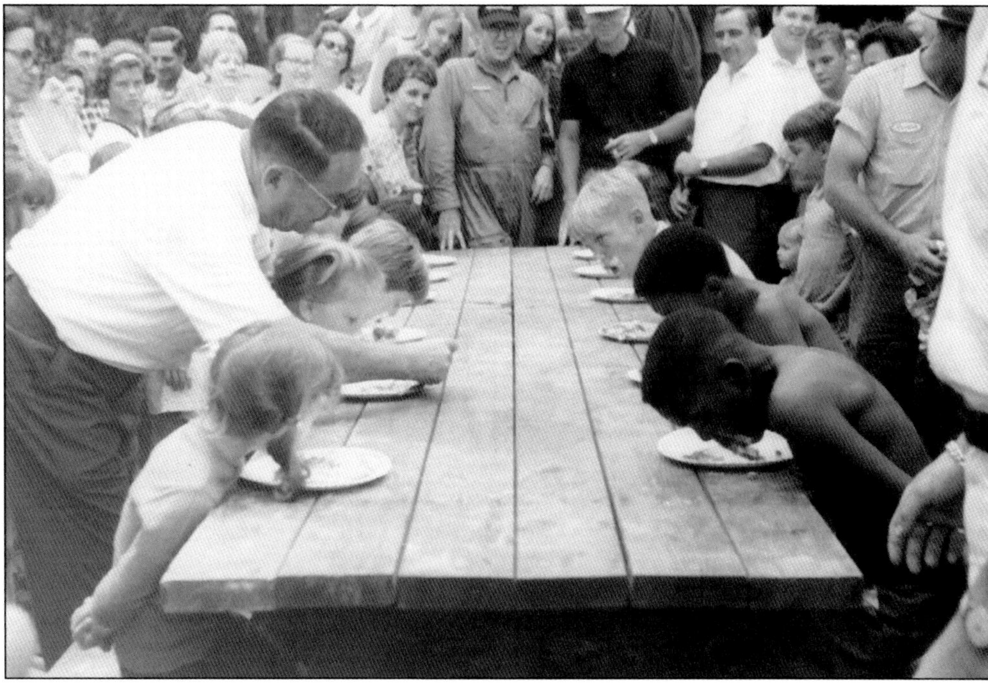

One of the big events for many years was the annual celebration of the Fourth of July at Aberdeen Lake. Crowds would gather to swim, eat, and enjoy the events. In this scene from the 1960s, the pie-eating contest was a hit with the youth who stuck their faces into pies and ate them without using their hands. Another eagerly awaited activity was climbing a greasy pole erected by the fire department for the occasion. Money was placed on the top of the pole, and whoever reached the top first claimed it. Today, the fun and games at the lake on Independence Day are more controlled and organized by the town parks and recreation department. (Both, courtesy of John Blue.)

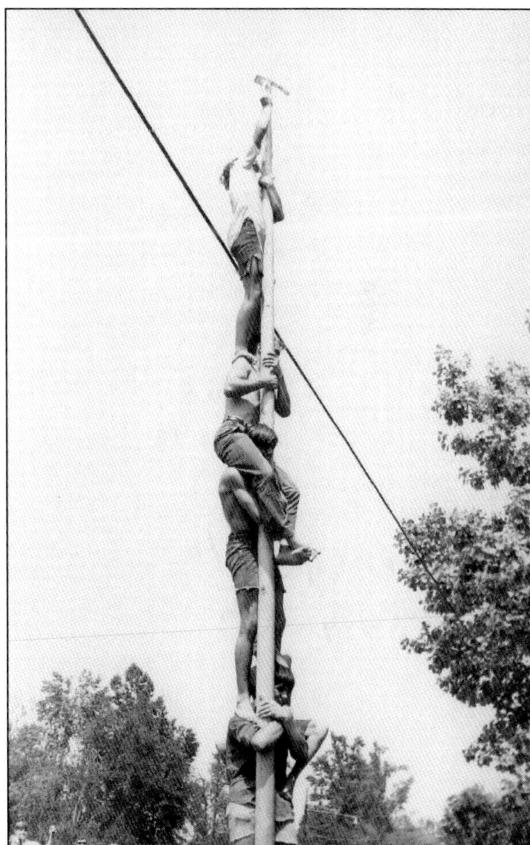

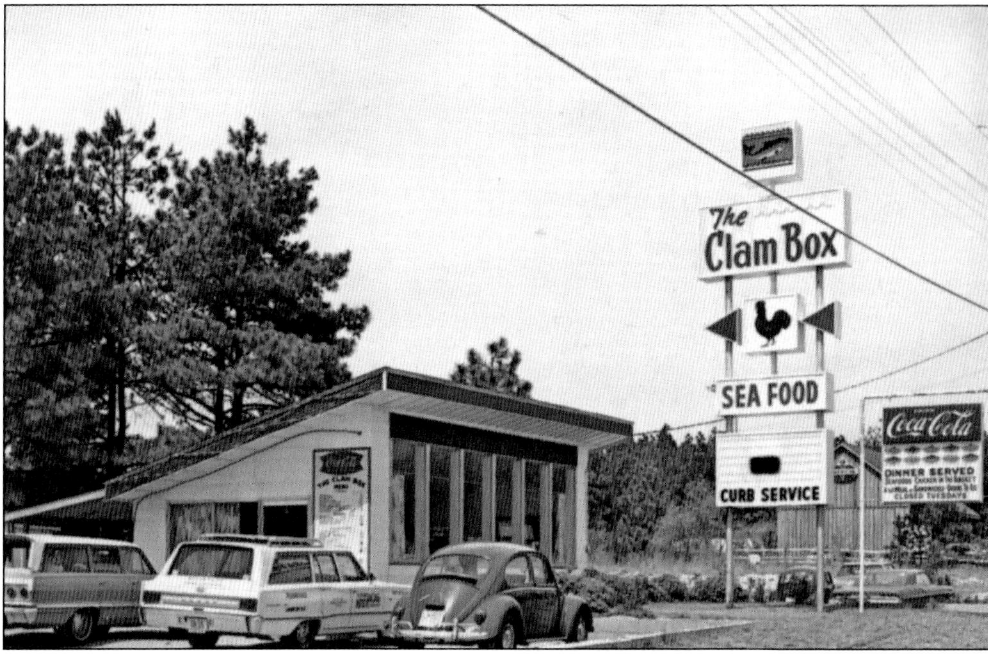

The completion of the Highway 1 bypass of Aberdeen and Southern Pines after World War II opened business opportunities between the two towns. One of the first to open was the Clam Box restaurant. Ernest and Julia Green bought the business from Dee Crowley, and it became a convenient stop for hungry travelers and a favorite hangout for high school students after school and on weekends. After the death of Ernest in 1964, the Green family continued to operate the restaurant as evident by the name cancellation on the business card. For more than 30 years, it served hamburgers, seafood, chicken baskets, and the famous 10¢ hot dog. Closed in 1972 to make way for a Wendy's restaurant, the tall sign survived, having been moved to a pizza restaurant several miles north. (Above, courtesy of John Blue; below, author's collection.)

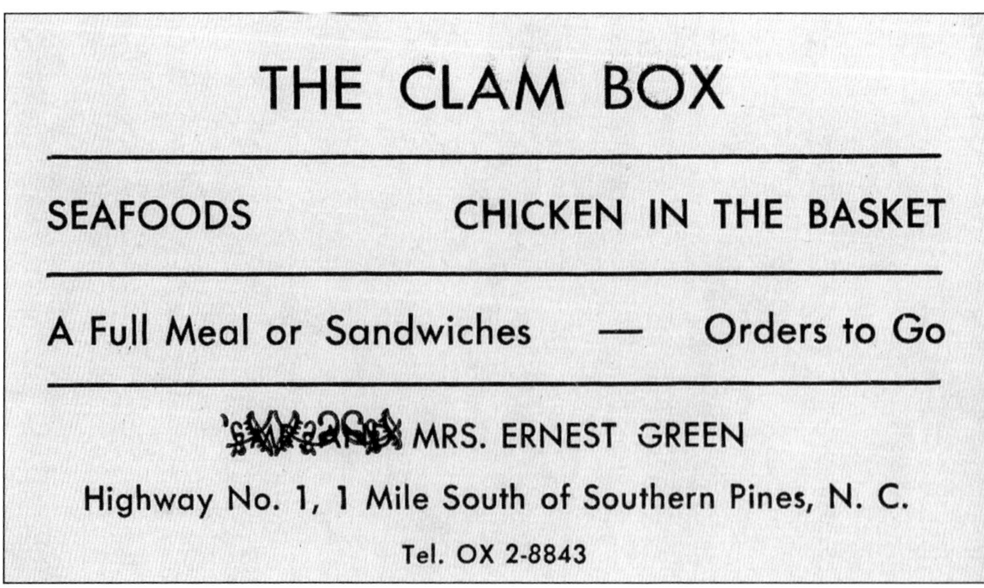
THE CLAM BOX

SEAFOODS CHICKEN IN THE BASKET

A Full Meal or Sandwiches — Orders to Go

MRS. ERNEST GREEN

Highway No. 1, 1 Mile South of Southern Pines, N. C.

Tel. OX 2-8843

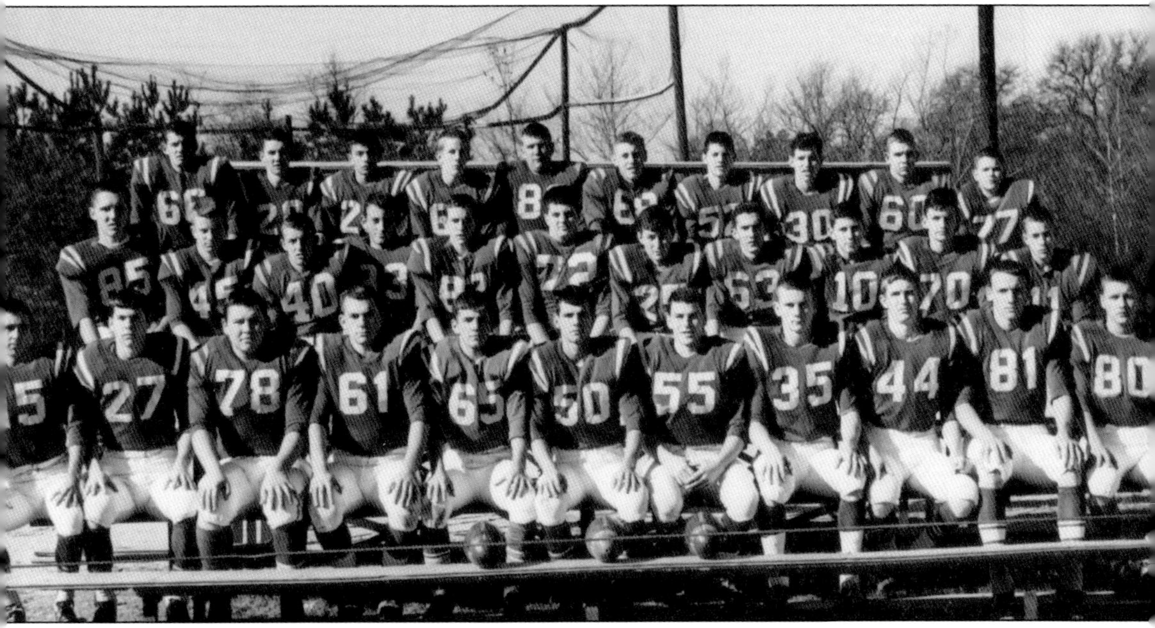

The Aberdeen High School football team poses in preparation for the 1963 season. From left to right are (first row) Johnny Burns, Dickie Walters, Bob Matthews, Larry Muse, Rodger Puckett, Danny Batchelor, Daryl Wynn, Gary Thompson, Gary Mofield, Wayne Lewis, and Lester Williams; (second row) Bill Yates, Gene Thompson, Andy Stoots, Lynn Monroe, Mike Adams, Mickey Melvin, Robert Garrison, Lewis Aycock, Charles Wicker, Gene Lewis, and Barry Craven; (third row) Joe Bilyew, Charles Swearingen, John Mims, Ben Wicks, James Styers, Tom Craven, Jimmy Robertson, James Mims, Mac Lathan, and Baxter Taylor. The Red Devils were state runners-up and won the Cape Fear Conference Championship. (Courtesy of John Burns.)

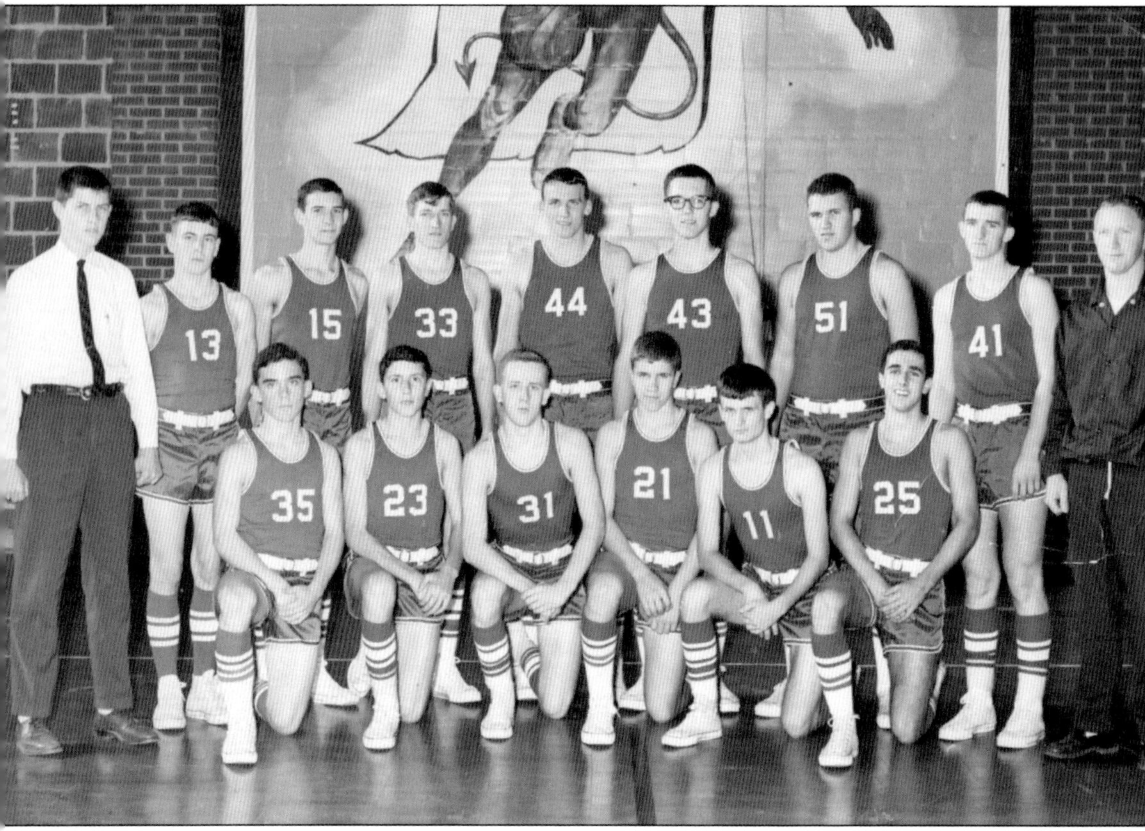

The 1964–1965 Aberdeen High School boys' basketball team was coached by Ben Utley (right), and the team manager was Jimmy Robertson (left). Posing in front of the Red Devil mascot painted on the gymnasium wall are, from left to right, (first row) Johnny Geer, Charles Wicker, Jimmy Bobbitt, Randy Sheffield, Tommy Veasey, and Johnny Burns; (second row) Robertson, Jimmy Tims, Wayne Luck, Jerry Brown, Wayne Lewis, Bill Yates, Eddie Sheffield, Billy Boyte, and Utley. (Courtesy of John Burns.)

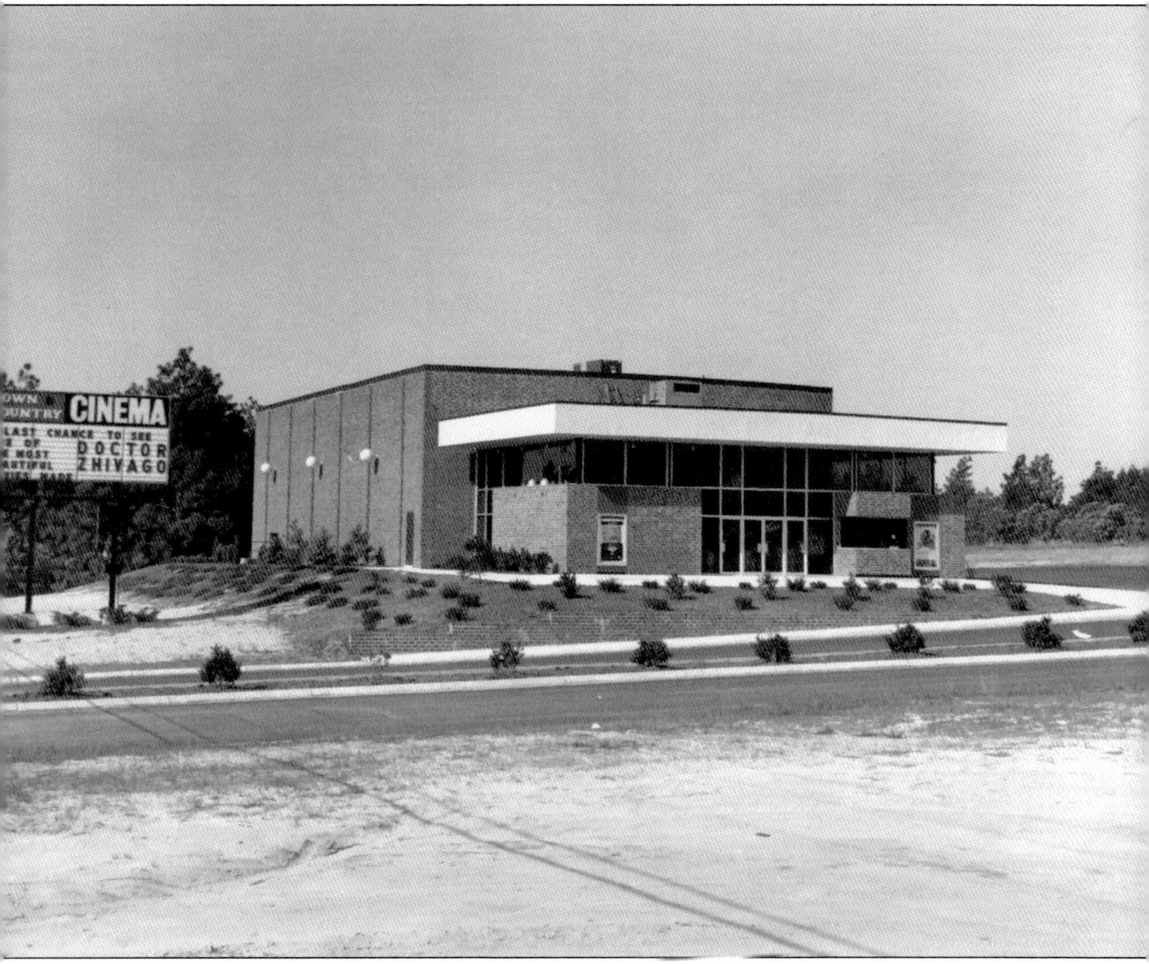

Town and Country Cinema, constructed in 1964, was the first modern theater built in Aberdeen. It was located adjacent to Town and Country Shopping Center. Patrons enjoyed amenities not found in older theaters in the area. It was razed in 2011 and replaced by a restaurant. (Courtesy of Moore County Historical Society.)

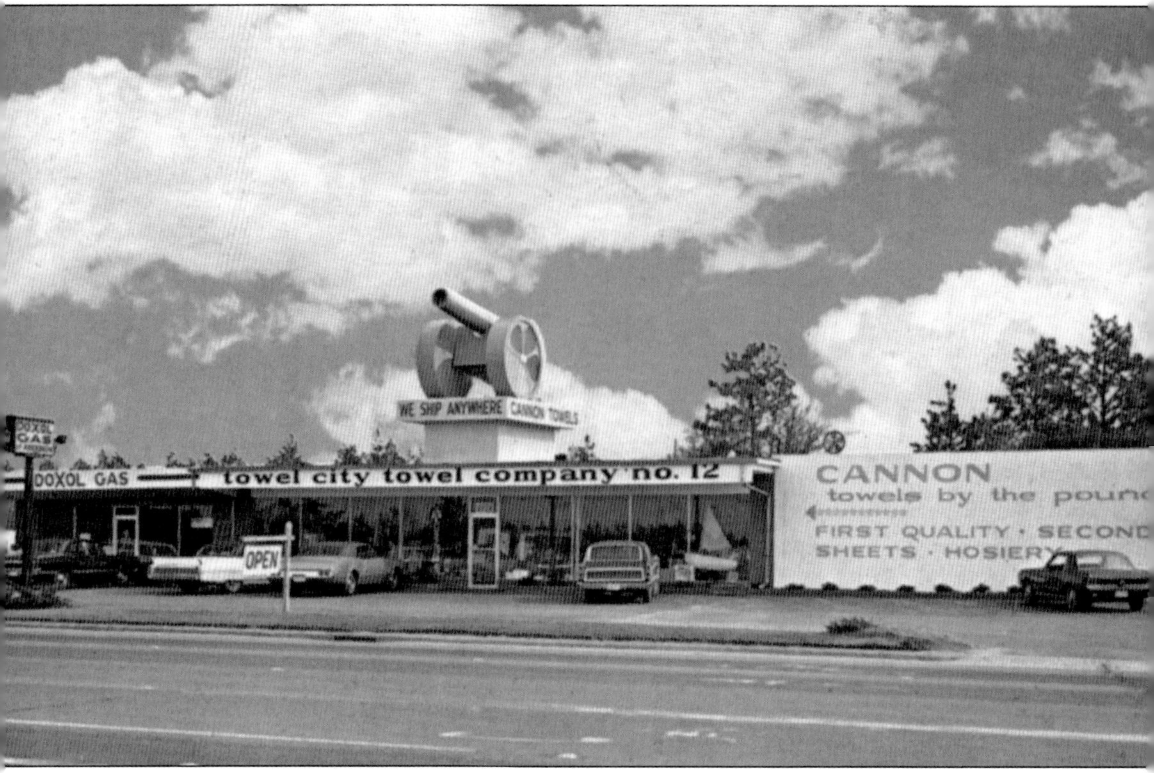

The Cannon Towel Outlet Store on Highway 1 North had a large wooden cannon on the roof for advertising. The wheels had colorful neon lights inside, and an electric motor turned the spokes that gave it the illusion the cannon was moving. It operated as a towel outlet from the late 1950s to the 1980s. Today, the iconic cannon is gone, and a golf equipment store occupies the building. (Courtesy of John Blue.)

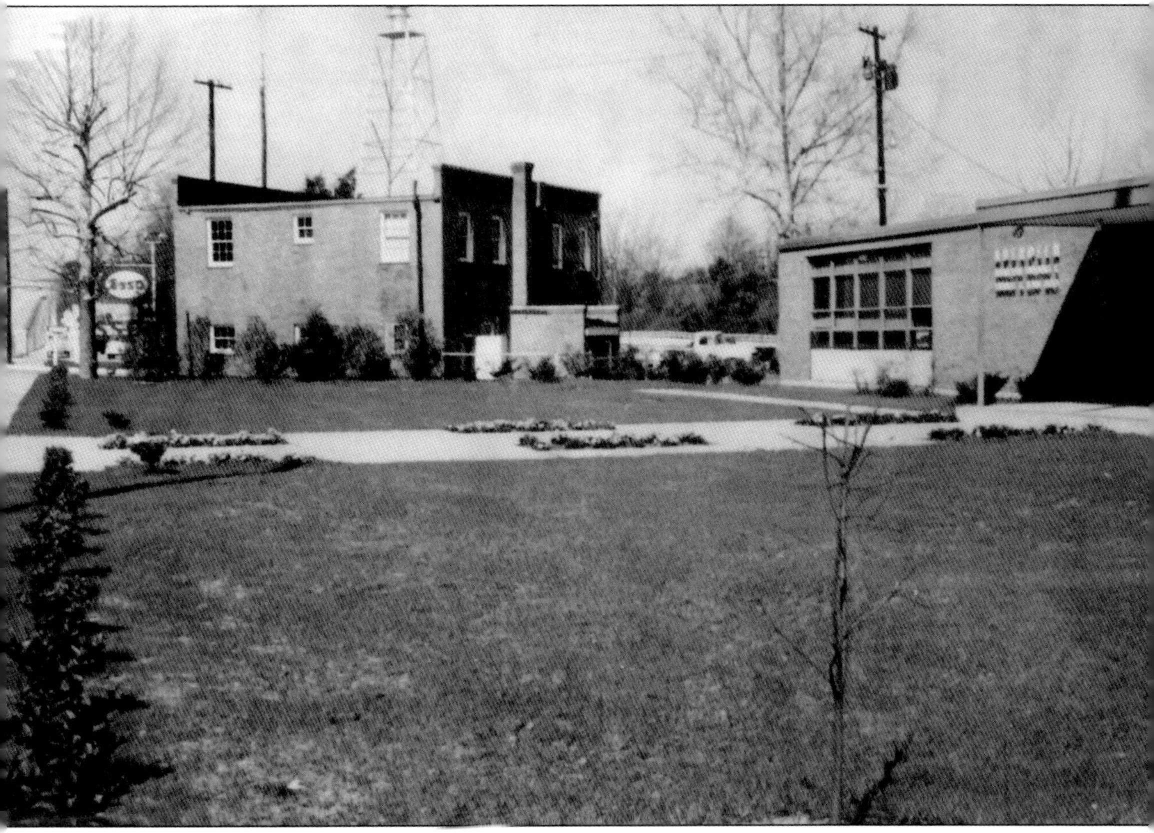

Looking north on Highway 1, this vintage c. 1960 view is of the 1930s-era fire department (left) and the Aberdeen Municipal Building (right). The two-story brick building had the town water and tax departments upstairs and the fire department downstairs. The fire siren to summon the volunteer firemen is seen on the tower above the roof. It also blew at 12:00 p.m. each day except Sundays. The new town hall and police department building was opened in 1957 replacing a small wooden police station. The new building had a courtroom, town offices, police department with two jail cells, and a savings and loan office. It was later sold, and a bank occupies the building today. (Courtesy of Page Memorial Library.)

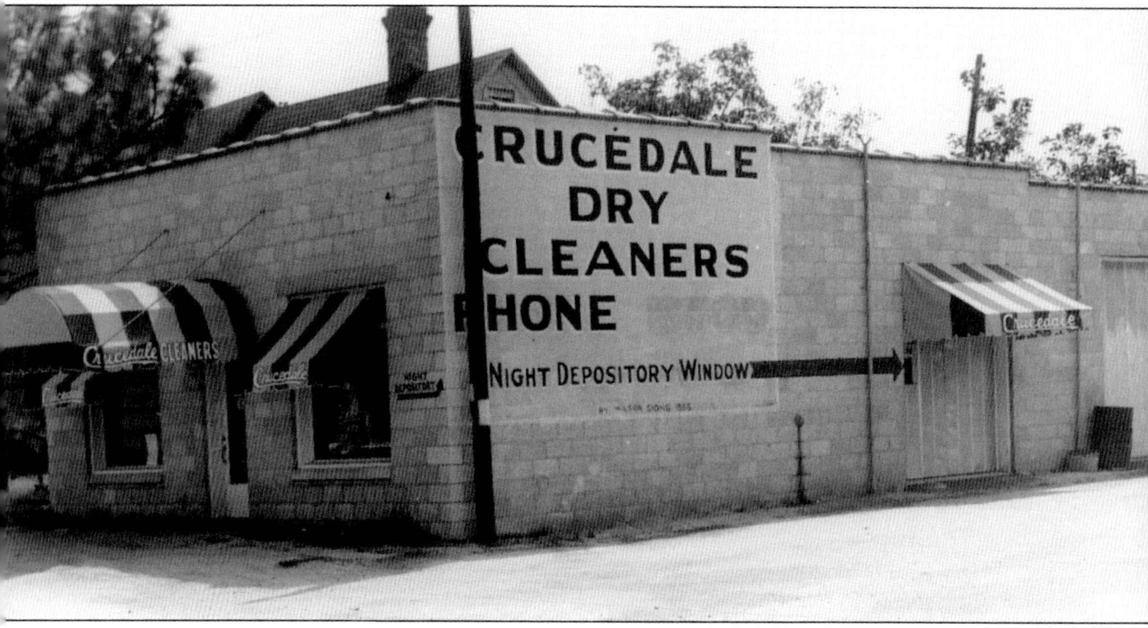

Located at 109 Knight Street, Crucedale Dry Cleaners was started in 1955 by Al Cruce. The family-run business was open at this location until 1974, when it was sold. Cruce was involved in civic activities for many years and was a member of the Aberdeen Board of Commissioners. A partial view of the roof and chimney of the Maggie Lewis boardinghouse can be seen behind the cleaners. Today, a window treatment company occupies the building. (Courtesy of John Blue.)

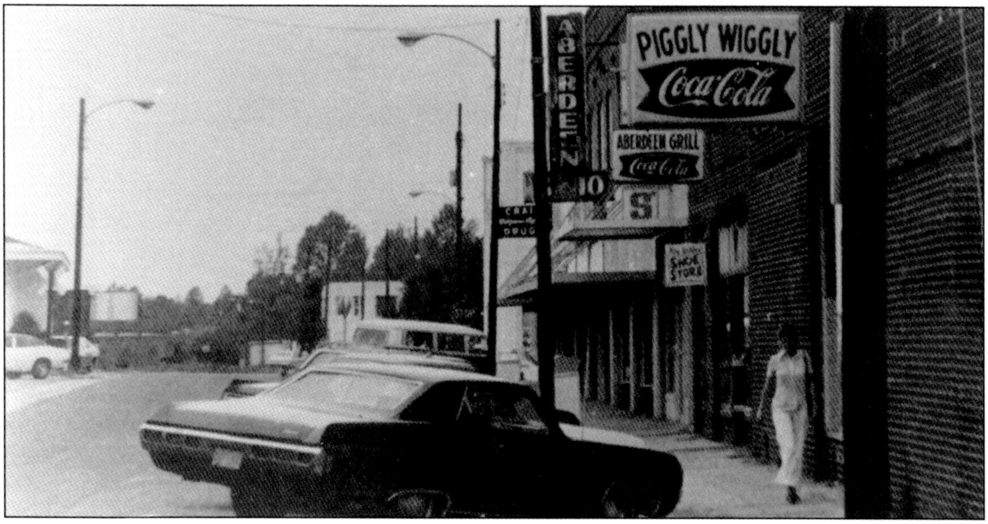

A lone pedestrian walks down Sycamore Street in this 1976 scene. The businesses pictured are, from left to right, Craig Drugs, Aberdeen Five and Ten, Roy Locklear's Shoe Store, Aberdeen Grill, and Piggly Wiggly. The Piggly Wiggly later became Davenport's Galaxy, which was built on the site of the Maggie Lewis boardinghouse. (Courtesy of John Blue.)

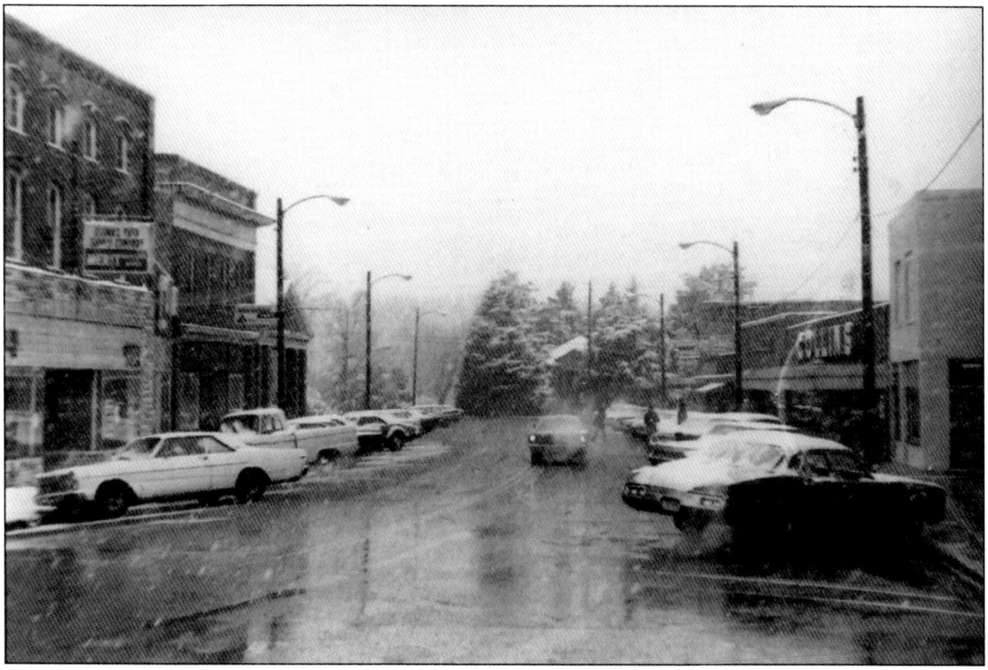

As snow accumulates on parked cars, Main Street, looking west, is seen in this 1970s image. Snow is not sticking to the road surface, so it is business as usual. The stores on the left side of the street are, from left to right, Browns Auto Supply Company in the former Keith Building, Aberdeen Hardware, and Carolina Bank in the former Page Trust Company offices. The stores on the right are, from left to right, Bryan Rexall drugstore, the Glitter Box jewelry store, Belk Hensdale Company, Collins department store, and the former hotel annex. Seen between two large trees at the end of the street, the roof of Page Memorial Library is covered in white. Located in a temperate weather zone, Aberdeen has mild winters and minimal snow each winter.

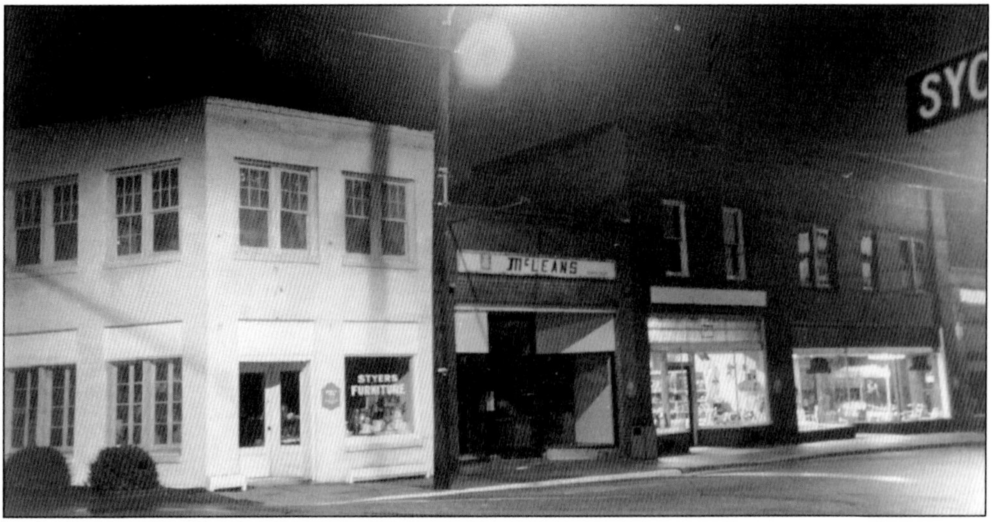

A night scene of South Street shows the five-sided Wiley Café Building (on the left), constructed in 1929 by H.L. Wiley. It has an angled side to allow clearance for trains to pass on the south leg of a railroad wye. Originally a five-and-dime store built by T.D. McLean, retired director of the Cotton Growers Association, McLeans Style Shop was operated by Susan McLean Bridgers for many years. The two adjoining buildings were constructed in 1924 as a grocery store and furniture store. The Economy Grocery Store Building had the second floor added in the 1930s. Today, new businesses occupy these storefronts. (Courtesy of John Blue.)

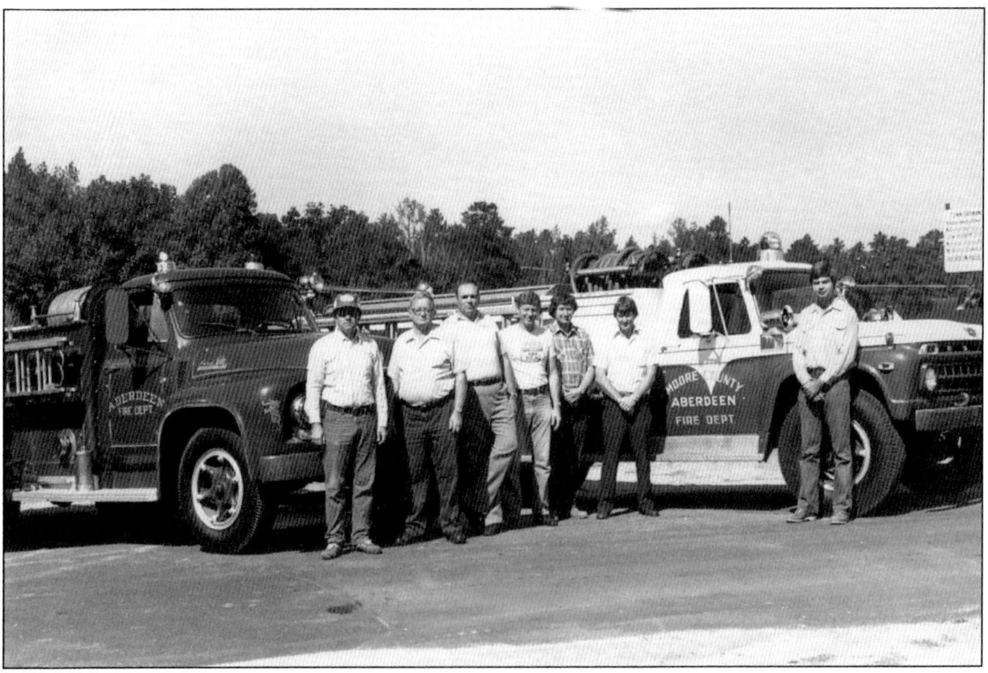

Aberdeen firemen pose in front of two of the department's fire trucks in the 1970s at Aberdeen Lake. Standing from left to right are James Davis, Randall Thompson, Tom Brock, C.F. Templin, Ray Bosworth, Gerald Stevens, and Arthur Parker. Chartered in 1921, the fire department acquired its first fire truck in 1922. Originally manned by an all-volunteer force, paid members have been employed by the department in recent years. (Courtesy of John Blue.)

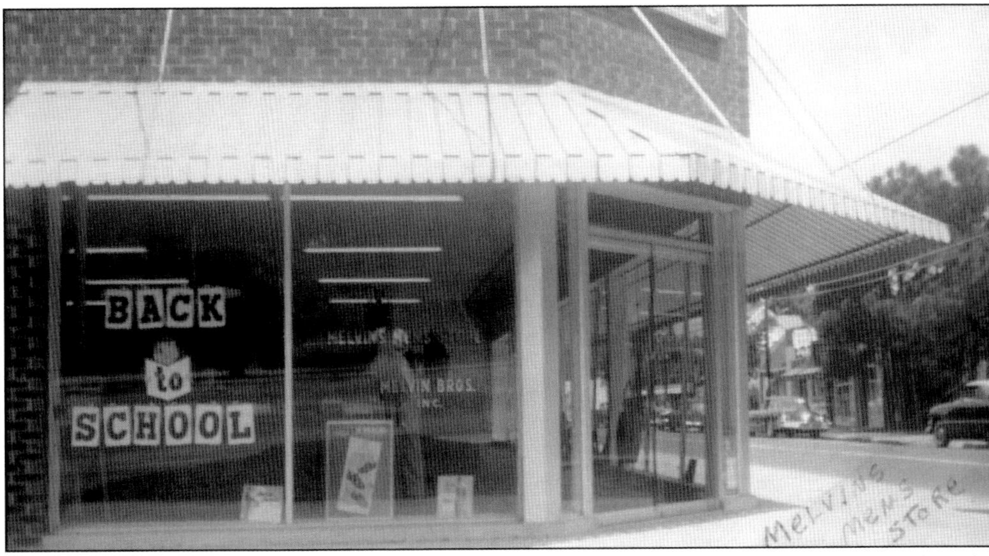

In April 1951, Melvin's Men's and Women's Store opened on the corner of West Main and Poplar Streets in a new building offering an expanded line of merchandise. John K. Melvin Jr. offered a variety of men's and boys' clothing, and Janie Melvin, widow of Thomas S. Melvin, sold ladies' and girls' clothing. The store was a popular destination for shoppers in Aberdeen and remained open until 1972. Today, the awning is gone, and a furniture store occupies the building. (Courtesy of Kay Crissman.)

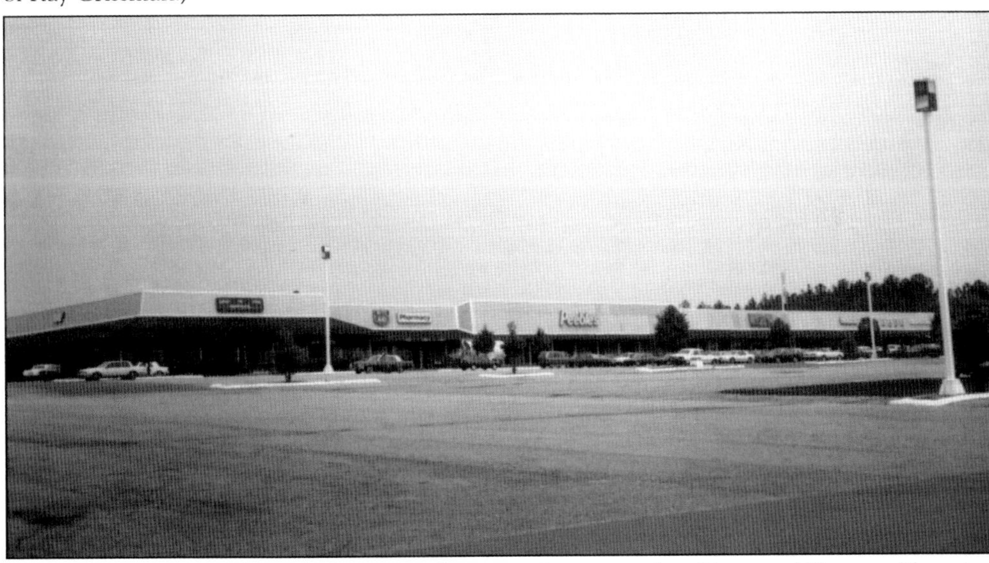

When constructed in the early 1960s on what was a former sandpit, Town and Country Shopping Center was heralded as a major office and retail center not only for Aberdeen but also surrounding communities. As the first true shopping center in the area, it drew tenants from their former locations in downtown Aberdeen and nearby communities in part because of the heavily traveled Highway 1 corridor and a convenient location north of town. In this 1980s view are, from left to right, Hallmark Gifts and Cards, Rite Aid Pharmacy, Peebles Department Store, the Dollar Store, and Sears. The shopping center today is showing its age with many empty storefronts, and Sears is the lone remaining business in the same location as depicted in this photograph. (Courtesy of the Town of Aberdeen.)

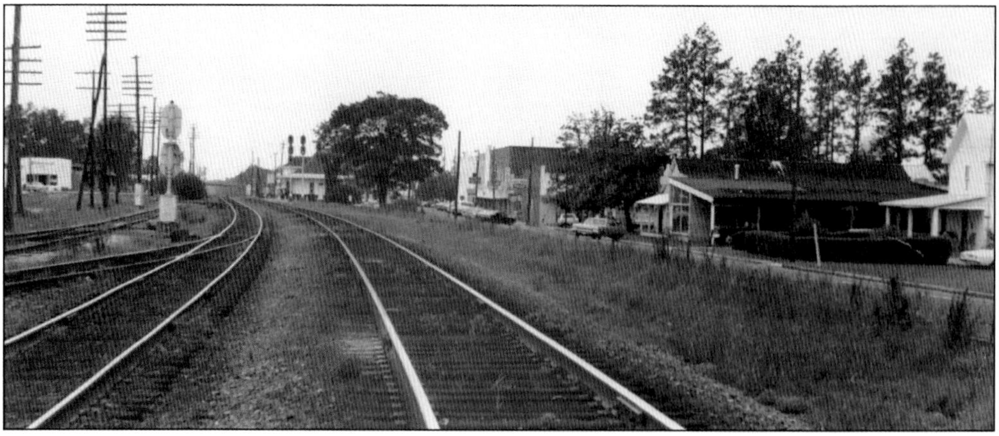

Here is a view of Aberdeen from the CSX Railroad tracks in 1976. The CSX Railroad was a merger of the Seaboard Systems Railroad and the Atlantic Coast Line Railroad, and the tracks through Aberdeen run from Richmond, Virginia, to Jacksonville, Florida. Looking south, pictured to the right, is Aberdeen Supply Company on the corner of Sycamore and Knight Streets. Union Station is pictured farther down the tracks on the left. (Courtesy of John Blue.)

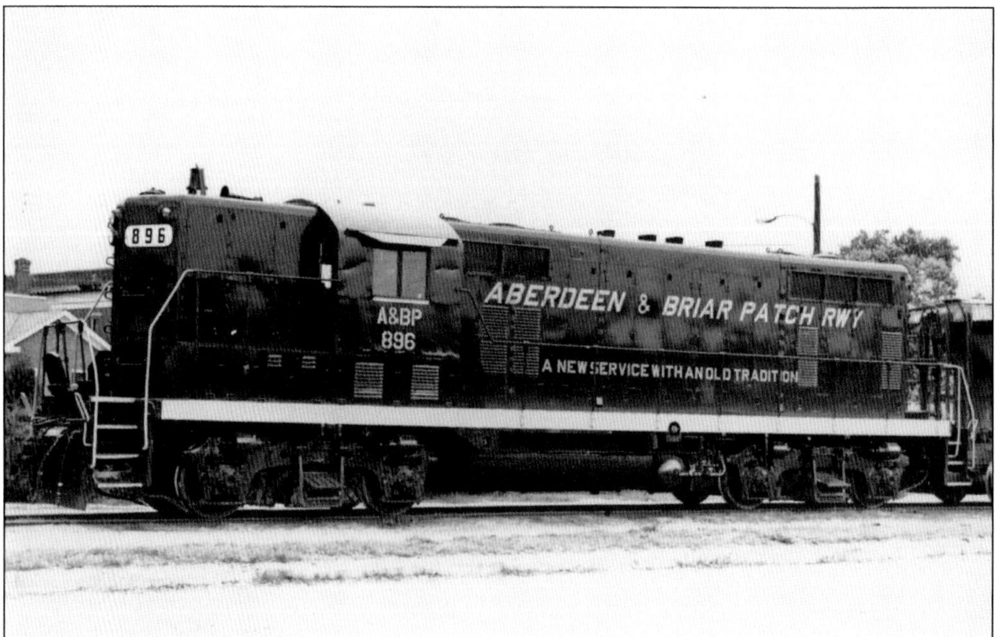

Aberdeen & Briar Patch Railway No. 896 stopped in downtown Aberdeen. Built in 1950 for the Seaboard Air Line Railway, it was acquired by the Aberdeen & Briar Patch Railway in 1982. The railway was sold in 1987 to the Aberdeen, Carolina & Western Railway, which continues to operate between Aberdeen and Star, North Carolina. (Author's collection.)

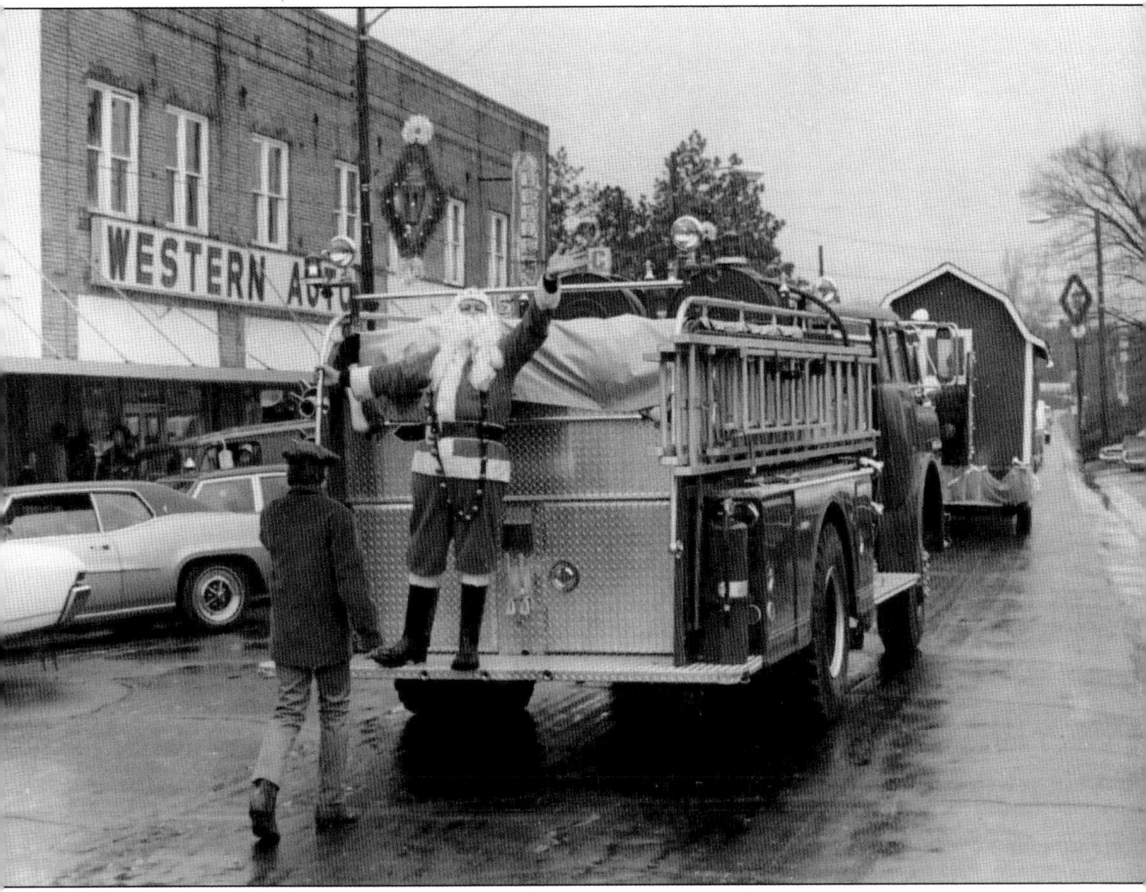

Aberdeen's Christmas parade, with Larry Boles as Santa Claus on the back of a fire truck, is pictured on Sycamore Street in the 1970s. Boles was proprietor of the Western Auto store, which can be seen on the left. He was also the owner of the Baron's Downtowner restaurant and was a past president of the Aberdeen Jaycees. (Courtesy of John Blue.)

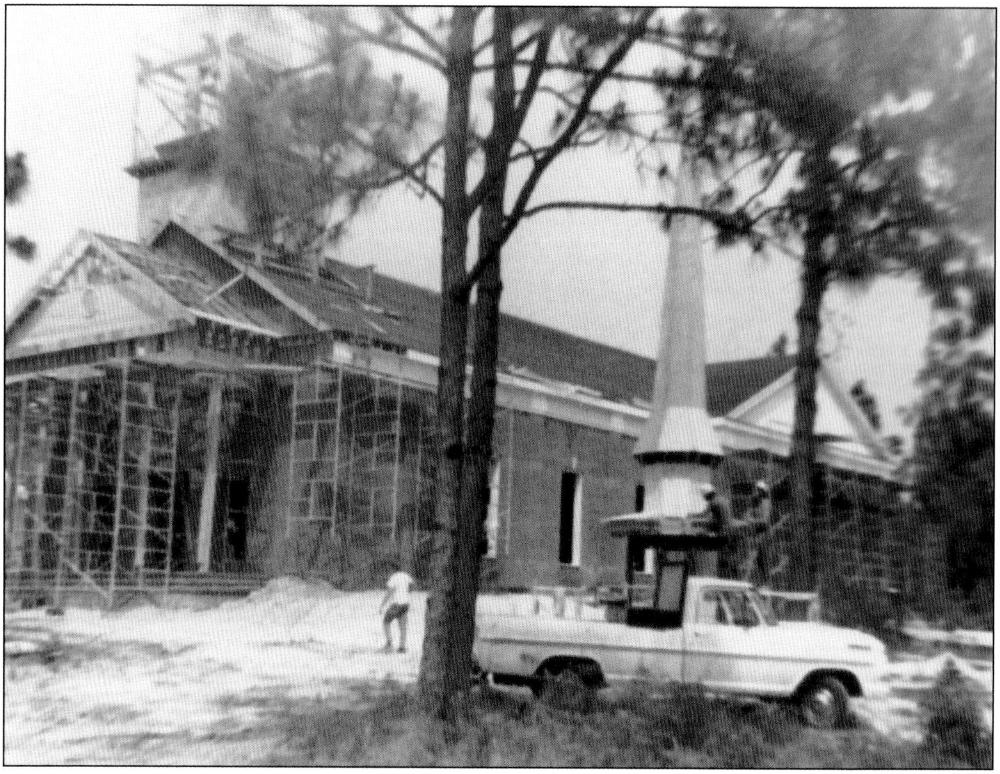

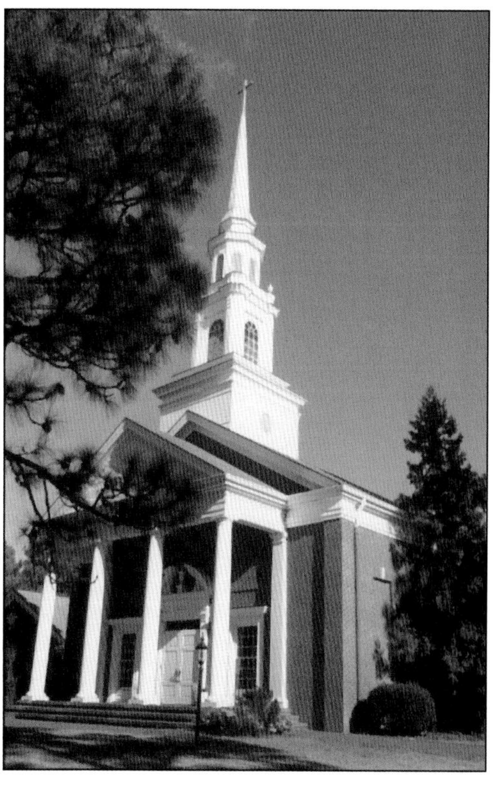

Seen under construction is the third Bethesda Presbyterian Church to be erected in Aberdeen. The congregation dedicated it in 1972. The first move was from the church built in 1862 on Bethesda Road to a larger sanctuary, erected in 1907, on High Street. After outgrowing that site, a new location across town was selected facing Highway 1, and construction began in the early 1970s. The lineage of a Bethesda church in the Aberdeen community goes back to Colonial times when early settlers to this area referred to it as the Bethesda community. Built in the Colonial style of architecture, this handsome church sits among stands of longleaf pine trees and faces a spring-fed lake. (Both, courtesy of Bethesda Presbyterian Church.)

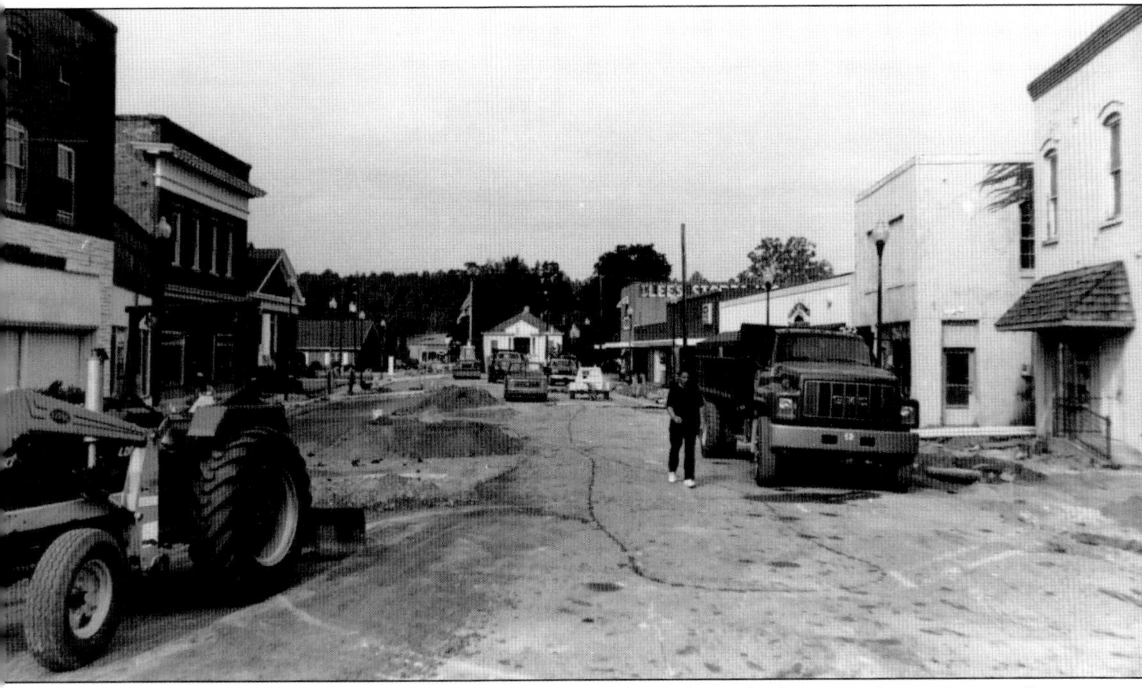

The town of Aberdeen received a state grant in the 1990s through the Main Street Project for upgrading and restoring Main and Sycamore Streets. Power lines were moved underground, and trees were planted. Decorative lampposts were installed, and brick pavers were laid in the sidewalks as part of the improvements. Above is a view looking west toward Page Memorial Library (center) as crews remove old asphalt in preparation of repaving the street. (Courtesy of John Blue.)

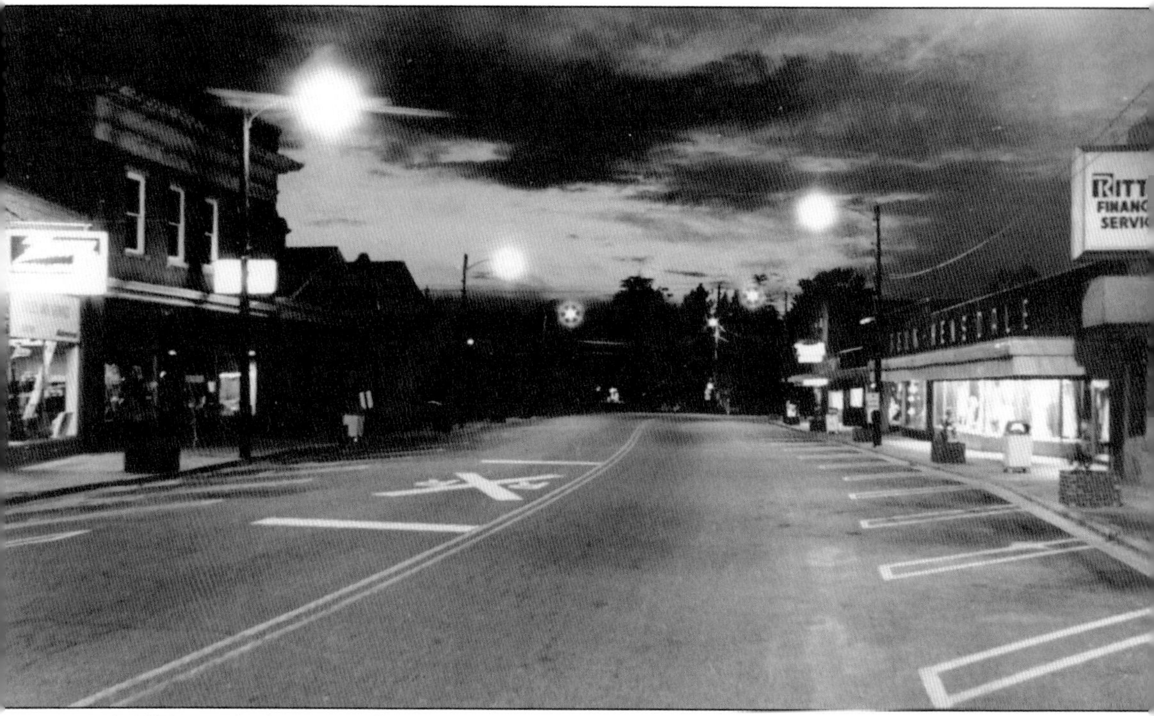

A 1979 view looks west as the sun sets over a deserted Main Street. Seen on the left are Flinchum's Television Service and Burney Hardware, and on the right is Ritter Financial Services, located in the hotel annex building. Lights glow in the Belk Hensdale department store display windows. Farther down on the right, the light from the Rexall Drugstore sign can be seen. Today, none of these businesses are located on Main Street. (Courtesy of John Blue.)

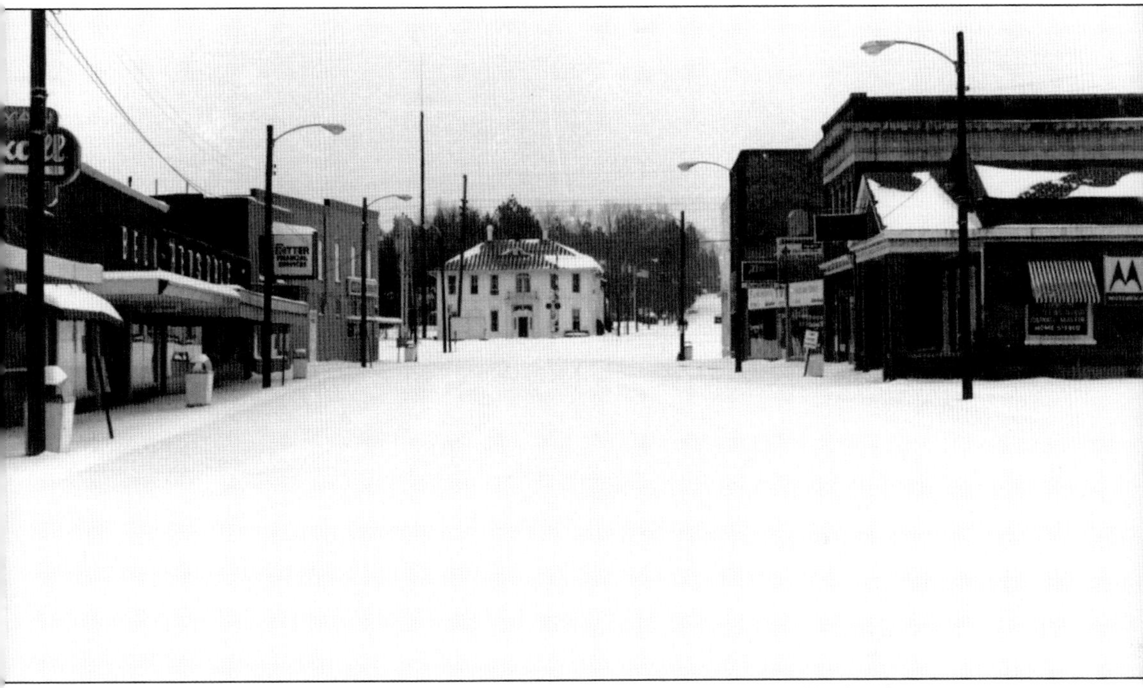

Main Street is seen after a March 1980 snowfall. Snows of this depth would often bring commerce and local schools to a halt until snowplows could make their way around town. Looking east in this view, the Aberdeen & Rockfish Railroad Building can be seen in the distance. (Courtesy of John Blue.)

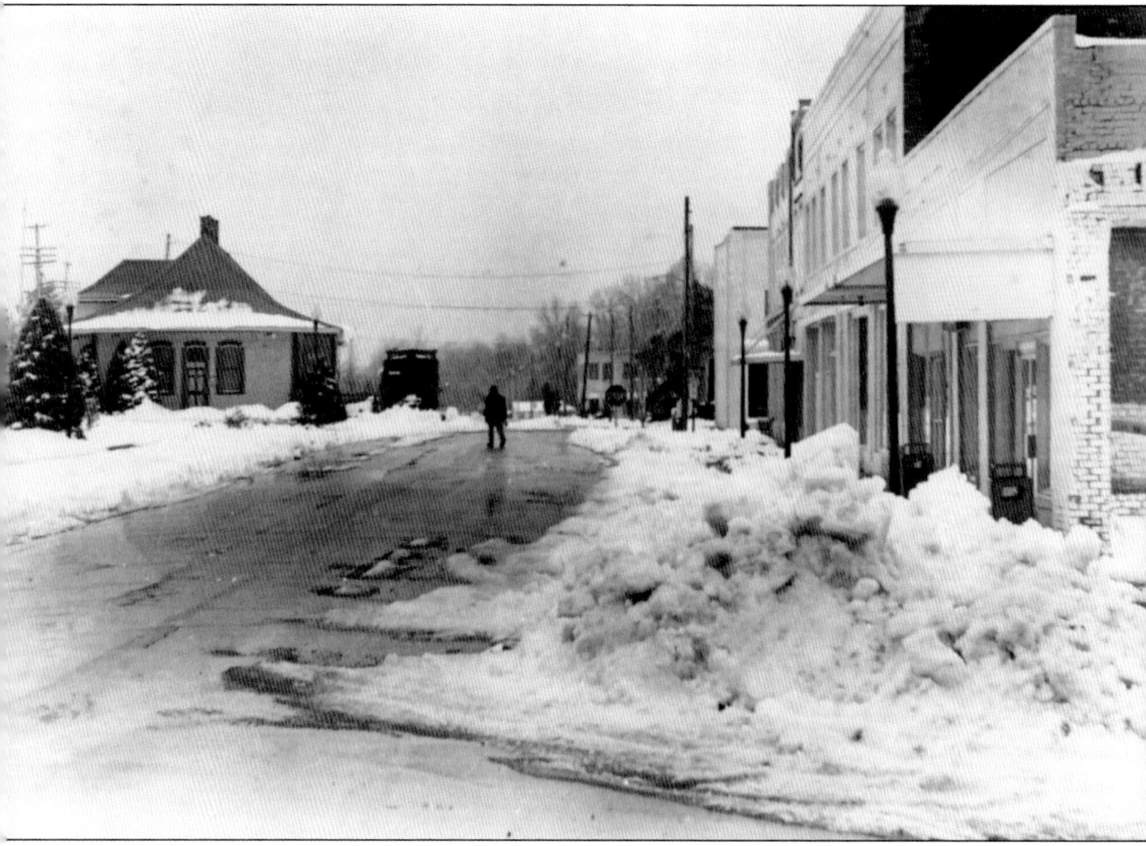

The big snow of January 2000 is pictured on Sycamore Street in front of Davenport's Galaxy. The deserted street has been plowed, and the storefronts and sidewalks are covered with snow. Landon Averitt, who painted murals on building walls downtown, can be seen crossing the street toward the Aberdeen Depot on his way home to Garrett Street. (Courtesy of John Blue.)

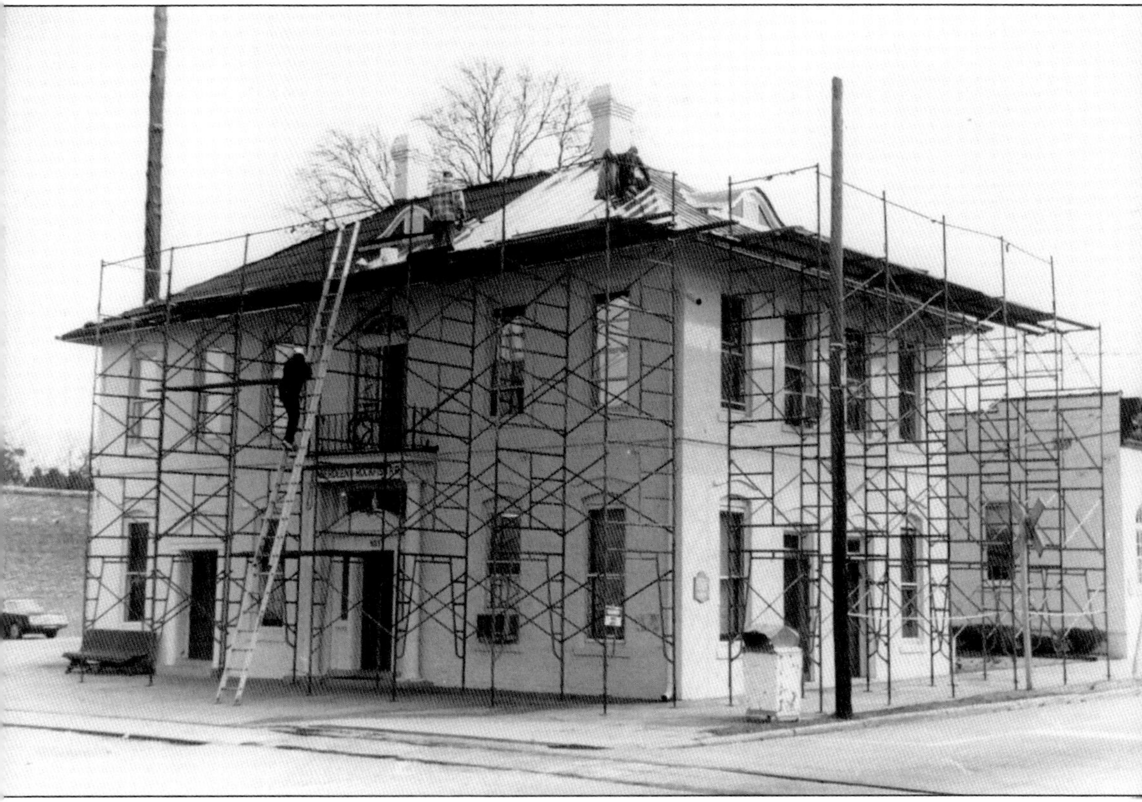

The Aberdeen & Rockfish Railroad headquarters was remodeled in the 1990s and received a new copper roof. Built in the Federalist style of architecture, the structure looks much as it did when constructed in 1904. The eastern terminus of the railroad in Fayetteville, North Carolina, has a similar office building. Known as the road of prosperous service, the Aberdeen & Rockfish Railroad has been in continuous service in the Sandhills of North Carolina since 1892. (Courtesy of John Blue.)

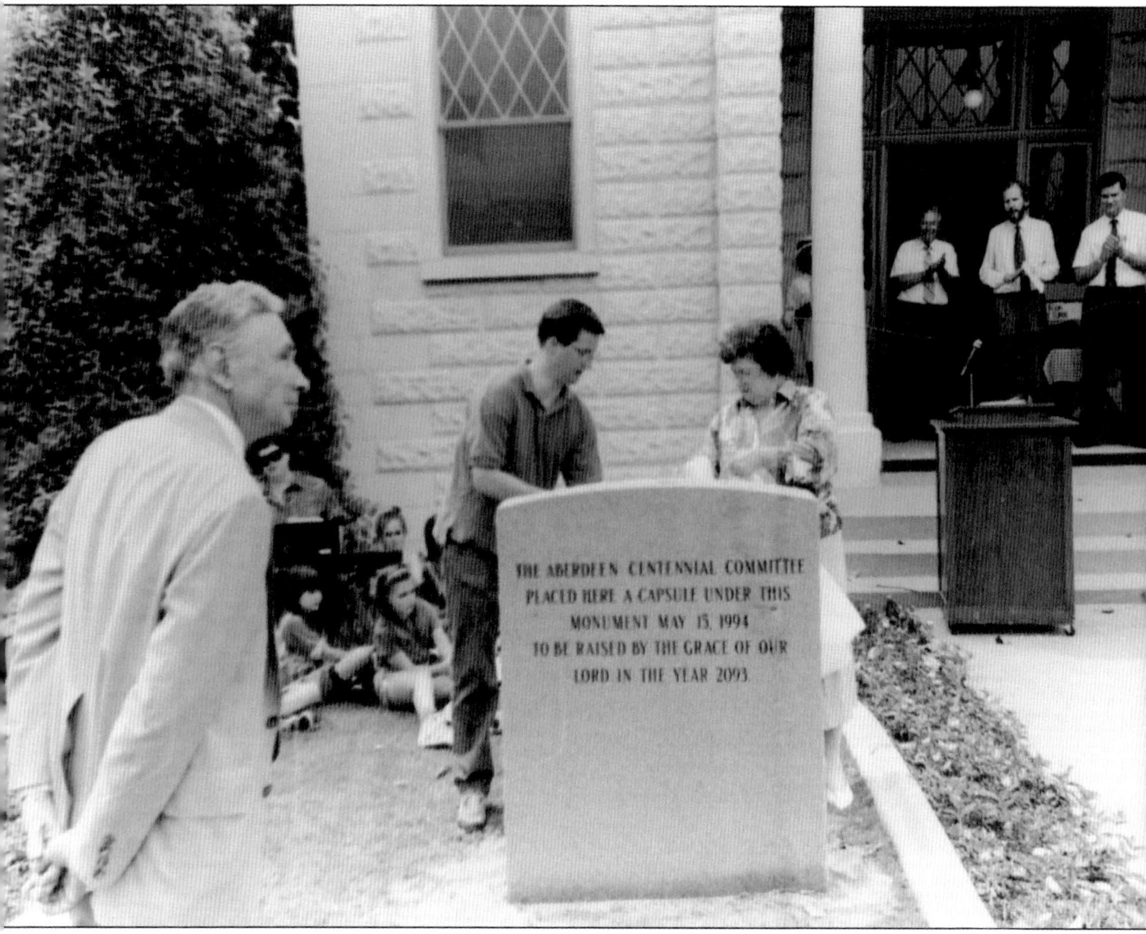

Aberdeen celebrated the centennial of its incorporation in 1993 by burying a 100-year time capsule in front of the Page Memorial Library. Mayor Robert N. Page III (left) watches as an unidentified person and Eldiweiss Lockey unveil the monument marking the location of the time capsule. The event created much pride, interest, and excitement in town. Mayor Page's grandfather Robert N. Page was the town's first mayor. (Courtesy of John Blue.)

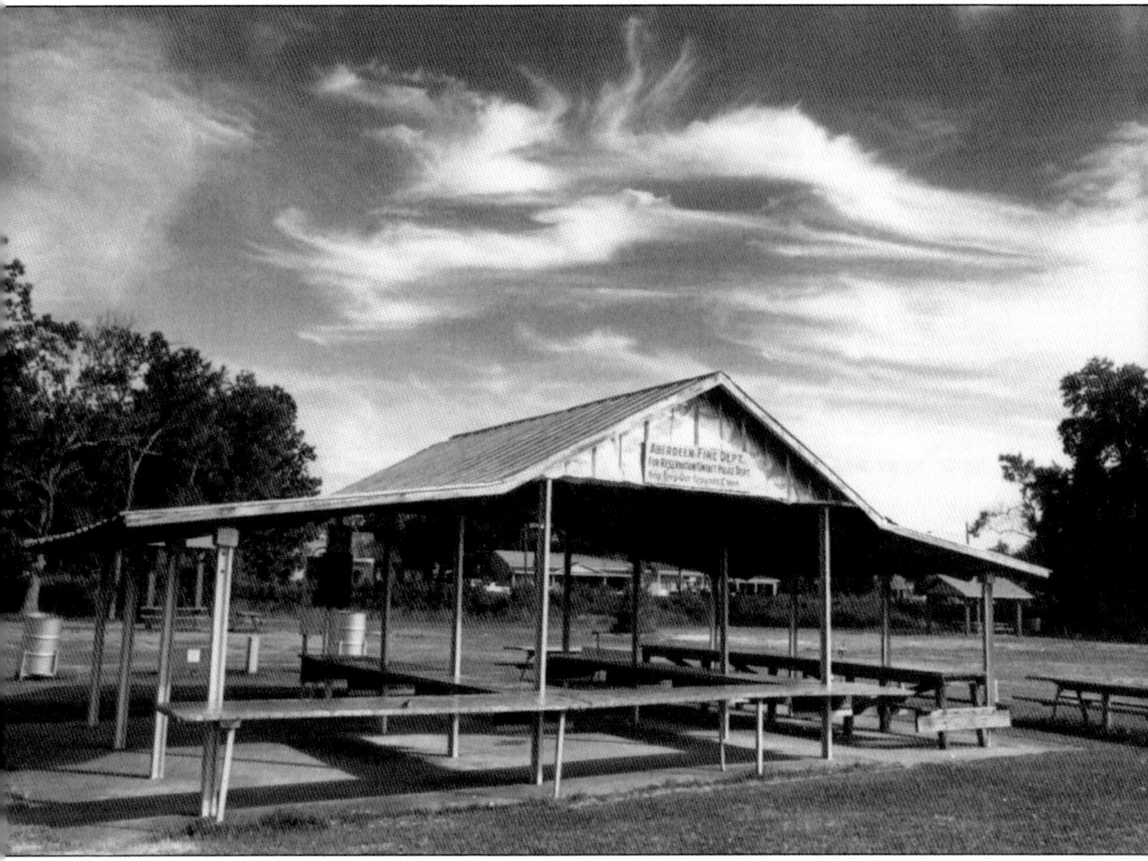

The firemen's shed was a fixture at Aberdeen Lake for more than 50 years. It was built by volunteers with the fire department from materials donated by John Dunk McLean and Curtis Lawhon. The shed was the scene of cookouts, birthday parties, and school trips and was used by cooks during the annual shad bake. Until recently, it was the site of the International Sardine Festival. The sign reads: "Aberdeen Fire Dept., For Reservation Contact Police Dept. and Help Keep Our Community Clean." The shed was torn down in 2006 during a major upgrade to the park. A modern facility was built on the site with a larger seating capacity. (Courtesy of the Town of Aberdeen.)

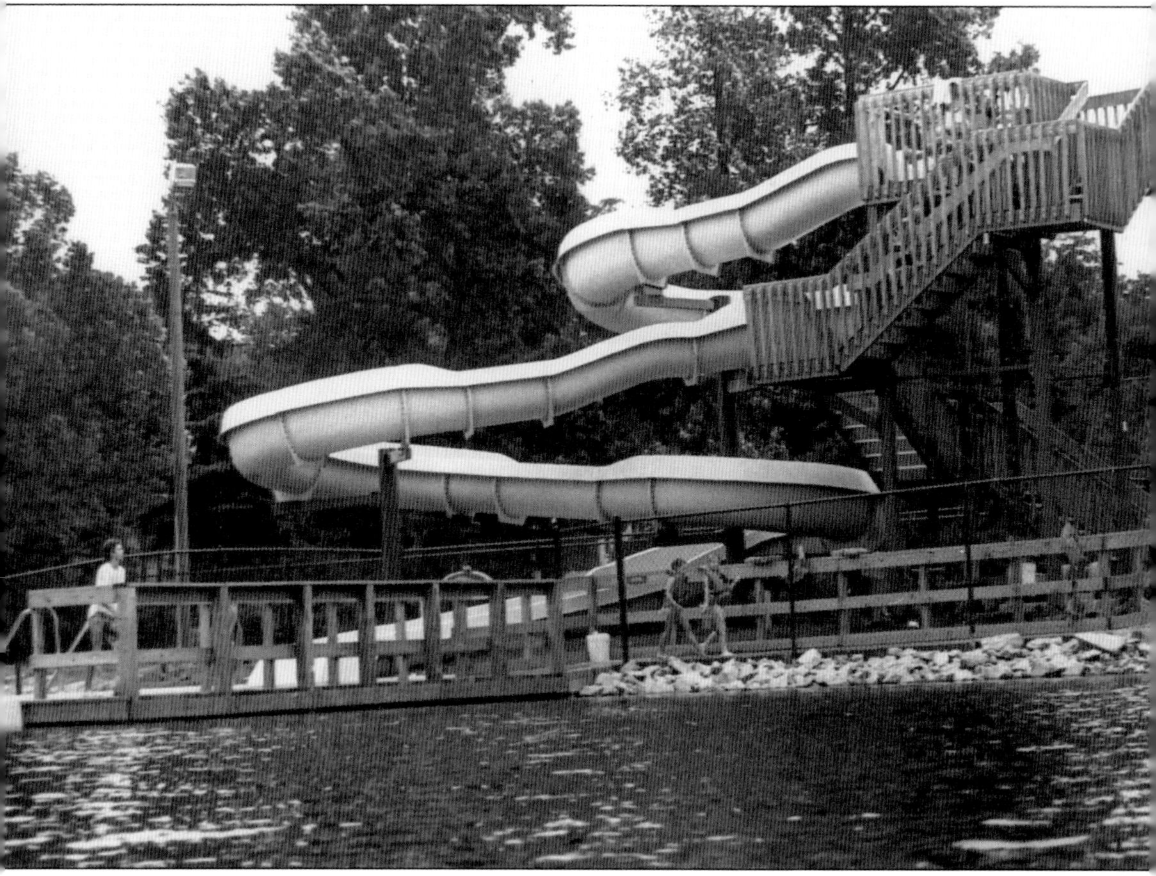

Summers became more fun for children of all ages when the Town of Aberdeen erected a waterslide and built a miniature golf course in 1992 as part of an upgrade at Aberdeen Lake Park. Operated by the parks and recreation department, the waterslide was dismantled within the decade, and the golf course was later removed in a conversion to a passive park. Today, a wooden gazebo occupies the waterslide site, overlooking the lake. Through a matching grant awarded to the town in 2004, a new recreation building and picnic shelter were opened at the park. (Courtesy of the Town of Aberdeen.)

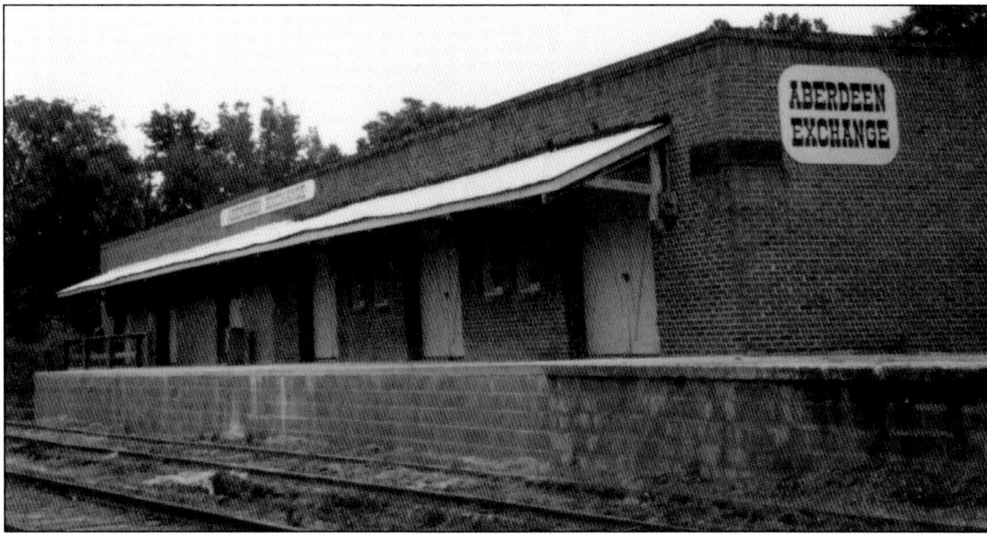

Originally built as a brick warehouse on an Aberdeen & Rockfish Railroad siding about 1920, a similar addition was added to the north elevation later in the 1920s. Used for general warehouse purposes for many years, the building was later leased from the railroad in 1989 by the Town of Aberdeen and named the Aberdeen Exchange. The exchange was a cooperative for local entrepreneurs to sell their produce and merchandise. In 1994, the nonprofit Artist League of the Sandhills leased the building. After extensive renovations, the facility houses 40 artist-in-residence studios, a gallery, and two large classrooms and offers exhibitions and art classes. (Courtesy of the Town of Aberdeen.)

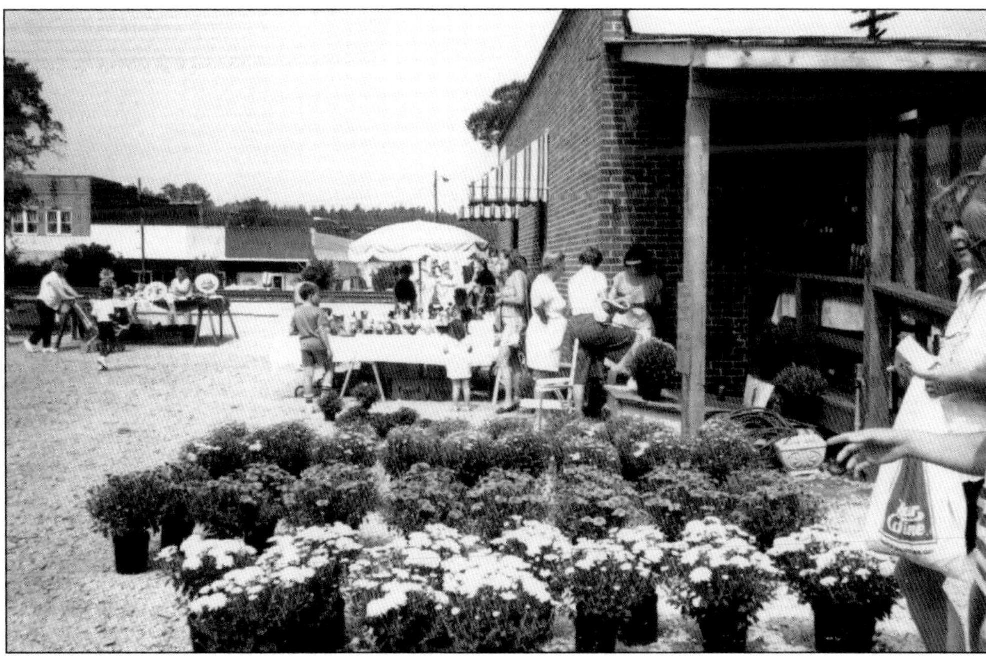

An outdoor farmers' market is seen beside the Aberdeen Exchange Building in the early 1990s. Opened as a local merchants and farmers' cooperative in an old warehouse, the market was managed by Martha Swaringen. The market was phased out when the building was leased in 1994 by an artist league. (Courtesy of the Town of Aberdeen.)

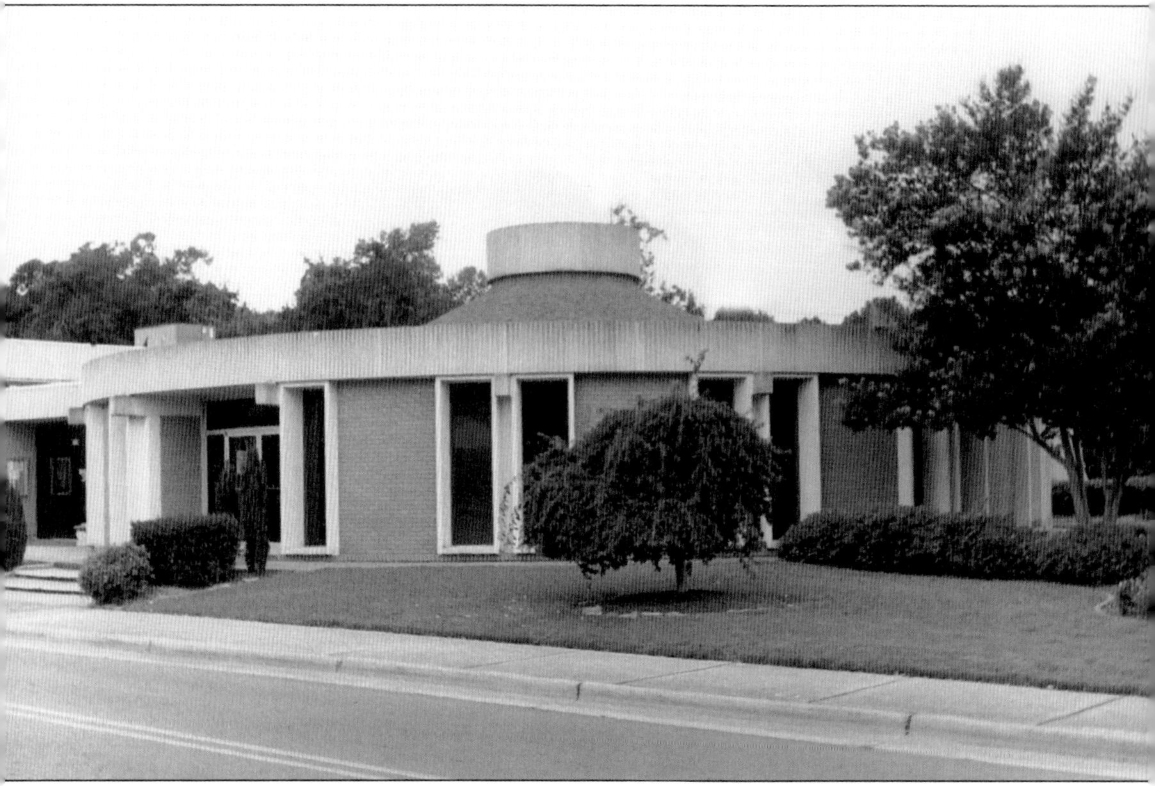

When Carolina Bank officials decided to move from their location on Main Street into a new building, they came up with a novel design. Opening in 1963 on Poplar Street, the bank was constructed as a circular building. It was the first round commercial building to be constructed in Aberdeen and was heralded for its innovation and design. Eventually, Carolina Bank merged with Branch Banking and Trust but continued at this location for a number of years. The bank later moved to a location on Highway 1, and in 1992, the Town of Aberdeen acquired the building and converted it into the town hall. On two occasions, the round portion has had additional offices added to the southern elevation; it is no longer completely round. Today, town council meetings are held in the rotunda. (Courtesy of John Blue.)

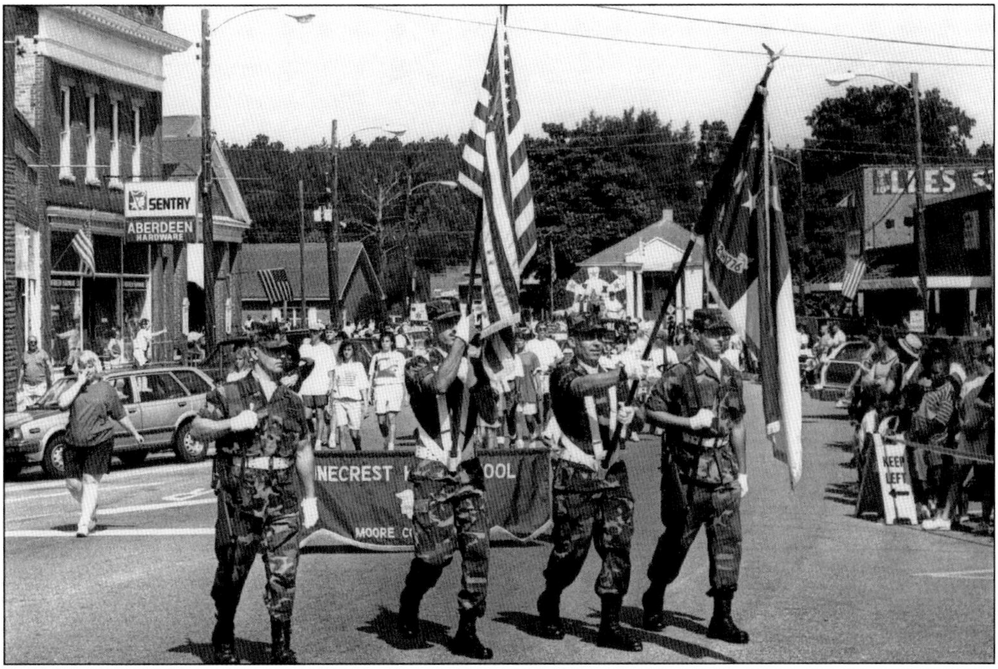

The Fourth of July parade was a festive celebration drawing large crowds to downtown Aberdeen. Seen in these 1992 images, the parade turns from Main Street onto Sycamore Street. Members of the color guard are from the local Army National Guard unit, followed by the Patriots marching band from Pinecrest High School providing stirring martial music. Local floats, fire engines, antique cars, and civic groups from Aberdeen and surrounding communities participated in the event. Later that night, large crowds gathered at Aberdeen Lake for a spectacular fireworks display. Today, the holiday is observed at the lake with music, food, games, and the largest fireworks show in the county. (Both, courtesy of the Town of Aberdeen.)

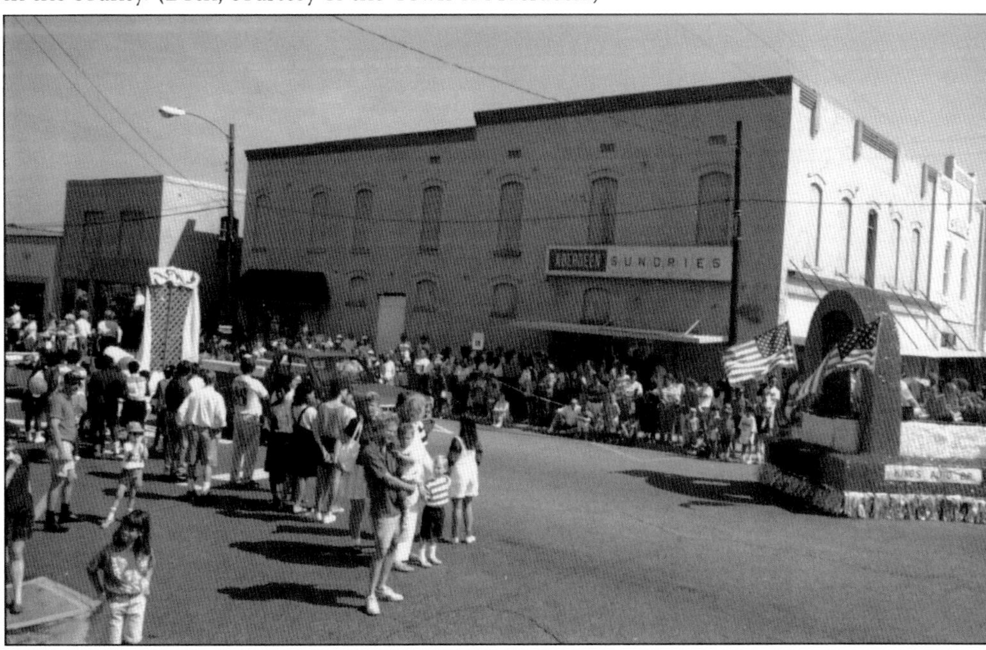

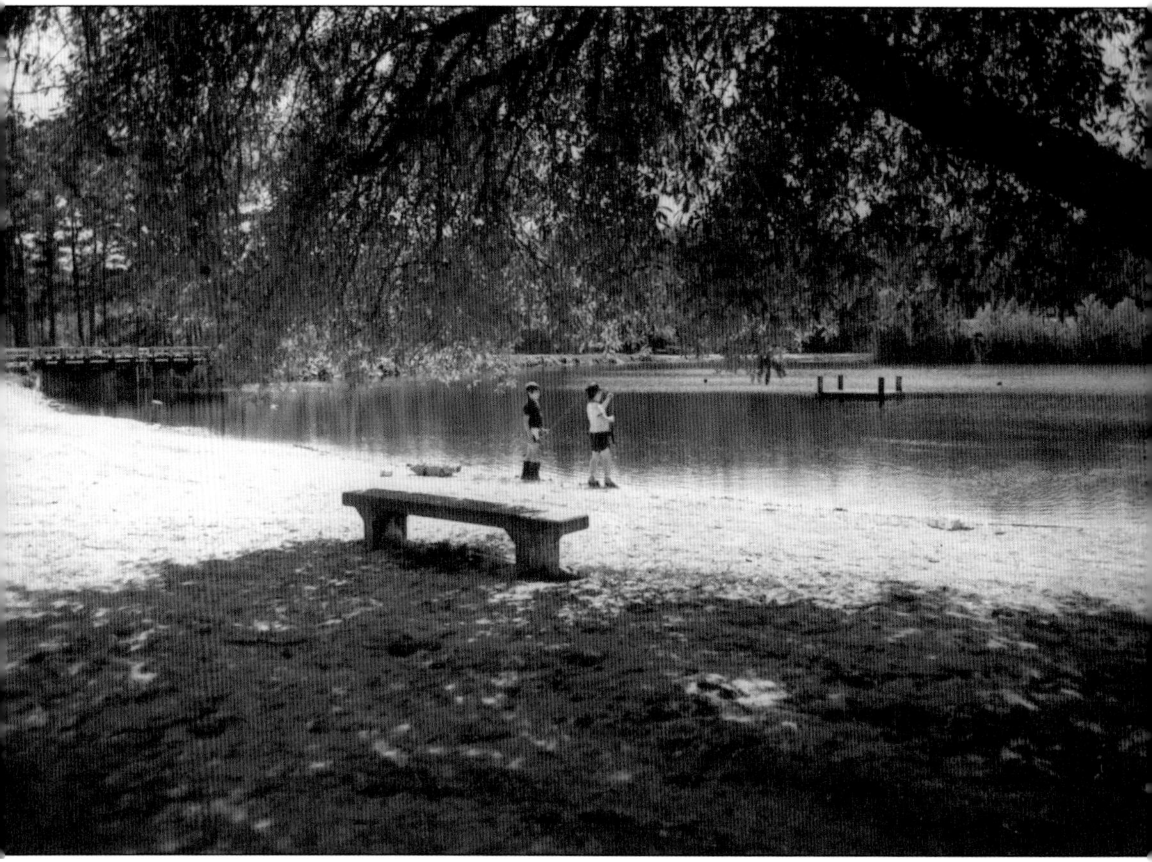

Two young boys try their hand at fishing from the bank of Aberdeen Lake. The dam and spillway can be seen to the left, and one of the platforms for diving is visible in the lake. The lake and dam were originally created to supply waterpower to a sawmill and gristmill. Originally known as Page's Lake, it was owned by the Jack Taylor family for a number of years before being acquired by the Town of Aberdeen as a municipal park. (Courtesy of the Town of Aberdeen.)

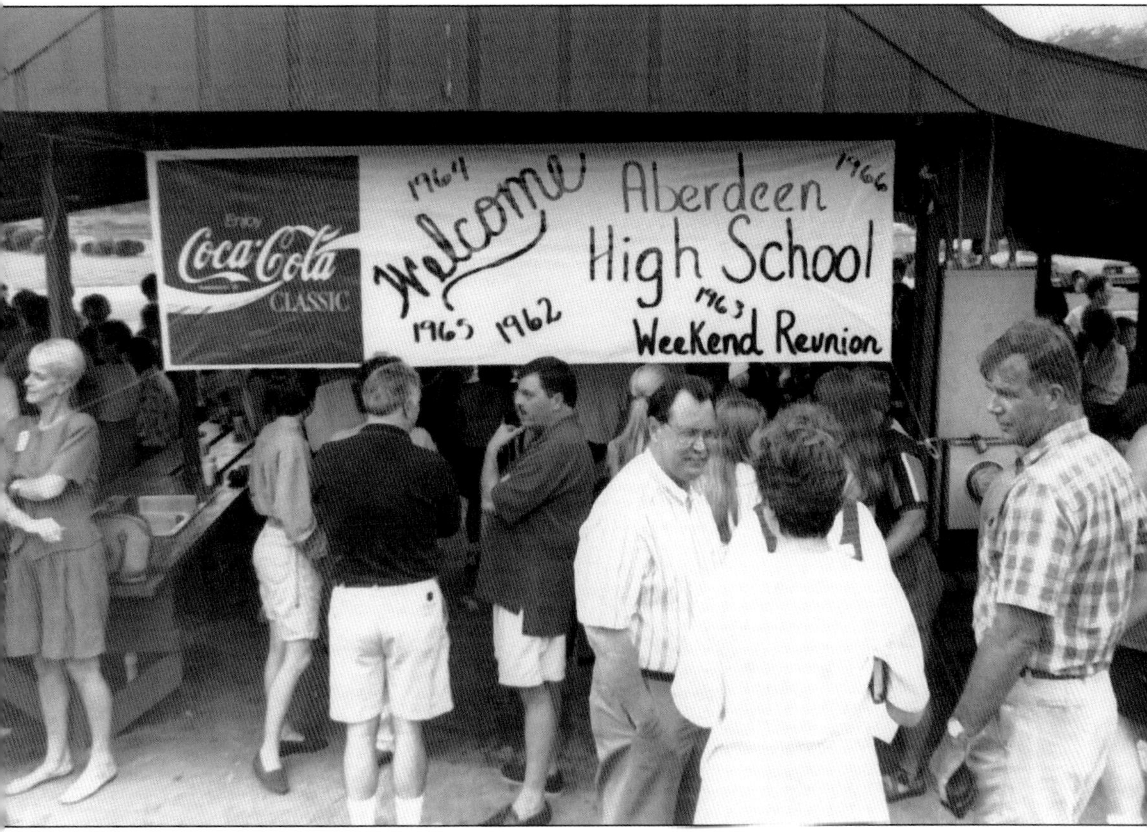

Aberdeen High School classes from 1962 through 1966 are enjoying a reunion gathering at Aberdeen Lake in this October 1995 photograph. The school had an enrollment during those years of approximately 300 students in four grades, which often meant a class reunion included more than one graduating class. Aberdeen High School was closed and torn down in 1969, and many organized reunions held today often invite everyone who attended the school. (Courtesy of John Blue.)

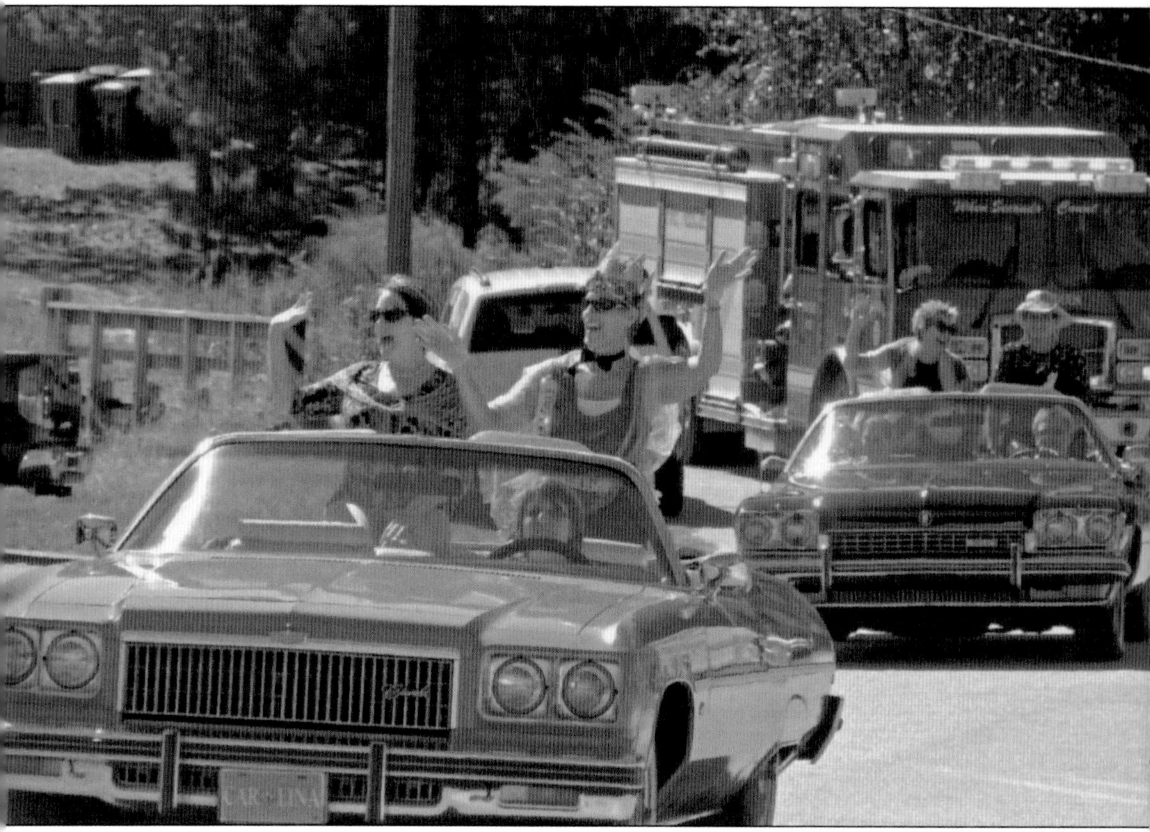

A highlight of the International Sardine Festival is the crowning of the queen. Past queens ride to the event in vintage automobiles while the new queen is escorted to the event in a fire truck. Each queen reigns for a year, and while the event is all in fun, those attending are anxious to see who steps out of the fire truck as the new queen of the festival. (Courtesy of David Powers.)

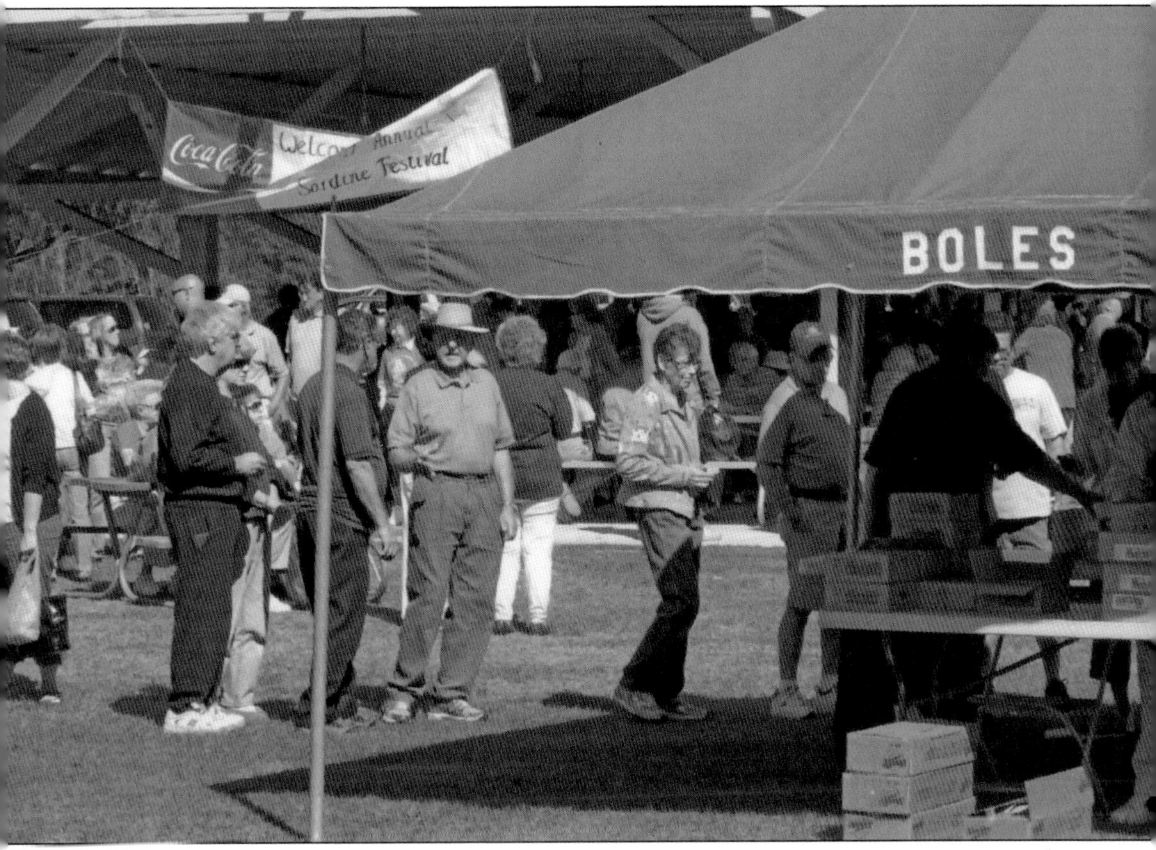

Crowds have been gathering at Aberdeen Lake since 1992 to enjoy the annual International Sardine Festival held each year in October. From a humble beginning by Randall Moss who was forced to go outside to eat his sardine sandwiches by his daughter and coworkers, Moss found others that enjoyed a can of the tiny fish, so they began meeting at lunch and thought up the idea of a festival to honor the sardine. While it is all in jest, the event raises money for local youth organizations and has attracted enthusiastic attendees from Aberdeen and surrounding communities. (Courtesy of David Powers.)

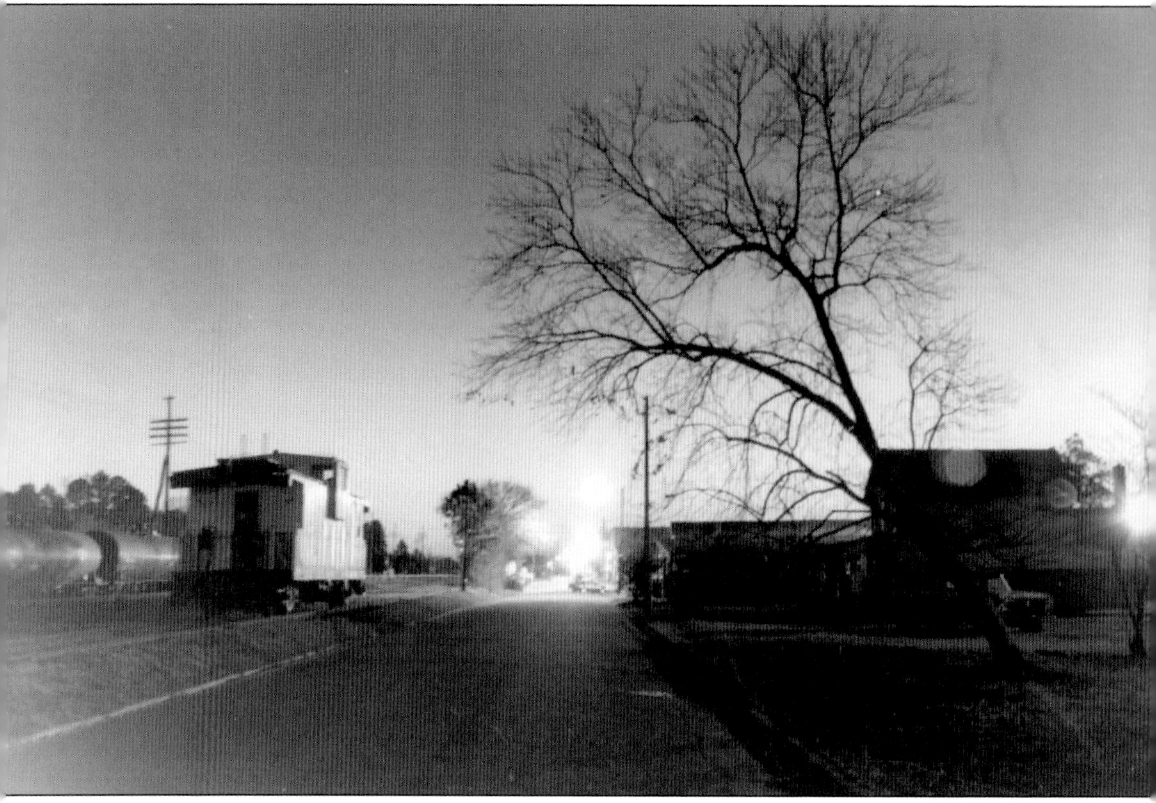

Sycamore Street is pictured as the sun sets in this 1990s scene. Aberdeen Supply Company (right) is silhouetted by the lights of town, and a caboose is pictured on the railroad tracks. Large poles with telegraph wires, seen in the background, were strung along the main line of the CSX Railroad tracks, but today, they have all been removed. (Courtesy of John Blue.)

Bibliography

Koster, Lawrence. *The Hotels and Boarding Houses of Moore County, NC, 1870–1950*. Whispering Pines, NC: self-published, 2008.

Ormsby, John. *The History of Six-Man Football in North Carolina*. Charleston, SC: self-published, 2010.

Richardson, Emma G.B., and Thomas C. Richardson. *History of Aberdeen*. Charlotte, NC: Delmar Printing, 1992.

Schloegl, Richard J. *Moore County*. Charleston, SC: Arcadia Publishing, 1997.

Stevens, Lowell, and Tom MacCallum. *Camp Mackall and Its Times in the Sandhills of North Carolina*. Rockingham, NC: Richmond County Historical Society, 2011.

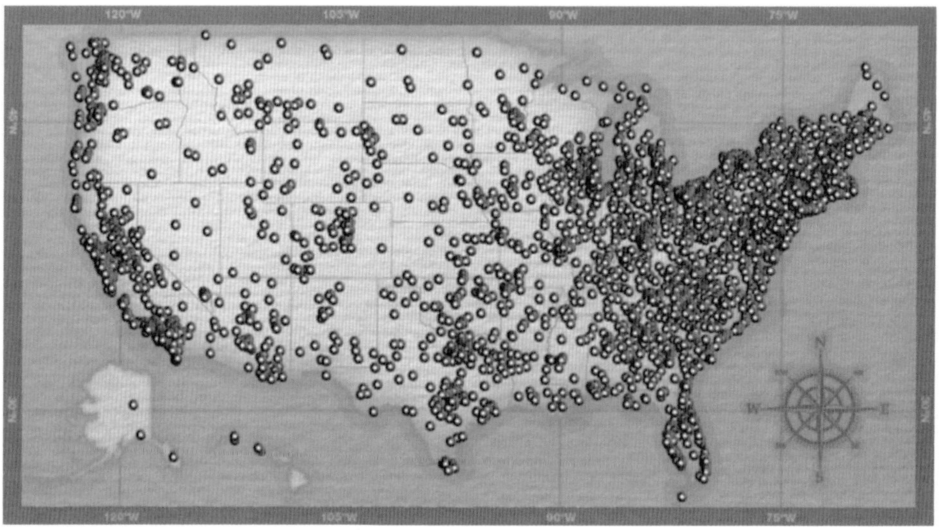

Consistent with our mission to preserve history on a local level, this book was printed in South Carolina on American-made paper and manufactured entirely in the United States. Products carrying the accredited Forest Stewardship Council (FSC) label are printed on 100 percent FSC-certified paper.

MADE IN THE USA